WARPATHS

WARPATHS

The Politics of Partition

Robert Schaeffer

HILL AND WANG • NEW YORK

A division of Farrar, Straus and Giroux

Library of Congress Cataloging-in-Publication Data
Schaeffer, Robert K.
Warpaths : the politics of partition / Robert Schaeffer.—1st ed.
Includes bibiliographical references.
1. World politics—1945–   2. Partition, Territorial.
3. Military history, Modern—20th century.
4. War.   I. Title.
D842.S32   1990
327′.09′045—dc20   89-19751

For Torry Dickinson

Contents

III · The Legacy of Partition

Acknowledgments

The idea that partition and war were related occurred to me when I was working at Friends of the Earth in 1984. Tom Turner encouraged me to devote time to an investigation of the history of divided states and the risks of war, particularly nuclear war, associated with partition. This work resulted in the publication of an essay on divided states that formed the basis for this book.

After reading this piece, Benedict Anderson, the director of the Southeast Asia program at Cornell University, suggested I write a book on the topic. I took his advice and benefited enormously from his thoughtful correspondence and from his own work on contemporary nationalism, particularly his book *Imagined Communities*. He reviewed my outline, helped me find a publisher, and went to great lengths on my behalf.

Torry Dickinson is greatly responsible for the completion of this project. She reviewed all my work and helped to develop ideas and think through problems at every stage. I relied on her global historical perspective, her understanding of ethnicity and politics, and her attention to intellectual detail. Without her enormous assistance, it would have been impossible to write this book.

In 1986, I circulated a descriptive outline to a number of people. Their suggestions and criticisms helped shape my research and direct my writing. I am indebted to Bill Smock, Bruce Coleman, Bruce Cumings, Urmilla Phadnis, John Judis, Elaine Draper, Jeff Escoffier, Vickie Smith, Steve McMahon, Bill Martin, Marcus Rediker, Kevin Kelley, Ken Barr, Earl D. Foell, Christopher and Eleni Hitchens, Joy MacCarthy, Paul Schaeffer, Sandra Kaiser, Evelyn Reilly, Iftikar Amad, Jessie Bunn, George Posner, and Immanuel Wallerstein for their comments and correspondence.

I am grateful to the assistance given me by Richard Healey at *Nuclear Times* and Andre Carothers and Peter Bahouth at Greenpeace. Richard Healey, John Judis, and Osama Mufta deserve my thanks for their help with computers and the myriad problems associated with electronic writing.

If one is not part of a university, it is difficult to obtain access to good research libraries. Librarians at the University of California at Berkeley, the University of Maine, and the Catholic University of America, particularly Adele Chwalek, generously allowed me to mine their resources.

Steve Wasserman encouraged me to write a provocative book and provided resources to do it. No one can ask more of a publisher. His suggestions, and the fine editorial work of Paul Golob, helped to focus the argument and make a long book more readable.

Credit should also go to Bill Friedland and James Houston. They taught me the discipline of writing when I was a student at the University of California at Santa Cruz. They argued that writing is as much a physical exercise as a mental one. After working on this book for five years, I'd have to agree.

Washington, D.C. ROBERT SCHAEFFER
April *1989*

Partition is the expedient of tired statesmen.

—Conor Cruise O'Brien

WARPATHS

Introduction

During this century, a number of countries around the world have been partitioned, resulting in the creation of separate states. After World War I, Ireland was partitioned. Then, in the decade after World War II, Korea, China, Vietnam, India, Palestine, and Germany were divided. The great powers responsible for partition, chiefly Great Britain, the United States, and the Soviet Union, promoted it as a peaceful way to devolve or transfer power to indigenous groups in countries that had been subject to colonial rule or military occupation. Government officials in London, Washington, and Moscow believed that the division of singular political entities and the establishment of separate states would create a home for majority and minority populations, satisfy the demands of independence movements that were then competing for state power, prevent the outbreak of civil war, and secure superpower interests in these regions.

But the division of countries into separate states has been a singular failure. Partition uprooted millions from their homelands and compromised the meaning of citizenship where they made their new homes. Partition undercut the meaning of sovereignty for newly independent states and sharpened the competition between divided or sibling states. And partition led to internecine war within and between divided states and drew superpower states into intractable regional wars. Not only was partition an immediate failure; it has proved to be an enduring problem. Decades have passed since these countries were divided, yet the conflicts between them have, in most cases, grown more bitter over time. And despite its failure, partition continues to be advanced as a political solution. Pakistan and Cyprus were divided in the early 1970s and a number of other countries—Lebanon, Sri Lanka, Ethiopia, and Israel—will probably be divided or redivided in coming years.

Because the problems endemic to divided states threaten both regional and global peace, it is important to understand the causes and consequences of partition. This book examines the political history of partition. It traces the events leading up to partition, examines how different countries were divided, and looks at the consequences and contemporary expression of partition around the world.

Although the history of partition is told chronologically, beginning in the 1880s and concluding in the 1980s, this work grew out of a concern about contemporary problems, the threat of nuclear war in particular. Of the approximately twenty times the United States has threatened to use nuclear weapons, two-thirds were directed at recently divided states engaged in conflicts with their sibling neighbors. The pattern of Soviet threats has been much the same. Three of the five or six known Soviet threats were directed at recently divided states.[1]

The relation between nuclear threats and conflict between recently divided states was striking and suggestive. A review of these countries' history indicated that many of them were habitually at war, engaged in either periodic or protracted wars with their neighbors. India and Pakistan fought three wars in the post–World War II period, Israel and its neighbors waged five. Korea and Vietnam have been the site of the two largest wars since 1945, the Korean War lasting three years and the war in Vietnam thirty. Periodic skirmishes between China and Taiwan have threatened wider wars, and global war loomed during disputes over Berlin and the division of Germany. Northern Ireland has been visited with a protracted irregular war that continues to this day. The martial résumés of recently divided states reinforced the observation that partition and war might be related in important ways. It was this connection that led to a more detailed examination of these and other divided states.

The subsequent investigation into the separate histories of contentious divided states revealed a number of patterns. First, partition is a relatively recent development. It was first practiced in this century and became widespread only after World War II. In the past, the victors of wars and arbiters of power frequently divided and redistributed conquered or unclaimed territory between already existing states. So, for instance, in the 1494 Treaty of Tordesillas, the Pope divided the New World between Portugal and Spain. Victors of wars between France and Germany periodically divided Alsace-Lorraine between them. Sometimes successful independence movements managed to detach themselves from European empires, as the United States did in the late eighteenth century and many Latin American countries did in the nineteenth century. Occasionally, victorious countries would break up defeated empires and devolve power to new political entities, as the Allies did after World War I, when they detached parts of Germany and Russia to create Poland and broke the Austro-Hungarian Empire into its constituent parts.

After World War I and again after World War II, the victors began dividing some of the world in a new way. Instead of dividing colonial or occupied territories and redistributing them between existing states, they frequently devolved power to indigenous successors. At the same time, they also divided power between competing groups within these countries. Thus, when the British tried to settle the Irish Question after World War I, they detached Ireland from the Empire, but did not permit its annexation by anyone else, and they divided the devolving power between two Irish states, north and south. And after World War II, the great powers devolved and divided colonial power or military authority in Korea, China, Vietnam, India, Palestine, and Germany. The simultaneous devolution and division of power is what distinguishes partition in these countries from the division of other countries in previous times.[2]

There have been other partitions, but they are not explored here because they were short-lived. Austria, like Germany, was divided after World War II, but it was peacefully reunited as a neutral country in 1955. The Congo was briefly divided into two separate states between 1960 and 1963, as was Nigeria between 1967 and 1970. But both were reunited. The two Yemens may at first appear to be divided states, but they were never united. They emerged as separate states with the same name, more like North and South Dakota than North and South Vietnam. These other countries are not without interest, but considerations of length preclude a detailed treatment in this volume.

Second, an examination of the divided states shows that they share much in common, more than a reading of their separate histories would suggest. In general, they all emerged through a wrenching political process over which they had little control. Put simply, none of the divided states divided itself. Independence movements in these countries participated in the process and may have wittingly or unwittingly contributed to its adoption, but partition could not have occurred without the intervention of great and superpower states.

When the partition of different countries is compared, it is evident that two separate but similar processes were at work. The partition of Ireland, India, and Palestine—all British colonies—proceeded along similar lines. In these countries, Great Britain more or less unilaterally devolved and divided power between indigenous independence movements along ethnic-religious lines. The partition of Germany, Korea, China, and Vietnam developed rather differently. In these countries, the United States and the Soviet Union, frequently in concert with other great states, devolved and divided power between indigenous independence movements along secular, ideological lines. But while the partition process differed in some respects, the consequences were much the same, for partition had extremely disruptive social and political consequences for most, if not all, of the divided states.

In the aftermath of partition, tens of thousands of people crossed Irish borders, hundreds of thousands crossed changing borders in Palestine, millions crossed frontiers in Korea, China, Vietnam, and Germany, and as many as 17 million crossed Indo-Pakistani borders in a migration that was probably the greatest, fastest human relocation ever. Yet, despite these unforeseen migrations, which divided families and dislocated whole economies, huge residual populations remained on the "wrong" side of the border. So, for instance, as many Moslems remained in India as called Pakistan their new home. Those who did not migrate to their assigned country became minorities in their homeland, even though they might have been part of a majority in an undivided state. At the same time, minority populations that assumed state power in divided states became members of ruling majorities.

After partition, newly empowered majorities moved to protect or enlarge their power. The attempt to guarantee continued majority rule typically came at the expense of minority inhabitants. Government officials constructed political and legal systems that restricted the ability of minority populations to select government authorities, observe their religions, or practice their customs. Minorities were frequently subjected to arbitrary military or paramilitary rule. These developments derogated the meaning of citizenship in divided states, and members of disenfranchised groups understandably resisted them. Some sought to reclaim lost rights by force, leading to internecine war within divided states and prompting war between divided states.

At the same time, partition has made it difficult for government officials to exercise sovereign rights and participate as equal members of the interstate system. Sovereign rights have been challenged by sibling states and their superpower allies, hampering the efforts of several divided states to conduct an independent diplomacy. For instance, it has proved difficult for many divided states to obtain entry or maintain their standing in the United Nations. Communist China was denied admission to the UN for more than twenty years, while Taiwan claimed a seat and a veto on the Security Council. And once China was admitted, Taiwan was unseated. The two Germanys joined the UN only in 1973; Vietnam was admitted only after it was forcibly reunited; and the two Koreas have never been permitted to join. Israel was quickly admitted, but it has continually had to fend off challenges to its membership. Government officials in divided states have resented and resisted developments that compromise their sovereignty. Their attempts to assert their sovereignty have resulted in civil war with indigenous populations and interstate war with their neighbors.

The derogation of citizenship and sovereignty created conflicts within and between divided states. The result has been war: irregular and conventional war, civil and interstate war. Since 1945, wars in the divided states have claimed nearly 13 million lives and have directly affected the lives of more than 2 billion people, two-fifths of the world's population.

Because superpower states played important roles in partition and formed alliances with divided states, post-partition conflict has frequently triggered superpower intervention. And when they have intervened, the superpowers have deployed conventional armies and have made nuclear threats to conclude these wars on favorable terms. In time, government officials in many of the divided states concluded that they should acquire nuclear weapons of their own. Proliferation and the *force de frappe*, or independent nuclear force, became the generic response to nuclear threats in divided-state conflicts. Because this proliferation has taken place in a context of ongoing conflict and superpower entanglement, it is an extremely dangerous development.

It would be difficult to analyze partition in each of these countries separately. Not only would such a study take up many volumes, but a case-by-case examination would suggest that each has had a unique history. They have not. The problems of particular divided states are not manifestations of individual maladies that can be understood and treated separately. Rather, their problems are endemic. They must be examined as part of a general phenomenon whose specific symptoms vary.

Still, while this book emphasizes what these countries share in common, there are some important discontinuities that should be mentioned at the outset. Partition emerged as a widespread political practice in the decade after World War II. The partition of Ireland after World War I had taken place nearly thirty years earlier, but despite this temporal hiatus, the partition of Ireland occurred in the same kind of time—immediately following a world war—with Great Britain playing a major role, as it would in several subsequent partitions. To some extent, Ireland was a model for the post-1945 partitions, though by most accounts its use as a model was unconscious.

The history of partition is marked by a second hiatus, between those that occurred after World War II and the division of Pakistan and Cyprus in the early 1970s. A third interlude separates these partitions from those of the contemporary period—Lebanon, Sri Lanka, Ethiopia, and Israel–Palestine—which are gaining momentum. These gaps, however, present no major difficulties for the chronology and will be explained in due course.

For the most part, partition was practiced in territories subject to colonial rule. Ireland, India, and Palestine were British colonies (Palestine was a "mandated territory"). At the end of World War II, Korea was a Japanese colony, much of China had been either annexed as a colony by the Japanese or subject to direct Japanese military rule, and Vietnam was a French colony. When colonial empires and superpower states devolved and divided power in these countries, they turned over their authority to indigenous movements that had been agitating for independence for many years.

Germany, of course, was different in this regard. It was not a colonial possession but a conquered empire, and it was subject, at war's end, to rule by military authorities from four great states. When the United States, Soviet Union, Great Britain, and France devolved and divided power in Germany, they acted not to promote the "independence" of two separate states so much as to diminish German autonomy. Because indigenous independence movements, if they may be called that, were extinguished before or during the war, political authority was transferred to movements that were only organized after the war. For this reason, there is little discussion of German independence movements in the first part of the book, which examines the rise of competing movements in colonial territories.

Developments in Germany differ in another respect. Although the two Germanys have had their share of conflict with each other, they have not themselves engaged in the kind of internecine and interstate wars that characterize other divided states. Conflict between the two Germanys is more an expression of superpower rivalry than it is in other divided states. Still, Germany has experienced many of the same problems that other divided states have. Superpower conflicts that resulted from its partition have periodically threatened world peace. And while the two Germanys, unlike most other divided states, have not waged war with each other, they both spend enormous energy preparing for it and host the largest permanent ready-to-use military encampments in the world. Partition in Germany, moreover, influenced and was itself shaped by the course of partition in Korea, China, and Vietnam. It would be impossible to understand partition in postcolonial Asia without examining its application in Central Europe.

Partition is not everywhere the same. But its expression in different countries is similar enough to warrant a collective treatment of it. The history of partition in some countries has been written, but there is no general treatment of partition as a contemporary global phenomenon. This work does not attempt an exhaustive account, though it does seek to provide an extensive and comprehensive examination.

It would be an act of hubris to claim that any study of partition and divided states could be objective and dispassionate. This is highly charged subject matter and its treatment will probably offend just about anyone who is party to partition. Partition is a subject over which people in divided states cheer, grieve, flee, fight, and die. The separation of family, the division of land, and the death of kin give partition a heightened importance and immediacy. In many countries, people refer to partition as if it occurred yesterday, so vivid is their memory of it. And these memories are fueled by contemporary events, particularly by war. As the Irish mystic and poet George William Russell said, "Great wars are the result of conflicting imaginations,"[3] and in the divided states, imaginations of what was and what might be clash regularly.

When one is attempting to discuss events that touch people so deeply, even simple tasks pose a problem. Take, for example, the names of divided states. The proper name for the state in northern Korea is the Democratic People's Republic of Korea, and the name for the southern state is the Republic of Korea. Although both states consider themselves "republics," neither state admits the other's right to claim that name. What's more, they refuse to recognize each other's legitimacy as a state and therefore deny the other's claim to any name, especially the name Korea. In some divided states, the press uses euphemisms to describe the sibling neighbor. Officials from the People's Republic of China once lodged a diplomatic protest with the Soviet Union simply because a Soviet magazine ran a picture of the flag of the Republic of China, which mainland authorities regard as an illegitimate regime.

In other divided states, the name of the country has changed or its meaning has changed. The Irish independence movement declared the creation of an Irish republic after World War I but named the new, post-partition state the Irish Free State. In 1937 the name was changed to Eire, and in 1949 it was changed again to the Republic of Ireland. Reference to these different names would no doubt add confusion in a book that covers the pre- and post-partition history of Ireland.

Like Ireland, Pakistan changed its name, becoming the Islamic Republic of Pakistan in 1956. But while it has since kept this name, the meaning has changed. Before East Pakistan seceded in 1971, becoming the People's Republic of Bangladesh, the Islamic Republic of Pakistan consisted of two territories, east and west, that were separated by a thousand miles of Indian territory. After 1971, the western territory kept the name the Islamic Republic of Pakistan, even though it no longer referred to the same territory.

It is difficult to sort through this mine field of politically charged names because the very definitions of "nation" and "state" are at issue in divided states. At stake is the meaning of citizenship and of sovereignty for people in different states. As a practical matter, it would be difficult to sort through changing, sharply contested names and present them clearly to an audience unfamiliar with the political baggage that names carry. For these reasons, this book adopts a generic approach to the naming of divided states. Throughout the text, reference will be made to the geographic location of divided states— North and South Korea, North and South Vietnam, East and West Germany, Northern Ireland and Ireland—or their commonplace English names: China and Taiwan, India and Pakistan. Palestine presents a particular problem. Before partition, it will be referred to as Palestine. After partition, it will be called either Israel, which refers to territory amalgamated into the Jewish state after the cease-fire of 1949, or Israeli-occupied Palestine, to describe the areas controlled but not annexed by Israel since 1967 (the West Bank and the Gaza Strip). Admittedly, these choices will be unsatisfactory for some people, but they may be less offensive and more readily recognizable than another system. The idea is to acknowledge that the definition of nation and state, of citizenship and sovereignty, is a contentious issue and, at the same time, to provide a way to move on to other issues.

Two kinds of explanations are usually given when conflict erupts in divided states. In former British colonies, conflicts are usually described as the product of centuries-old struggles between implacable indigenous enemies. Writing in *The New York Times* about the "roots of conflict" in the Middle East, Marc Charney argued: "In the West Bank, Gaza and Jerusalem, the conflict between Israeli and Palestinian is being shaped by a fratricidal agony: competing, centuries-old claims to the same precious strip of land between the Jordan River and the Mediterranean, and the right to exist there as a nation. The rivalry is as old as the conflict between Moslem and Jew for the legacy of their common father Abraham."[4]

A rather different explanation is usually given for divided-state conflict in Asia and Central Europe. There, conflict is seen through a Cold War prism and events are treated as an expression of superpower rivalry, with indigenous actors as surrogates for their superpower allies. In 1950, Dean Rusk, who participated in the partition of Korea and Vietnam, told the U.S. Senate Foreign Relations Committee that the war then raging between the French and Vietminh in Indochina was not simply a local contest: "This is a civil war that has been in effect captured by the [Soviet] Politburo and, besides, has been turned into a tool of the Politburo. So it isn't a civil war in the usual sense. It is part of an international war. . . . We have to look at it in terms of which side we are on in this particular kind of struggle."[5]

Both kinds of explanation are fundamentally mistaken.

If conflict in Ireland, India–Pakistan, and Israel–Palestine were the product of centuries-old feuds, then there would be little or nothing contemporary political actors could do to settle them. Given the protracted and obdurate character of violence in these countries, this explanation is understandable, but it is also deeply cynical and historically inaccurate.

Conflict in ethnically divided states has contemporary roots. As we shall see, independence movements that organized Catholic and Protestant, Hindu and Moslem, Arab and Jew emerged only in the late nineteenth century. These movements sought to become independent from the British Empire and assume power in sovereign states, not to conduct feuds and settle ethnic vendettas stretching back centuries. The attempt to achieve independence would subsequently bring different independence movements into competition and conflict with each other, usually as the prospect of independence drew near, but this struggle is a relatively recent development. The conflict between the Indian National Congress and the Muslim League, both allied against the British for many years, emerged only in the late 1930s. It does not date back to the arrival of Moslem armies in India in 1192. Much the same is true for movements in Palestine and Ireland.

Because these conflicts have recent origins—dating back decades, not centuries—they *are* subject to change by contemporary political actors. The attempt to shrug them off as implacable feuds obscures their roots and cripples any attempt to address their differences constructively. The ahistorical cynicism that is prevalent in the literature on divided states produces questions but not answers. Whole books are written about the Irish Question or the Palestinian Question. But in them the question is rhetorical, because no answer usually follows. This approach leads to a dismissal of the problem as insoluble, in the same vein as British Prime Minister Lord Palmerston's cynical comment on the Schleswig-Holstein Question: "Only three people ever understood it. One died, one went mad, and I've forgotten."[6]

The description of divided-state conflict in East Asia and Germany is given to a different kind of ahistorical cynicism. It imagines, for example, that the Vietminh, which Rusk described as a "tool of the Politburo," would fight completely at its superpower ally's behest. The idea that indigenous independence movements in Korea, China, or Vietnam would fight bitterly, sometimes for decades, on behalf of foreigners is a conceit. It is difficult enough for movements or states to persuade their citizens to fight and die for their own cause, their own country, much less for the geopolitical goals of another country. Although the superpowers played important roles in post-partition conflict, independence movements and state officials are not mere superpower mercenaries. They have their own differences to settle.

Nor can conflict be understood simply as a product of the Cold War. Throughout this period, the superpowers frequently sought geopolitical accommodations with each other that worked to the detriment of their own allies. This kind of behavior cast a very different light on contemporary conflict. Divided states have not been particularly amenable to superpower control. Their relative autonomy from superpower control makes the conflict between them simultaneously more and less dangerous. Because they are relatively autonomous, they are more likely to wage regional wars on their own. But because they do so on their own initiative, these conflicts are less likely to provoke the kind of superpower confrontation that could lead to global war.

Taken together, conflicts in divided states are neither expressions of centuries-old animosities nor manifestations of Cold War machinations. Indigenous and exogenous political forces contribute to conflict, but they do not always act in expected ways. And while conflict within and between divided states is obdurate and protracted, it is also subject to change.

In analyzing the historical framework that has given rise to such persistent conflict, I have divided this book into three parts. "The Background to Partition" examines organizational and ideological developments that preceded and set the stage for partition, from the end of the nineteenth century to 1945. "Devolution and Division" looks at the process of partition in the aftermath of world war. And "The Legacy of Partition" analyzes the consequences of partition in the contemporary world, including a brief account of partition's re-emergence in the 1970s and 1980s.

In the years prior to partition, two sets of political actors emerged that would participate in the partition process. Within countries that would be divided, political parties organized mass movements that demanded "independence." At the same time, officials in great and superpower states began promoting "dominion" or "self-determination" as a way to devolve power and secure their own interests. Leaders of independence movements and officials in powerful states had different ideas about how power would devolve and to whom. The clash between and within these groups would set the terms of partition.

The first part of the book will examine these groups, their politics, and the events that led to partition. Chapters 1 and 2 will explore the social origins and political aims of movements that demanded independence and vied for popular support and political power. The different movements that emerged shared a common political approach. They adopted a simultaneously cosmopolitan and parochial political orientation and used modern and traditional methods to achieve a contemporary goal: state power.

Chapters 3, 4, and 5 examine the strategies developed by powerful states to address the challenges posed by independence movements. Two rather different strategies emerged: leaders in the United States and the Soviet Union advanced "self-determination" as a way to promote the devolution of power to independence movements and the creation of new nation-states, while officials in the British and French Empires argued that devolution should take place within the context of empire and result in what they called "dominion" or "union." After World War II, the rise of the United States and the Soviet Union as global superpowers resulted in the adoption of their devolution strategies and the creation of a new interstate system to which newly divided states would belong.

The devolution and division of political power is analyzed in the second part of the book. The partition of British colonies—Ireland, India, and Palestine—along ethnic-religious lines is treated in Chapters 6 and 7. The ideological partition of Germany, Korea, China, and Vietnam by the United States and the Soviet Union is examined in Chapter 8.

Although the course of partition differed, its results were much the same. The third part of the book examines the various social and political consequences of partition. Chapter 9 surveys the immense social dislocations and political repercussions that resulted from partition. In most of the divided states, political institutions emerged that disenfranchised minority populations and compromised the meaning of citizenship and democracy. Chapter 10 reviews the ways in which the sovereignty of divided states was abridged by partition.

These developments contributed to social conflict and war within and between divided states. The emergence of civil and interstate war, of irregular and conventional war, and of nuclear threats and the proliferation of nuclear weapons is examined in Chapter 11.

The organization of second-generation independence movements and the partition of Pakistan and Cyprus in the early 1970s is examined in Chapter 12. This chapter also includes a discussion of partition in the contemporary period and in the near future, in Lebanon, Sri Lanka, and Israel–Palestine.

Finally, Chapter 13 explores the lessons of partition and possible alternatives to it.

Partition corrupted the meaning of citizenship and sovereignty in divided states. It also corrupted the meaning of independence and frustrated the aspirations of movements that sought to wrest power from colonial and military authorities. It is appropriate, therefore, to begin with the independence movements, whose ideologies and strategies would subsequently clash with those of rival movements and with those of great and superpower states. For the independence movements, partition would simultaneously realize their best hopes—the devolution of power—and their worst fears—the division of power.

· I ·

THE BACKGROUND
TO PARTITION

· 1 ·

The Independence Movements

Ho Chi Minh, like the leaders of independence movements in Korea, China, India, Palestine, and Ireland, was a "nationalist." He celebrated the history, language, and culture of the people living in Vietnam and argued that because they constituted a "nation" they should be accorded the same rights as other nations—particularly the right to form representative institutions to govern their own state, which would become a full-fledged member of an interstate system composed of "nation-states."

But Ho Chi Minh did not discover his nationalism at home. He found it abroad.

In 1911, at the age of twenty-one, Ho left Vietnam as a cabin boy on a French freighter. His work as a seaman took him to Europe, Africa, and the United States, where he labored as a gardener. For a time he washed dishes and shoveled snow in London before moving to Paris, where he worked as a pastry chef and photographer. He burst onto the political scene in 1919, when he petitioned Woodrow Wilson, who was then presiding over the Peace Conference in Paris, asking him to assist the creation of a constitutional government, democratic freedoms, and other reforms in Vietnam.[1]

Issued in France, Ho's appeal made him a hero among fellow Vietnamese expatriates there and brought him to the attention of French socialists, who asked him to attend their party's 1920 congress in Tours. Wearing a hired suit and standing amid a crowd of mustachioed socialists, Ho took the opportunity to denounce French imperialism and to ask the socialists to "support the oppressed natives" in Vietnam.[2]

Debate at the congress focused on whether the French Socialist Party should dissolve its association with the Second (Socialist) International and join the Third (Communist) International, which had been formed the previous year by Bolshevik revolutionaries in Russia. During the debate, Ho wanted to know the answer to only one question: Which International sided with the peoples of colonial countries? After listening to the debate and reading Lenin's *Thesis on the National and Colonial Questions*, Ho decided that the cause of Vietnamese independence would be better served by Lenin's followers, and he voted with the majority of delegates to affiliate with the Third International.[3]

In many ways, Ho discovered his "nationalism" or the "path to [Vietnamese] liberation" in Tours, France, not in his home province of Nghe An. During his extensive travels, before and after the congress at Tours, Ho met people, learned languages, and developed ideas that he would not have acquired if he had stayed in Vietnam. He read Shakespeare, Zola, Dickens, and Hugo; learned English, French, Russian, three Chinese dialects, and Siamese; consorted with Fabians, anarcho-syndicalists, Vietnamese expatriates, socialists, French literati, Indian, Chinese, and Indonesian nationalists, and Russian and Chinese Communists.

These experiences shaped Ho's approach to the problem of Vietnamese independence and gave to the movement he organized a cosmopolitan character. He acted as an importer of ideas and organizational strategies from abroad. Of colonialist France, Ho once said, "It is a strange country. It is a breeding ground of admirable ideas, but when it travels, it does not export them."[4] Ho, the peripatetic organizer, would himself be the importer of "admirable ideas" from France and other countries.

The leaders of independence movements in other countries would play a similar role. By importing worldly, cosmopolitan ideas into their countries, they organized movements capable of mobilizing the masses and winning state power from colonial administrators. Cosmopolitan ideologies would supply both organizational methods and political goals for these independence movements.

Cosmopolitan ideas were typically imported by cadre in the leadership of independence movements. Traveling abroad, they studied European and American ideas, attached themselves to "international" movements, and drew support from expatriate communities. Like passengers carrying steamer trunks covered with stickers from exotic ports of call, movement leaders returning home carried baggage full of illicit ideas and international connections. Unpacked in an indigenous setting, these cosmopolitan ideas then shaped and informed the development of independence movements.

For Ho Chi Minh, the path to Vietnamese liberation would lead in the early 1920s through Moscow, and then China, where he worked as a translator for Mikhail Borodin, the Comintern's representative to the Chinese Communist and Nationalist Parties. He returned to Vietnam briefly, but spent much of the 1920s and 1930s shuttling to Hong Kong (where he was reported to have died), to China (where he was imprisoned for two years), to Moscow (where he worked with the Comintern), and to Europe (where he met independence-movement leaders like Madame Sun Yat-sen, Jawaharlal Nehru, and Mohammad Hatta, an Indonesian nationalist who would become Prime Minister of that country in 1948).[5] Ho said of his role as political tourist: "I have always thought I would become a scholar or a writer, but I've become a professional revolutionary. I travel through many countries, but I see nothing. I'm on strict orders and my itinerary is carefully prescribed, and you cannot deviate from the route, can you?"[6]

Ho's political passport was impressed with the stamp of diverse political ideologies: the democratic ideas of Abraham Lincoln and Woodrow Wilson,[7] the socialism of French workers, and the revolutionary Communism of Lenin and the Third International. When he announced the foundation of the Vietnamese republic on September 2, 1945, Ho paraphrased the American Declaration of Independence: "We hold the truth that all men are created equal. They are endowed by the Creator with certain inalienable rights; among these are life, liberty and the pursuit of happiness."[8] At the same time, Ho attributed many of his ideas to socialist sources. "When drinking water, remember its source," he told a Vietnamese audience in the 1950s. "With gratitude to the Soviet Union, our party and people have always believed that they must make every effort to fulfill their tasks regarding the nation and fulfill their international obligation to the peoples of other countries."[9]

Ho's journeys left a lasting impression on him and his country, and the same was true for other anti-colonial activists. The leaders of independence movements in Korea, China, India, Palestine, and Ireland were, like Ho, a well-traveled group. Their journeys not only afforded them opportunities to study the source of oppression firsthand but also introduced them to revolutionary ideas. New contacts with expatriate communities also provided important financial and political aid that could then be imported into the "home" country.

Syngman Rhee, who led one of the Korean independence movements in exile and later became South Korea's first President, was introduced to cosmopolitan ideas by U.S. missionaries, who converted him to Christianity and helped him journey to the United States after he had been imprisoned for his opposition to Japanese colonialism in Korea. Rhee's studies at American University and at Princeton introduced him to liberal democratic thought and Wilsonian internationalism. Whereas the Third International assisted Ho's travels, the Young Men's Christian Association (YMCA) helped Rhee return to Korea in the 1920s to organize the anti-colonial movement and then obtained his release from custody after he was arrested for subversive activities. In the Korean context, the YMCA was no less a subversive international organization than the Third International. Colonial administrators viewed them as equal threats to Japanese rule.[10] Rhee then returned to the United States until the end of World War II, organizing Korean expatriates and hounding State Department officials as a "Minister Plenipotentiary" of a Korean government in exile.[11]

While Rhee's travels took him to the United States, Kim Il Sung, the first Premier of North Korea, traveled to China and the Soviet Union, where he was introduced to Communist, as opposed to Christian, internationalism. There he participated in movements against Japanese colonialism and returned to Korea during World War II as a guerrilla leader.

In China, two independence movements emerged in the 1920s. But while Nationalist and Communist movements competed for political power, their leaders traveled in similar circles and drew ideas from similar sources. Nationalist leader Chiang Kai-shek and Communist leader Mao Tse-tung were both introduced to cosmopolitan ideologies by Sun Yat-sen, a revolutionary who spoke English, studied Western medicine, traveled extensively abroad, and returned to China promoting nationalism, democracy, and the non-Marxist socialism of American economist Henry George.[12] Both Mao and Chiang traveled to the Soviet Union and employed Soviet political and military advisers during the interwar years. Although the two men did not themselves sojourn extensively abroad and did not master other languages, as did so many other contemporary independence-movement leaders, their colleagues and relatives did. Mao's right-hand man, Chou En-lai, like Ho Chi Minh, studied in France; Chiang's wife, Mayling Soong, was the U.S.-educated daughter of a Christian Shanghai banking family; and Chiang's son, who would succeed him as President of Taiwan, spent twelve years studying in the Soviet Union. As a result, notes John King Fairbank, Chiang developed an eclectic ideology drawn from diverse cosmopolitan sources: "Tseng Kuo-Fan's view of moral purpose . . . Lenin's interpretation of imperialism, the Methodist piety of a practicing Christian, influences from Japan, Russia, America and the Axis powers, all within the framework of a conservative nationalism."[13]

While leaders in East Asian countries infused independence movements with Communist and Christian ideologies (Ho's anti-Communist counterpart, Ngo Dinh Diem, studied Catholic theology in the United States and France), leaders in South Asia and the Middle East imported secular legal and scientific traditions.

The leadership of Indian independence movements—Mahatma Gandhi, Jawaharlal Nehru, and Muhammad Ali Jinnah—all went to England for their education. There, Gandhi and Jinnah studied and practiced law, an endeavor that shaped their subsequent anti-colonial activity in India. Although the jurisprudence practiced in British courts is not usually thought of as a cosmopolitan ideology like nationalism or socialism, it was one of the principal ideological exports of the British Empire. For Gandhi and Jinnah, jurisprudence was their International. Their work as barristers—Gandhi spent twenty-one years in British South Africa organizing and representing a nonviolent movement that resisted unjust racial laws—probably explains why the movements they organized in India refrained from "extralegal" activity, such as riot or rebellion, and restricted themselves to "illegal" agitations, for which they accepted punishment by British courts. They challenged particular laws, but not the rule of law. Indeed, the devolution of British power in India was remarkably legalistic. British officials and independence movements spent considerable energy on "constitutional" questions, proposing legal and administrative structures that could accommodate the movements' political demands and also retain order.[14]

Science, like law, is another grand cosmopolitan ideology. For Chaim Weizmann, the leader of the Zionist movement after the death of its founder, Theodor Herzl, science was an important reference. A chemist by profession, Weizmann suggests in his autobiography, *Trial and Error*, that the Zionist political experiment was subject to the same scientific laws that governed his work in the laboratory. He promoted Jewish immigration to Palestine on the grounds that it contributed to the scientific, intellectual, and industrial development of the region, and he consistently downplayed the mystical, religious, and emotional reasons for establishing a Jewish state in Palestine.[15]

Like most other independence movements in this period, Zionism discovered its nationalism abroad, in Europe and in American Jewish communities and intellectual circles (where diverse cosmopolitan ideologies flourished), and not in Palestine, its eventual "homeland." The Arab Palestinian movement, which emerged somewhat later, mobilized through pan-Arabic independence movements and through the British-based "youth international"—the Boy Scouts.[16]

Like Weizmann, Eamon De Valera, the leader of Ireland's Sinn Fein movement, had a scientific bent and taught mathematics before he picked up a gun, drilled with the Irish Volunteers, and joined the 1916 Easter Rebellion. De Valera, who would be Prime Minister of Ireland for twenty-one years and President for fourteen more, was an expatriate by birth. The fact that he was born in New York and could claim U.S. citizenship saved him from a British firing squad after the rebellion and made it possible for him to fund-raise effectively in Irish communities in America. But like other leaders, he took pains to disassociate himself from his foreign roots and he denied that he was anything but Irish. When criticized in a parliamentary debate for being less than Irish, he replied, "My mother and father were married in a Catholic church. . . . I was baptized in a Catholic church. I was brought up in a Catholic home. I have lived amongst the Irish people and loved them and every blade of grass in this land. I do not care who says, or who tries to pretend that I am not Irish."[17]

Although cosmopolitan ideologies were essential to independence movements, leaders of these movements insisted that they were home-grown rebels, not foreign-influenced agents, and understood that the success of their movements depended on their ability to translate these ideas into an indigenous vernacular. As the historian Tom Nairn observes, "The middle-class intelligentsia of nationalism had to invite the masses into history, and the invitation card had to be written in a language they understood."[18]

De Valera thus made his case before the Irish parliament by emphasizing his Catholicness—Catholic parents, baptism, home, and country—even though, by his own account, he was not a religious man. This practice may at first seem disingenuous, but it should be seen more as a translation of cosmopolitan values into a local idiom that could be widely understood than as an attempt to fabricate or deceive. All the independence movements sought to translate cosmopolitan ideas, values, and languages into vernaculars that could be understood by indigenous populations and used to mobilize them.

Cosmopolitan ideas like independence and self-determination had to be translated into ideas that could be understood in city and hamlet. Whereas self-determination had a commonly understood, universal meaning in cosmopolitan circles, its parochial rendition often had different meanings, inflections, and nuances. When the leaders of these movements addressed colonial administrators, petitioned great-war victors, and courted world opinion, they spoke of "independence" or demanded the right to "self-determination," a term coined by Lenin and Woodrow Wilson during World War I. "Independence" and "self-determination" were words that administrators, statesmen, and the media the world over could understand. But because these terms originated from European and American usage, they had to be translated into a local vernacular. At the Indochinese Communist Party's 1935 congress, for example, a resolution reminded party members "of their task of explaining to the Vietnamese masses and to the national minorities the important significance of the watchword 'self-determination' and of close unity against the imperialists. The Communist Party recognizes the right of all nationalities to full liberty. It opposes all colonial systems and all forms of oppression and exploitation . . . of one nationality by another."[19]

Thus, when speaking to an indigenous audience, leaders of independence movements used words that drew on commonplace metaphors that could be grasped easily by literate and illiterate people alike. In the countryside, leaders typically likened independence to everyday processes that could be easily visualized. Instead of trying to explain that independence meant the devolution of foreign political power to indigenous successors and the creation of a sovereign nation-state—a difficult, abstract set of concepts—leaders described it as a process of waking from a deep sleep, standing up on one's own two feet, or being swept off one's feet.

For most movements, independence was an "awakening" from a colonial-induced stupor. Leaders of these movements set for themselves the task of rousing the masses from their slumber, what Vietnamese Communist Party historians call the "long night of slavery."[20] Thanh Nien, the Vietnamese Revolutionary Youth Association (founded by Ho Chi Minh in 1925), circulated pamphlets warning that "if the Vietnamese people continued in their deep slumber" they would be destroyed, and calling upon the populace to "wake up" (*thuc tinh*) and fight the French colonialists.[21] Later the Indochinese Communist Party resolved "to employ an especially stirring method of appeal to awaken the traditional nationalism in the people."[22]

Communist and non-Communist movements alike used this imagery to press for independence. Arabs meeting in Cairo in 1914 issued a manifesto that sought to awaken the masses: "O Sons of Qahtan! . . . Are you asleep? And how long will you remain asleep? How can you remain deep in your slumber when the voices of nations around you have deafened everyone? Do you not hear the commotion all around you? Do you not know that you live in a period when he who sleeps dies, and he who dies is gone forever? When will you open your eyes and see the glitter of the bayonets which are directed at you . . . ? Arise, O ye Arabs! Unsheathe the sword from the scabbard . . . !"[23]

Compare this to a speech given three years later by Annie Besant at an All-Indian Congress committee meeting in April 1916. "I quite realize that when people are asleep," she said, "they do not like the tomtom that goes on all the night through, beating and beating and never stopping. I am an Indian tomtom, waking up all the sleepers so that they may wake and work for their Motherland. That is my task. And they are waking on every side, and the young ones, even more than the old ones, are waking to the possibilities that lie before them."[24]

Colonial administrators often used the same language, though for them the prospect of independence was itself a nightmare. The British political economist Nassau Senior wrote of Ireland in 1843: "When the Irish questions, or when the Irish Question (for there is but one), has been forced on our attention, we have felt, like a dreamer in a nightmare, oppressed by the consciousness that some great evil was rapidly advancing—that mere exertion on our part would avert it, but that we had not the power to will that exertion."[25]

After rousing the masses from their slumber, their leaders then tried to get them to stand up for themselves. The image of standing up for oneself and one's country is common to most independence movements throughout history. (In the United States, people stand to recite the pledge of allegiance or to sing the national anthem.) In 1897, one Indian propagandist argued: "What we want is strength. . . . We have wept long enough. No more weeping, but stand on your two feet and be men."[26] Similarly, when Ho Chi Minh announced the foundation of the Vietnamese republic, he used the term *doc lap*, which means "to stand alone," to describe what had taken place.[27] And in "The Coming of the Fenians," the Irish poet Douglas Hyde described the implication of a collective "standing up" for independence:

> There is a big change coming, a big change!
> And riches and store will be worth nothing;
> He will rise up that was small enough,
> And he that was big will fall down.[28]

Independence quickly came to be associated with a rising, in the sense of a collective "standing up" or an "uprising," as in a revolt to overthrow the existing government. In his description of the "Quit India" agitation of 1921–22, Jawaharlal Nehru captures both meanings: "The extraordinary stiffening-up of the masses . . . filled us [the Congress leadership] with confidence. A demoralized, backward and broken-up people suddenly straightened their backs and lifted their heads and took part in a disciplined, joint action on a countrywide scale."[29]

The Korean expression *sinparam* provides another evocative gloss on the vernacular meaning of independence. As the Korean writer Chong Kyong-mo explains, the word *sinparam* "expresses the pathos, the inner joy, of a person moved to action not by coercion but by his own volition. *Param* is the sound of the wind; if a person is wafted along on this wind, songs burst from his lips and his legs dance with joy. A *sinparam* is a strange wind that billows in the hearts of people who have freed themselves from oppression, regained their freedom, and live in a society of mutual trust. This word, redolent with a shamanistic mystique, has a talisman-like appeal for Koreans."[30]

The "wind" of independence blew across other countries as well. In his autobiography, Nehru says that in 1921–22 "*Swaraj* [which he describes as "national freedom"] was very much in the air and in people's thoughts."[31] And he describes the political situation this way: "There was still thunder in the air, and the atmosphere was tense and pregnant with revolutionary possibilities."[32]

Social movements seeking "independence" gave two kinds of meaning to their goal. They used the term "independence" to demand the devolution of state power from London, Paris, or Tokyo. And they used terms like *doc lap, swaraj,* and *sinparam* to mobilize the inhabitants of village, hamlet, and town. By making this two-sided or "Janus-faced" appeal, independence movement organizers hoped to create a community of people that could join the global community of nation-states as an equal member and, at the same time, divorce themselves from it and set up a separate state.[33]

Organizers of independence movements had to be politically bilingual. The language they spoke had to be understood in both London and Bhiwandi, Washington and Kyongju, Moscow and Pingxiang, Paris and Nghi Loc. To be understood in the provinces, to make headway among urban and rural masses, independence movements issued appeals to parochial religious, ethnic, linguistic, cultural, and customary identities. After insisting that these parochial characteristics make the inhabitants of one nation different from all others, movement organizers then argued that they were similar to other "nations" who were "different in the same way." The insistence on the separate, parochial characteristics of a group of people was essential to support the claim to self-government.

To mobilize rural and urban masses, independence movements spoke local languages and steeped themselves in parochial traditions and social conventions. To appeal to illiterate peasants in rural India, Indian National Congress leaders donned Nehru jackets or loincloths, spoke in dialect, placed a symbol of the cow—an animal venerated by Hindus—on election ballots to identify party candidates, and affixed a rendering of the multi-spoke Indian handloom to their flag.[34]

At the local level, independence movements in British colonies— Ireland, India, Palestine, Cyprus—tended to have a strong religious-ethnic character at the parochial level (Protestant and Catholic Irish, Hindu and Moslem Indians, Jewish Zionists and Moslem Arabs, Christian Greeks and Moslem Turks), while movements in East

Asia—in Korea, China, and Vietnam—were organized on a more "secular, ideological" basis, though the religious element was not absent (Rhee, Chiang, and Diem saw themselves as Christians fighting a war against an "atheistic religion"—Communism). But all these movements were very much alike in their cosmopolitan parochialism.

By using existing parochial languages to mobilize indigenous support, the movements transformed the meaning of language, religion, and ethnicity for their peoples. Because a particular group of people have long spoken a language, practiced a religion, or married people with similar physical characteristics, their group identity is often regarded as permanent. Independence movements encouraged this interpretation because they wanted their followers to think of themselves in the same way—as having existed together as a long-standing cultural-linguistic-religious-ethnic-national unit.

But in fact, these characteristics and social categories change all the time. And the movements' attempts to use them to mobilize support for independence changed them further. Contemporary "Indians," inhabitants of the subcontinent, can no more understand ancient Sanskrit than untutored English schoolchildren can understand the Middle English of Chaucer. Until the introduction of print media in the eighteenth and nineteenth centuries, which "standardized" regional languages that had previously been spoken in diverse dialects, Indians in one part of the subcontinent could not understand the languages spoken in a neighboring province.

In China, the "standardization" of the Chinese language was a conscious political program. Both Nationalist and Communist movements sought to change the way Chinese was written. The classical written form, which was developed in 200 B.C. and is still used by scholars and administrators, does not correspond to the language spoken by inhabitants of China in the twentieth century. So, as John King Fairbank notes, independence movements "advocated the use of pai-hua or Chinese spoken language as a medium for scholarship and all purposes of communication."[35]

Much the same is true of religion. Although contemporary Irish Catholics practice the same "faith" as Spanish Catholics of the sixteenth century, it could hardly be said to have the same "meaning" for Irish volunteers as it had for the "praying, preying conquistadors."[36] For the conquistadors, Catholicism served to justify the proselytization, conversion, or extermination of the unfaithful. For contemporary Irish revolutionaries, Catholicism was used to rally the already faithful. They made no attempt to convert Irish Protestants. The Irish independence movement bent Catholicism to a different purpose and changed its meaning in the process.

Similarly, the Zionist movement changed the meaning of Jewishness. Zionist leaders argued that contemporary Zionism and historical Judaism are coterminous. As Chaim Weizmann said, "The obstinacy and persistence of the movement cannot be understood except in terms of faith. This faith was part of our make-up; our Jewishness and our Zionism were interchangeable; you could not destroy the second without destroying the first."[37] Yet prior to the late nineteenth century, the goal of establishing and maintaining a state for a Jewish nation in Palestine was not one of the characteristics used by Jews or Gentiles to define what it meant to be Jewish. Quite the opposite. Many Jews, particularly Orthodox Jews in Central and Eastern Europe, opposed the inclusion of this "secular" goal into the definition of Jewishness. Walter Laqueur notes that when Herzl's *Der Judenstaat* appeared, Vienna's chief rabbi, Moritz Gudemann, attacked Herzl "in a pamphlet in which he protested against the 'Kuckucksei of Jewish nationalism,' maintaining that Jews were not a nation, that they had in common only their belief in God, and that Zionism was incompatible with the teachings of Judaism."[38]

In recent decades, however, the Zionist movement has argued fairly successfully that its secular goal—the creation of an Israeli state for the Jewish people—has become part of what it means to be Jewish. But as critics in the Jewish community make clear, this has not always been the case, and the definition of what it means to be a Jew is not immutable or uncontested.[39] Despite Weizmann's claim, the Zionist movement is itself responsible for changing the meaning of Jewishness. By grafting cosmopolitan ideas onto parochial religious stock, it has changed the meaning of religion and ethnicity for Jews around the world.

The movements that emerged to demand independence from colonial empires constructed a cosmopolitan and parochial politics to advance their cause at home and abroad. Expanding on this dual approach, these movements sought to use history to their advantage as well. Because the independence movements were new political constructions, the oldest dating back only to 1885, their leaders sought to legitimize their claim to rule by simultaneously claiming to represent past traditions and future goals. They argued that their youth should not prevent them from assuming power, and to demonstrate their maturity, they presented themselves as the heirs of long-standing political traditions. But because they also wanted to break with the past, which was associated with a slumbering colonialism, and rouse the masses, they adopted modern political conventions and promised to practice a new kind of government in the future.

· 2 ·

The Uses of History

The emergence of nationalist independence movements is a recent development. Indeed, the idea of "nation" is relatively new, born in the late eighteenth century. Benedict Anderson argues that its birthday should be regarded as 1787, when delegates to the U.S. Constitutional Convention drew up a document "which was meant to 'constitute' a wholly novel sovereign polity, the Republic of the United States of America."[1]

On the eve of partition, the independence movements that took power were really quite young. The oldest political organization, the Indian National Congress, sixty years old at the end of World War II, was founded in 1885. But even this age must be qualified. For its first twenty years, the Congress promised "unswerving loyalty to the British Crown."[2] The All-India Muslim League, the main rival of the Congress, was founded in 1906. But the League, which was created by Islamic princes and nobles "to foster a sense of loyalty to the British government among the Muslims of India," would not become an independence movement until the 1930s. Prior to that, independence-minded Moslems joined the Congress Party.[3]

The Zionist movement got underway in 1896 with the publication of Herzl's *Der Judenstaat*, though some Jewish intellectuals and rabbinical scholars had advocated the creation of a Jewish state prior to the publication of Herzl's book. The first Arab National Congress, which contained Palestinian elements, met for the first time in Paris in 1913. (Like the Muslim League, however, it was for some time more a political action committee for princes and notables than a mass political movement.)

In 1905 Arthur Griffith organized a non-violent movement for Home Rule in Ireland and called it Sinn Fein (Gaelic for "Ourselves"). Irish Protestants began organizing in the same period and in 1912 "signed a Solemn League and Covenant binding Irish Unionists to resist Home Rule with every means at their disposal."[4] Irish Unionists, who wanted continued "dependence" on Great Britain, cannot really be described as an independence movement, though they did shape the course of Irish "independence."

The 1917 Russian Revolution provided the impetus for the formation of independence movements in Korea, China, and Vietnam. Meeting at a YMCA in Tokyo in 1919, a group of Korean students began organizing the first *mansei*, or "long live Korea," demonstrations against Japanese colonial rule. A number of independence movements grew out of the subsequent wave of Korean protests in March 1919.[5] At about the same time, in Manchuria, the All-Korean Communist Party was formed. This group grew out of the Korean Socialist Party (founded in 1918) and would become the Korean Communist Party in 1925.[6] The Chinese Communist Party was founded in 1921, and Sun Yat-sen's reorganized Nationalist Party was launched with help from the Communist International (Comintern) a year later. And in Vietnam, Ho Chi Minh organized Thanh Nien, the Revolutionary Youth Association, in 1925; but Vietnamese Communists celebrate his founding of the Indochinese Communist Party in 1930 as their movement's birthday.

Independence movements regularly enlist the past to serve the present and to construct a future in which they can play a major role. In India, the discovery of an Indian past occurred at the same time that political activists were searching for an all-Indian future. In the late nineteenth and early twentieth centuries, European scholars began to translate ancient Indian literature and to write histories about pre-colonial Indian civilizations based on archaeological evidence. Indian scholars and activists immediately began comparing ancient

Hindu scribes and civilizations to European societies. During the course of this evaluation, one scholar observed, "Kalidasa, the great Sanskrit dramatist, was first hailed [by Indian activists] as the Shakespeare of India; later when the Hindu renaissance became more aggressive, Shakespeare was called the Kalidasa of Britain."[7]

The Indian National Congress immediately seized upon evidence of India's past greatness to make the case that a people with such a glorious past deserved a great future. Congress leader Annie Besant reminded audiences, "You must remember that 3,000 years before the time of Christ, India was great in her commerce, great in her trade. . . . You have no need to be ashamed of India's past, no need to be ashamed of being born an Indian. There is no living country in the world with such a past, no country that can look forward to such a future. For the value of the past is that it shows you how to build a future . . . the value of the past is to remind you of what you are; the value of the past is to awaken self-respect; the value of the past is to *make* that feeling of national pride, without which no nation can be, and no national greatness can accrue."[8] An inhabitant of "India" in 1916 is treated as being a member of the same "India" that existed some three thousand years before Christ. Five thousand years of history between Sanskrit and British India leaves "India" and its inhabitants more or less unchanged. Besant treats this condensation of history as if it were unremarkable and regards the British colonial intermission (from 1765 to the time of her speech in 1916) as inconsequential. What is 150 years of British colonial rule, she asked, "in the 5,000 years . . . of Indian greatness, Indian wealth and Indian culture?"[9]

She also passes over the period of Moslem rule (1192 to 1765) without comment, not stopping to consider whether Moslem invaders were as Indian as the people they conquered. And while arguing that the contemporary Indian is born to be a member of this great historical family, she admits that "national pride" has to be "made" with the help of the past. Again, the "awakening" metaphor is instructive. Besant assumed that the body politic had a prior, wakeful existence, which, after a Rip Van Winkle–like, 5,000-year sleep, needed only to be roused by the Congress.[10]

The historical imagery of the Indian National Congress is found in other independence movements as well. Herzl's *Der Judenstaat*, which launched the contemporary Zionist movement, used the same kind of language to argue that contemporary Jews and ancient Jews belonged to one and the same nation: "The Maccabees [of biblical times] will rise again. We shall live at last [as we did before] as free men on our own soil, and in our own homes peacefully die."[11]

This trans-historical identity was used to rouse the masses and to impress colonial administrators with the legitimacy of a movement's claim for independence. In 1906, Chaim Weizmann, Herzl's successor as the leader of the Zionist movement, met with British Conservative Party leader Arthur James Balfour. Balfour had suggested to Herzl that the British government might find a homeland for the Jews in Uganda, a proposal that Weizmann had rejected in Zionist congresses.[12] Balfour asked Weizmann why this offer had been so bitterly opposed. Weizmann replied, "Mr. Balfour, supposing I were to offer you Paris instead of London, would you take it?"

Balfour sat up in his chair, looked at Weizmann, and answered: "But Dr. Weizmann, we have London."

"That is true," rejoined Weizmann, "but we had Jerusalem when London was a marsh."[13]

What is remarkable about this exchange is that Weizmann's remark, "we had Jerusalem when London was a marsh," assumes that Jerusalem belonged to the same "we." Weizmann's assumption that contemporary Zionists were synonymous with pre-Diaspora Jews was accepted without comment by Balfour. Yet many Jewish contemporaries of Weizmann would quarrel with his claim that Zionists were the legitimate heirs and executors of a Jewish legacy that included title to Jerusalem.

Weizmann's attempt to identify a contemporary movement with an ancient people, despite the many centuries that separated them, is not unique. Almost all independence movements attempt to establish legitimacy by tracing their genealogy back to an antique, more glorious past. Legitimacy for contemporary movements is often found in past exploits.

In 1925, Ho Chi Minh's compatriot Nguyen Thuong Huyen wrote a pamphlet on revolution for Thanh Nien called *Cach Menh*. The title itself, which entered the political vocabulary in the first decade of the century, means "to take away the [heavenly] mandate of colonial rulers."[14] But Huyen's title does not explicitly refer to Thanh Nien's aim of creating a socialist state in Indochina. Instead, he uses language familiar to those Vietnamese who might want to reestablish a Vietnamese monarchy and reclaim *its* "heavenly mandate" from French usurpers. Huyen uses the pro-monarchist term *cach menh* to enlist monarchist support for the creation of an independent socialist state.

In his pamphlet, Huyen refers to various historical rebellions against outside authority as examples of *cach menh*. Contemporary Vietnamese revolutionaries are thus portrayed as belonging to the same tradition as that of the Trung sisters, who in A.D. 40 threw out the Chinese, briefly set up an independent state in Hue, and committed suicide rather than submit to foreign rule when the Chinese reconquered the territory; or that of Le Loi and Nguyen Trian, a fisherman-turned-general and a poet-turned-revolutionary, who together defeated the Chinese in 1426 and established an independent kingdom.[15] Huyen presumes that the contemporary Vietnamese struggle has a long history stretching back to a distant and heroic past. Despite the fact that the Trung sisters fought for monarchy, Huyen enlisted them as honorary members of a socialist movement; despite the defeats inflicted on them by colonial French forces, Vietnamese socialists could claim past victories as their own. Like Herzl's Maccabee-Zionists, Vietnamese revolutionaries could see themselves as reincarnated warriors from ancient and feudal times.

A second remarkable feature of this pamphlet is that Huyen dated it "the nineteenth of the twelfth month, the Year of Giap Ti." He did not date it January 3, 1925, the equivalent date in the Christianized French calendar.[16] Revolutionary independence movements frequently reckon dates according to nationalist time. In a massive non-violent countrywide protest against Japanese colonial rule, the leadership of the Korean independence movement issued an exhortatory pamphlet and dated it "the 4252d Year of the Kingdom of Korea, 3d Month, 1st Day," in lieu of March 1, 1919. This symbolic dating repudiated the calendar of the colonialist Japanese, who had effectively liquidated the Kingdom of Korea in 1910.[17]

One of the *mansei* demonstration organizers was Syngman Rhee. Like other independence movement leaders, Rhee promoted the idea that the 4,000-year history of Korea rightfully belonged to the anticolonial movement. When looking back at his nation's history, Rhee probably viewed it in much the same way that his father, a scholarly genealogist, viewed the Rhee family tree. Independence movement leaders were, in a sense, political genealogists, tracing their ideological roots back to ancient figures and movements that might have had very different motives and aims—the defense of monarchy instead of republic—but that could nonetheless provide a model of patriotism.

But social movements do not have genealogies the same way families do, though they frequently make that claim. The argument that people not related by blood or marriage belong to the same national family is also a modern phenomenon. Prior to the nineteenth century, only aristocracies and a few religious groups made this kind of claim. Christians, Moslems, and Buddhists believe that one might become a member of a giant, global family, but membership in these families is not automatic. One has to be converted or baptized to join these faiths; one is not born to them. Nationalist movements revived the notion that one is born to the nation. Membership, or citizenship, in a nation depended simply on the location of one's birth. As Thai van Giai, a member of the Indochinese Communist Party, said in 1931, "Patriotism is inborn."[18]

Zionist, Vietnamese Communist, and Korean nationalist movements all traded on the past to lay claim to the future. When colonial administrators wanted to denigrate a movement's claim to power, they did so by attacking the movement's historical claims. As Balfour said of Irish historical claims, which were used to advance the republicans' case for independence: "Ireland never had an organic political past as a single great community, and when an Irishman asks us to restore to Ireland Irish institutions . . . you will always find an English institution. It is not the fault of the Irish; it implies no inferiority on their part. It does imply that the contact between England and Ireland took place at a time when the civilization of England . . . was far more advanced than the tribal system that prevailed in Ireland. But it is a fact that there are no Irish institutions, there are no Irish laws, there is nothing in existence at this moment that could possibly be restored to Ireland which is of itself of pure nationalist Irish origin."[19]

Just as Balfour denied to republicans the existence of a usable Irish past, so other colonial administrators denied to independence movements the existence of a useful history. The attempt to rebut colonial administrators animated independence movements and prompted them to search for and promote a legitimate past. But it is nonetheless clear that the memory of these contemporary movements was frequently faulty or incomplete. The emphasis on historical continuity, on an unbroken link with past revolutionary movements, no matter what their political or social character, neglects many social and political discontinuities. So when Weizmann reminded Balfour of Jewish ownership of Jerusalem in biblical times, he was silent about the nearly two thousand years of the Diaspora, when Jews did not "possess" the city in any meaningful secular way. As Benedict Anderson notes, "The jump-cut periodization of much nationalist historiography is quite revealing in this regard. Vietnamese historians insist on an umpteen-thousand-year-old history of the Vietnamese nation, but little time is wasted on the 900 years (between 40 and 939 AD) in which 'Vietnam' was a more or less peaceable part of the [Chinese] Celestial Empire. A fast-forward rushes the reader from the heroic resistance of the Trung sisters to the founding of the independent Ngo dynasty."[20]

Likewise, the Indian National Congress passed quickly over the period of Moslem and British colonial rule, as if it were an unpleasant nightmare that was best forgotten. And Koreans, looking back at "their" long history as a nation, viewed the periods of foreign rule as a discontinuity that could, after independence, be forgotten as well.

In many ways, independence movements resemble Walter Benjamin's Angel of History, which faces the past and backs into the future.[21] Instead of being resolutely "forward-looking," contemporary independence movements have regularly looked back to the past for inspiration and legitimacy. As Karl Marx observed in *The 18th Brumaire:* "Just when [movements for radical social change] seem engaged in revolutionizing themselves and things, in creating something that has never yet existed, precisely in such periods of revolutionary crisis they anxiously conjure up the spirits of the past to their service and borrow from them names, battle cries and costumes in order to present the new scene of world history in this time-honoured disguise and this borrowed language."[22] For example, the proclamation announcing the establishment of a provisional government by the Irish Republican Army at the end of World War I begins, "Irishmen and Irishwomen: In the name of God and of dead generations from which she receives her old tradition of nationhood, Ireland, through us, summons her children to her flag and strikes for her freedom."[23]

While recognizing the tendency of movements to bend the past to serve the future, Marx argues that new revolutionaries must depart from this traditional use of history: "The social revolution of the nineteenth century cannot draw its poetry from the past, but only from the future. It cannot begin with itself before it has stripped off all superstition in regard to the past. Earlier revolutions required recollections of past world history in order to drug themselves concerning their own content. In order to arrive at its own content, the revolution of the nineteenth century must let the dead bury the dead."[24]

The Communist movements of the twentieth century, however, are unwilling to face the future without a reassuring look backward. Independence movements adopt a "traditionally modern" view of their place in time: they invent a useful, "traditional" past that will enable them to lay claim to a "modern" future. They invent a past that members of the nation—born to a given territory—can claim as their own. As George William Russell, Irish mystic and poet, says, "What is a nation but an imagination common to millions of people?"[25]

There are, however, some movements afflicted with an amnesia about their past. Independence movements that emerged in Germany after World War II did not legitimize their claims to power by referring to a German past. It was too odious. So instead they denied any claim to being the political heirs of Wilhelmian Germany, the Weimar Republic, or the Third Reich. Indeed, German politicans often refer to 1945 as *Stunde null* ("zero hour"), "a moment in time when history has been obliterated and everything began from scratch."[26]

None of the other independence movements has ever abandoned its claim to a history. Movement organizers fabricated useful histories to substantiate their claims for independence because colonial rulers—who based their own right to rule on the same kind of historical claims—accepted such appeals to history as legitimate. Thus Balfour rejected the Irish movement's historical case but accepted the Zionist's brief.

Although "traditionally modern" independence movements may have seen themselves as contemporary incarnations of previously existing movements, they distinguished themselves from their putative predecessors by adopting modern means and modern ends.

Independence movements typically had modest beginnings and did not immediately command widespread public support. In Asia and Ireland, small groups of determined partisans met in secret to organize modern movements. Initially, there was little to distinguish these clandestine organizations from the brotherhoods and secret societies that characterized political activity in many nineteenth-century settings. In the late 1880s and 1890s, the program of many of these secret political societies consisted of attempts to assassinate heads of state. Some "terrorist" groups were rather successful at this—the Czar of Russia was murdered in 1881, the President of the French Republic was killed in 1894, the Empress of Austria was assassinated in 1898, the King of Italy was killed two years later, and the President of the United States a year after that—but they accomplished little else.[27] In China, Sun Yat-sen, revered by both Nationalist and Communist Chinese as the founder of their respective independence movements, organized innumerable secret societies, but these failed to accomplish any lasting political purpose or attract widespread public support. It was only when he turned to the Comintern, which provided organizers skilled in developing mass-based organizations that adopted democratic forms, that he achieved any real success: the creation of the Nationalist Party, the Kuomintang.

The adoption of democratic forms and the development of mass-based organizations eventually distinguished independence movements from secret societies, clandestine fraternities, and spontaneously created mobs. Instead of plotting assassinations and organizing conspiracies, these groups began organizing public demonstrations, gathering petitions, electing delegates and holding congresses to review their tactics and debate their goals.[28]

At one time or another, though, independence movements in Korea, China, Vietnam, Palestine, and Ireland operated in secret or formed clandestine military organizations to avoid detection and destruction by colonial administrators or rival independence movements. But even these sub-rosa organizations—from Sinn Fein brotherhoods to Communist Party cells in Korea, China, and Vietnam, to the Zionist Haganah—departed from secret-society behavior in that they adopted democratic norms and bent themselves to the task of assisting the creation and defense of mass-based political movements.

Organizers of independence movements consciously adopted democratic conventions to advance their cause. When the Indian National Congress convened its first meeting in Bombay on December 27, 1885, the seventy-two delegates, who were "well-acquainted with the English language," assembled "in their morning coats, well-pressed trousers, top hats and silk turbans" to discuss the issues of the day.[29] Twelve years later, Theodor Herzl convened the first World Zionist Congress in Basle, Switzerland, in an effort to turn Zionist ideas into a mass movement. He urged delegates attending the congress to wear formal black dress to observe the solemnity of the occasion.[30] It is significant that from the outset these movements adopted democratic conventions and norms: they elected delegates and sent them in morning coat and top hat to attend a congress where the strategy and tactics of the movement might be deliberated. They did not call their meeting a parliament, assembly, or convention, but a congress. At that time, only the United States styled its body of elected representatives a congress, and it is likely that the independence movements sought to emulate the republican tradition in the United States.

The widespread adoption of democratic conventions by independence movements is also remarkable. Indian nationalists, Jewish Zionists, Korean, Chinese, and Vietnamese Communists all regularly sent delegates to attend party congresses. The degree to which delegates actually represented anyone but themselves, or the extent to which issues were freely discussed, varied widely. But these movements attempted, under difficult circumstances (many were subject to arrest by colonial administrators), to practice some version of democracy and to adhere, as best they could, to democratic norms and conventions. Membership in their movements may not have been open to everyone, but they all attempted to create popular, mass-based organizations and political parties that could assist them in the drive for independence.

Delegates attending these congresses frequently decided to adopt force as a means of achieving independence. And when they did, they typically relied on modern military means—guerrilla, irregular warfare—to advance their cause. Movement leaders in Korea, China, Vietnam, Palestine, and Ireland all organized paramilitary and guerrilla units. (India remained staunchly committed to non-violence during the colonial period.)[31] And these forces were drilled in modern military methods. Korean Communists trained with Chinese Communists, who fought Chinese Nationalists and invading Japanese colonial forces; the Vietminh fought the French, the Japanese, and the Americans under Vo Nguyen Giap's command; socialist Zionists in Palestine organized the Haganah, and other Zionist parties created military units such as the Betar, Etzel, Stern Gang, and Irgun to fight the British and Arab Palestinian groups; Arab Palestinians organized various paramilitary and irregular forces such as the Green Hand Gang to do the same; and the Irish Volunteer Army was organized as an irregular military wing of Sinn Fein to fight the British and, after partition, would fight itself in a factional civil war.[32]

It is sometimes said that guerrilla warfare is an ancient art, a way for the weak to defeat the strong.[33] But its practitioners in contemporary independence movements retheorized guerrilla warfare as both a military and a political strategy. Although they were often referred to as "bandits" by the colonial administrators and the press, modern-day guerrilla units that were part of larger independence movements shared little in common with their *bandito* predecessors. They trained their forces not to loot the rural populace but to protect them against colonial forces so they could in turn feed guerrillas in the field. Friendly relations with rural producers required contemporary guerrilla units to adopt an entirely different mode of behavior.

And previous bandit-guerrilla units were not armed, as it were, with the thought of Mao Tse-tung.

During the "Long March," when Chinese Communists escaped from the attacking Kuomintang armies by marching some six thousand miles across China, the Communist leadership insisted that illiterate soldiers learn to read and write as well as fight. As Jean Fritz explains, all the soldiers were "learning as they marched. In a new China, it was agreed, everyone should be able to read. So why wait? Each soldier wore a white cloth on his back with a character (or word) written on it so the soldier behind could learn as he marched. Each day the character was changed. The longer they marched, the more words the soldiers knew, and soon they were able to read the rules and slogans they had memorized, which they chanted in order to keep them fresh in mind. After all, they were expected not only to preach revolution but to remember the rules so well that they would practice them."[34]

Nor did guerrilla units act autonomously. They were guided by their political parties, which attached political cadre to military units. In Vietnam, for instance, the subordination of military units to the party was real and symbolic. The party called the commando and irregular forces assembled by Vo Nguyen Giap "Armed Propaganda Teams."[35] Previous guerrilla forces would not have carried literacy campaigns into battle or stuffed political manifestos into their rucksacks along with their ammunition. The fusion of military and political tasks distinguished contemporary armed independence movements from their predecessors.

Sometimes the military arms of independence movements did act unilaterally—for example, the Irgun attack on the King David Hotel in Jerusalem on July 24, 1946—but this kind of episode was infrequent and exceptional. For the most part, military arms were subordinated to mass-based political parties that employed force as one of the means they used to achieve a modern end: state power.

In their early years, the Indian National Congress, the Muslim League, and Sinn Fein pressed the British for some kind of home rule that would enable them to obtain a measure of self-government. Home rule typically meant being able to elect representatives to an indigenous parliament or assembly that could take up domestic affairs, but remaining within the British Empire as a "dominion," with Britain retaining control of military, trade, and foreign affairs. It took some years before these movements adopted the more "republican" goal of independence as a wholly sovereign state. The Congress only began urging the British to "Quit India" in the late 1920s. The Muslim League joined the call for independence after 1937, and began pressing for a separate, independent Moslem state only in 1940.

In his protracted campaign for sovereign state power, Eamon De Valera persuaded the Dail (the Irish parliament) to move toward full independence only after partition in 1921. After opponents of the Anglo-Irish Treaty (which gave Ireland home rule and dominion status) were defeated in a civil war, De Valera returned to office as Prime Minister in 1932, withdrew Ireland from dominion status in 1937, insisted on Irish neutrality during the Second World War, and finally withdrew from the Commonwealth in 1948.

From the outset, Communist independence movements in Korea, China, and Vietnam, as well as the Zionist movement, boldly announced their intention to seek power in an independent, sovereign state. But they retreated rather quickly from this "revolutionary" goal and adopted more pragmatic aims for long periods of time. Asian Communists were advised to adopt more modest goals by the Comintern (the Third International). Asian Communist parties were formed in the years after World War I, a period in which the Bolsheviks made a successful revolution in Russia and socialist movements staged unsuccessful uprisings throughout Europe. During this period, the Comintern initially called for Communist Parties to revolt and seize state power, but when it became evident that the revolutionaries had been exhausted or crushed, the Soviet-controlled Comintern began advising Communist Parties in Asia (and throughout the world) to abandon state power as a goal. In China, the Comintern urged the Communist Party to join forces with Sun Yat-sen's Nationalist Party and work together for the unification of China, which meant the overthrow of the indigenous warlord government in Peking, not the ouster of foreign colonial powers. At the same time, the Comintern advised Vietnamese Communists to abandon their call for independence and work instead to fight the indigenous bourgeoisie, be they French or Vietnamese. It was only after the failure of this policy in the late 1920s—the near-destruction of the Chinese Communists by its Nationalist "partner" led by Chiang Kai-shek and of Vietnamese Communists by French security forces—that the Comintern abandoned these modest aims and permitted Communist Parties in the 1930s to renew their demand for independence from colonial rule and the creation of wholly sovereign states.

The Zionist movement followed a similar trajectory. After adopting the creation of an independent Jewish state in Palestine as their goal, Herzl and then Weizmann moderated this aim in order to appeal to the Turkish administrators of Palestine before World War I. During the war, they sought to enlist the support of British officials, who might cede some territory—in either Uganda or Palestine—for the creation of a Jewish national home,[36] and to assuage the Arab inhabitants of Palestine who feared that Jewish immigration would lead to the creation of a Zionist state in Palestine. Because the British were then unwilling to consider Irish or Indian demands for independence, they were not prepared to discuss the creation of a sovereign Zionist state. And Zionist leaders were not eager to press the matter. It was only in the late 1920s and early 1930s, after British administrators began to reassess their commitment to the Zionists as a result of growing opposition to Jewish settlement by Arab Palestinians, that leaders like David Ben-Gurion began advocating a return to the original Zionist aim. Ben-Gurion defeated Weizmann's policy of moderation and persuaded Zionists to adopt independence in a sovereign Jewish state as their goal.[37]

Independence movements adopted sovereign state power as a goal rather slowly, in part because the seizure of state power had only recently become identified as a necessary component of social change. The international socialist movement had adopted the seizure of state power as a goal only in the late nineteenth century, and then only after the rancorous debate between anarchists and Marxists which dissolved the First International in 1876.[38]

Although independence movements used history to portray themselves as the legitimate heirs of long-standing political traditions, they were really quite modern. They mobilized rural and urban populations to create mass-based political parties, observed modern conventions and practiced congressional politics, trained modern guerrilla armies, and sought to seize state power itself. They were not content simply to conduct strikes or urge reform on existing authorities. Such efforts distinguished these movements from their political predecessors and also from many of their political contemporaries.

As the devolution of power drew near, independence movements would be drawn into increasing conflict with powerful foreign states and with each other. These conflicts would produce a bitter political legacy, as we shall see. But this bitterness would stem not from age-old antagonisms but from the struggles associated with the devolution and division of power by great and superpower states.

· 3 ·

Self-Determination

Woodrow Wilson, a reformist Democrat, and Vladimir Lenin, a revolutionary Communist, seem unlikely political partners. Yet despite their many differences, they developed a common approach to the devolution of power in colonial empires, an approach that would simultaneously assist independence movements and advance the American and Soviet position in the world.

Wilson, a minister's son, spent most of his adult life in academic cloisters, teaching, writing books on American government, and wrangling over educational reforms in Ivy League schools. In 1910, he left his job as president of Princeton University to become a reform-minded Democratic governor of New Jersey. Two years later, the Democratic National Convention nominated him as its presidential candidate on the forty-sixth ballot, and he was elected to the presidency when his opponents—William Howard Taft and Theodore Roosevelt—split the Republican vote.

As President, Wilson promoted business and financial reforms and maintained U.S. neutrality during the first half of World War I. Reelected in 1916 on a peace platform, Wilson subsequently took the United States into the war on the Allied side. A determined anticolonialist, Wilson sought to establish a peace that would provide collective security through the League of Nations and promote the "self-determination" of oppressed minorities in Europe and colonial peoples around the world.

By contrast, Lenin devoted his adult life to revolution, not reform. After his older brother was executed for participating in a plot to execute the Czar, Lenin became active in clandestine revolutionary circles. Occasionally jailed and frequently exiled, Lenin wrote books on the development of capitalism in Russia, maintained a voluminous correspondence with radical socialists across Europe, and penned blistering pamphlets designed to incite the masses and antagonize his opponents. He returned to Russia to participate in the revolutions of 1905 and 1917. Like Wilson in 1912, Lenin benefited from his opponents' disarray, and in 1917 he maneuvered past liberal and socialist rivals to seize power in a Bolshevik *coup d'état*.

Whereas Wilson was applauded as a peacemaker for his motives in bringing the United States into the First World War (he won the Nobel Peace Prize in 1919), Lenin was condemned for taking Russia out of the war. Nevertheless, both men's opposition to war grew out of an antipathy to colonialism, which they believed contributed to economic and military rivalry. Thus they sought to reshape the existing interstate system, promoting self-determination and collective security as alternatives to colonialism and war. Self-determination would permit oppressed peoples or "nations" to secede from colonial empires. Then, as political power passed from colonial empires to indigenous peoples, it would be possible to create a new interstate system based on independent nation-states, which would participate as equals in the global community. Because diplomacy is conducted by states, not nations (hence the term "international" is misleading because some states are themselves multinational), Wilson and Lenin sought to reform the interstate system of diplomacy.

Wilson and Lenin also advanced self-determination as a means of breaking up the imperialist-dominated interstate system, which confined and frustrated U.S. and Soviet interests. Their philosophy thereby served the needs of colonial independence movements and would-be superpowers in the interwar years. To facilitate this development, Wilson and Lenin advanced separate institutions to promote the dissolution of the old interstate system and to create a new one. Wilson designed the League of Nations for this purpose and Lenin organized the Communist or Third International. But before long their calls for self-determination succumbed to domestic exigencies in the

United States and the Soviet Union and to continuing opposition by still-strong European empires. By 1921, the prospect for devolving colonial power to indigenous independence movements and world power from European empires to American and Soviet successors had receded.

In the long run, however, Wilson's and Lenin's lieutenants would revive the notion of self-determination and together would promote a single institution—the United Nations—to reconstitute the interstate system shattered by World War II. The war weakened first-generation British and French colonial empires and wrecked second-generation German, Italian, and Japanese imperialists. During the war Franklin Roosevelt and Joseph Stalin would then be able to sweep aside the weakened and the wrecked, dissolving the old interstate system. Their new system would simultaneously assist the movements seeking independence from colonial rule and advance both the U.S. and Soviet positions in the world. What Wilson and Lenin began, Roosevelt, Truman, and Stalin would complete. And it would be in this context that devolution and division would occur.

Wilson and Lenin practiced what some historians have called the "New Diplomacy," which opposed colonialism, war, and the balance of power, and supported self-determination.[1] Although Wilson supported capitalism and Lenin was a Communist, both men were the product of anti-colonial political traditions and shared an animosity toward the British-dominated interstate system. Wilson belonged to an American anti-colonial tradition that stretched back to the war of independence against imperial Britain. These anti-colonial sentiments were kept alive throughout the nineteenth century as post-revolutionary Americans time and again bumped up against the limits set by European colonial powers—the French in Louisiana, the British in Canada and later in Hawaii, the Spanish in the South, the Russians in Alaska—during the westward continental expansion of the United States. During this period, U.S. policymakers typically supported independence movements in European colonies, particularly in Latin America, directly assisting them in Cuba, Puerto Rico, and the Philippines.

In the view of many American leaders, colonialism constrained the westward growth of the republic, stifled the development of popular sovereignty, and obstructed the expansion of U.S. trade and industry. These leaders wanted to do away with imperial trading policies and open colonial markets to American manufactures and agricultural products. Independent nation-states, they believed, were more prepared to adopt liberal trade policies than colonial dependencies yoked to the economies of European empires. During his first presidential campaign, Wilson told the Virginia General Assembly that "we are making more manufactured goods than we can consume ourselves . . . and now, if we are not going to stifle economically, we have got to find our way out into the great international exchanges of the world."[2]

When the United States itself acquired, annexed, or seized adjacent continental or overseas territories, U.S. leaders were anxious not to describe them as colonies. Wilson sought to distance himself from European imperialists and from domestic rivals like Theodore Roosevelt, who had departed from the American anti-colonial tradition and openly embraced British-style imperialism. In a break from Roosevelt's policies, Wilson negotiated a treaty compensating Colombia for detaching Panama and creating a state more sympathetic to U.S. canal builders. He later told an audience that "the United States will never again seek one additional foot of territory by conquest."[3]

Lenin belonged to a rather different anti-colonial tradition: that of the socialist movement. Whereas American liberals opposed colonialism because it obstructed the political and economic expansion of the republic, socialists opposed colonialism because it exploited the working class and led to war. Nineteenth-century socialists watched in dismay as the inter-European competition for colonial territories escalated into economic and military rivalry. And they viewed war between rival imperialists as particularly injurious to workers, who would bear the brunt of any fighting. Lenin shared the socialist movement's condemnation of imperialist war, and his anti-colonialism was stiffened by the fact that Russia participated in this interimperialist rivalry but did not directly benefit from it, possessing no overseas colonies of its own.

Both Wilson and Lenin resented the fact that British-orchestrated balance-of-power diplomacy, often conducted in secret, assigned their countries a subordinate role in the interstate system. In Wilson's view, the balance-of-power system "had never produced anything but aggression, egotism and war," insisting instead that "there must not be a mere balance of power but a league of powers, a universal, organized peace instead of organized rivalries."[4] A system based on equal representation would promote the interests not only of small states but also of those large ones—like the United States and Russia—that were denied an equal share of power in the existing system.

As an alternative to colonialism, Wilson and Lenin advanced a novel political idea: the right of all nations to self-determination. And in place of the existing interstate system, which was based on a balance of power among unequal states, they suggested a new international order consisting of equal states that would join together and provide for their "common security."

Although they agreed on the principles of a new system, Wilson and Lenin each urged the development of a separate organization to express it: the League of Nations and the Comintern. But at the same time, these institutions were organized along very similar lines. Their simultaneous rise and fall suggests that they shared much in common, enough, in fact, that U.S. and Soviet leaders could agree without much difficulty to create during World War II a single institutional expression of self-determination and common security—the United Nations.

Central to Wilson and Lenin's "New Diplomacy" was the idea of national self-determination. Although some historians trace the concept back to the sixteenth century, the term first found popular expression in the socialist movement during the late nineteenth century. The Second International, meeting in London in 1896, passed a resolution declaring "that [the International] stands for the full right of all nations to self-determination," which it rendered in German: *Selbstbestimmungsrecht*.[5]

Prior to the First World War, Lenin debated the interpretation of self-determination with socialists like Rosa Luxemburg, a Polish-German leader of the German Socialist Party,[6] but the phrase was popularized by Wilson, who argued that "all nations have a right to self-determination" and incorporated it into the League of Nations Covenant. In 1918, Wilson told Congress, "Self-determination is not a mere phrase. It is an imperative principle of action, which statesmen will henceforth ignore at their peril."[7]

Although the term has been given different meanings, Wilson and Lenin subscribed to the same usage. For them, self-determination meant the right of secession. As Lenin put it, "The right of nations to self-determination implies exclusively the right to independence in the political sense, the right to free political separation from the op-

pressor nation," or "the self-determination of nations means the separation of [national movements] from alien national bodies, and the
formation of an independent national state."[8] And in one of their first
declarations after seizing power in 1917, the Bolsheviks proclaimed
"the right of the peoples of Russia to free self-determination, even to
the point of separation and the formation of an independent state."[9]

Wilson, like Lenin, believed in secession. Raised in the South as a
Democrat after the Civil War, Wilson believed in popular sovereignty
and sympathized with the right of sovereign states to secede. Although reconciled to union in America, he believed that oppressed
peoples in other countries should have the right to secede. In Article
III of the League's Covenant, Wilson drafted the following language:
"The Contracting Powers unite in guaranteeing to each other political
independence and territorial integrity." To which he added this secessionist proviso: "But it is understood between them that such territorial readjustments, if any, as may in the future become necessary
by reason of changes in present racial conditions and aspirations or
present social and political relationships, pursuant to the principle of
self-determination, and also such territorial readjustments as may . . .
be demanded by the welfare and interest of the people concerned,
may be effected, if agreeable to those peoples."[10]

The anti-colonial thrust of Wilson and Lenin's call for self-determination was clear to the colonial powers. But the secessionist meaning Wilson and Lenin imparted to it gave even their supporters pause.
In a confidential memo in 1918, U.S. Secretary of State Robert Lansing
argued that self-determination is a "phrase simply loaded with dynamite." His reservations about the concept anticipate many of the
problems with a secessionist formulation:

> The more I think about the President's declaration as to the right of
> "self-determination," the more convinced I am of the danger of putting
> such ideas into the minds of certain races. It is bound to be the basis of
> impossible demands on the Peace Congress and create trouble in many
> lands.
>
> What effect will it have on the Irish, the Indians, the Egyptians, and
> the nationalists among the Boers? Will it not breed discontent, disorder,
> and rebellion? Will not the Mohammedans of Syria and Palestine and
> possibly of Morocco and Tripoli rely on it? How can it be harmonized
> with Zionism, to which the President is practically committed?
>
> The phrase is simply loaded with dynamite. It will raise hopes which
> can never be realized. It will, I fear, cost thousands of lives. In the end

it is bound to be discredited, to be called the dream of an idealist who failed to realize the danger until too late to check those who attempt to put the principle in force. What a calamity that the phrase was ever uttered! What misery it will cause![11]

In 1919, Wilson himself admitted to the Senate some second thoughts about his formulation of self-determination: "When I gave utterance to those words, I said them with the knowledge that nationalities existed, which are coming to us day after day. . . . You do not know and cannot appreciate the anxieties that I have experienced as a result of many millions of people having their hopes raised by what I have said."[12]

For his part, Lenin defended secessionism, which he viewed as akin to divorce, and tried, unsuccessfully, to distinguish it from what he called "separatism": "To accuse those who support freedom of self-determination, i.e., freedom to secede, of encouraging separatism, is as foolish and hypocritical as accusing those who advocate freedom of divorce of encouraging the destruction of the family. Just as in bourgeois society the defenders of privilege and corruption, on which the bourgeois marriage rests, oppose freedom of divorce, so, in the capitalist state, repudiation of the right to self-determination . . . means nothing more than defense of the privileges of the dominant nation and police methods of administration, to the detriment of democratic methods."[13]

But despite their own reservations, Wilson and Lenin adhered to the secessionist interpretation of the concept. Given their long-standing anti-colonialism and the recent bloodshed of an interimperialist war, both men used self-determination to urge colonial peoples to secede from colonial empires and to form independent nation-states. Lenin said of self-determination that in Western Europe it was "a thing of the *past* . . . [in] Eastern Europe . . . a thing of the *present* . . . [and in] semi-colonies and colonies . . . largely a thing of the *future*."[14]

In Wilson and Lenin's view, newly independent nation-states would become the building blocks, the constituent political units, of a new interstate system. The old interstate system consisted of heterogeneous states possessing unequal status within a complex global hierarchy. At the end of World War I, the interstate system was quite motley. It consisted of imperial European states and their dominions, colonies, overseas departments and territories (which were assigned an unequal and complicated status within each empire), together with democratic and socialist republics, dynastic kingdoms and military states. Wilson and Lenin wanted to reform the interstate system so that it consisted of more homogeneous units, preferably nation-states. In the new system, sovereign nation-states would meet as equals, not as superiors and subordinates. As Wilson said before the United States entered World War I, "The equality of nations upon which peace must be founded if it is to last, must be an equality of rights; the guarantees exchanged must neither recognize nor imply a difference between big nations and small, between those that are powerful and those that are weak."[15] Still, neither man believed that the new system would be completely egalitarian. It would have an implicit hierarchy, a hierarchy based on the moral political standards set by the United States of America or the Union of Soviet Socialist Republics.

In the new interstate system, standards would be applied equally. As to whose standards would be applied, Wilson was clear. He told an audience in 1919 that the United States "was the only idealistic nation in the world," the only one, presumably, able to set moral standards.[16] Lenin came to his analogous conclusion more slowly. During World War I, he said, "It would be absurd to set up our revolution as the ideal for all countries."[17] But within a few years, he had changed his mind: "We now possess quite considerable international experience, which shows . . . that . . . our revolution [has] a significance that is not local, or particularly national, or Russian alone, but international."[18]

Wilson and Lenin each believed that his country should lead the way for others because it was already an egalitarian republic. Until other states reached the American or Soviet egalitarian ideal, they would be inferior and their relations with the standard-bearer unequal. This inequality, however, would be merely temporary. Instead of assuming positions of permanent superiority—as imperialist powers had done—the United States and the Soviet Union would attempt to move other states along the road to independence and full equality within the new interstate system. As Wilson said of countries in Asia and the Middle East, "Nations and peoples which have stood still the centuries through are to be quickened, and made part of the universal world of commerce and of ideas which has so steadily been a-making by the advance of European power from age to age. It is our peculiar duty [to secure for them] the free intercourse and natural development which will make them equal members of the family of nations."[19]

Lenin likewise argued that, while he supported the equality of all nation-states, "the aim of socialism is not only to end the division of mankind into tiny states . . . it is not only to bring nations closer but to integrate them."[20] And this could be more easily done by big states. "Other things being equal," he adduced, "big states can solve the problems of economic progress and of the struggle between the bourgeoisie and the proletariat more effectively than small states."[21]

Taken together, Wilson and Lenin advocated the construction of what might be called an egalitarian hierarchy of states on a global scale. In Lenin's view, equality and hierarchy were not contradictory but complementary. Socialist movements in particular nation-states were equal, but because some were more advanced than others, they also existed in a hierarchy. The less advanced should be subordinated to the more advanced in order to promote the cause of world revolution: "Proletarian internationalism requires, first, the subordination of the interest of the proletarian struggle in one country to the interests of the proletarian struggle on a universal scale."[22] Increasingly, however, it would be the Soviet Communist Party that would subordinate the interests of proletarian struggles in other countries to its struggle for socialism in one country.

Although hierarchy is implicit in their conception of self-determination, it became explicit in the institutions Wilson and Lenin used to promote the new interstate system. Wilson founded the League of Nations in 1919. Lenin organized the Communist International the same year. Although membership in one precluded membership in the other, both were designed to promote self-determination and develop a new interstate system, which would provide common security. Wilson and Lenin believed that an "international" organization could provide the kind of collective security that individual political units could not. The political associations of the late nineteenth century—leagues of voters, chambers of commerce, and trade unions—had all been based on the idea that a collectivity could better protect and defend the interests of its members than an individual could alone. But despite their initial promise, these organizations eventually succumbed to global and domestic political forces. The League, which in 1934 had some sixty members, met regularly in Geneva throughout the interwar period. It collapsed in 1939 and formally dissolved itself in 1946. The Comintern met regularly during the early 1920s, but after Lenin's death in 1924, Stalin convened it infrequently. He dissolved it unilaterally, without consulting its members, in 1943, at President Roosevelt's request.[23]

Although neither institution distinguished itself during the interwar period, Wilson's and Lenin's lieutenants—Roosevelt and Stalin—drew upon the early history and ideas of the League and the Comintern to fashion the United Nations, the foundation of the interstate system after World War II. In their separate ways, both the League and the Comintern adopted the nation-state as the unit upon which membership was based. The League recognized existing non-Communist governments of nation-states as members; the Comintern recognized only the Communist Parties of various nation-states.[24] Formally, these units would be permitted equal representation in their respective internationals. Governments of great states would sit side by side with representatives of small states to settle disputes and keep the peace; members of the successful Bolshevik Party would sit down with party members for whom revolution was only a distant prospect and together determine the course of world revolution.

But despite formal equality, some governments and some parties would be "more equal than others." The League and the Comintern both developed a hierarchical structure that assured a preeminent position for certain states, certain parties. In the League, hierarchy was created by its membership provisions and by the mandate system. Non-independent colonial states could not be members, though Britain managed to obtain membership for several of its dominions. This established a hierarchy between member and non-member states. The League's mandate system then created a hierarchy for member states. Territories and peoples freed from colonial or military rule as a result of the war would be placed under the protection of a great state, which would be given a League mandate to administer it and prepare it for eventual self-government. The League graded these mandates into classes, each with different provisions for its duration and its terms, depending on the League's assessment of the territory's ability to govern itself. It was assumed that only great states—Britain, France, Italy, the United States, Japan—would receive and administer mandated territories.

Implicit in Wilson's design was the assumption that the United States would take a leading role in applying the principles of self-determination to territorial questions, classifying these territories, assigning mandates, reviewing their administration, preparing them for self-government. But because the United States did not join the

League, the colonial empires acquired mandated territories and then refused to promote their independence or to relinquish them. The League's hierarchical system ossified.

Many critics of the League in the U.S. Congress opposed it because it did not go far enough toward creating a hierarchy in which the United States would be the preeminent actor. One of the Senate's reservations was that the League would supersede the Monroe Doctrine and permit other countries to interfere in Latin America, a region in which the United States had already established its hegemony. A system that was too egalitarian and did not allow the United States to construct an informal hierarchy or exercise its hegemony was unacceptable to many senators.[25] Roosevelt would later allay these fears by making certain the United Nations would not be too egalitarian, winning recognition for the Monroe Doctrine and continued U.S. supremacy in Latin America as a matter of right in the UN Charter.

In the Comintern, representatives of parties from various countries met as equals. But Lenin insisted that these parties be admitted to the Comintern only if they adhered to the twenty-one conditions adopted by the Comintern's second congress in 1920.[26] These conditions mandated that existing Socialist Parties, which had belonged to the Second International, reconstitute themselves as Communist Parties, adopt a Communist program, expel opponents of the new program within their ranks, extricate themselves from alliances with non-Communist Parties, and, most important, draw up new programs and submit them for ratification by the Comintern or its executive.[27] This last condition meant that Communist Parties around the world would have to accept discipline from the Comintern and, by extension, from Moscow. Lest there be any doubt about Bolshevik domination, the second congress also passed a resolution saying that the Bolshevik path to power would be its model.[28]

Like the League's mandate system, which empowered great states to determine the ability of people within their charge to govern themselves, the Comintern took on the responsibility of determining which parties were ready to make their own revolution. And under Stalin, the hierarchy of Communist Parties within the Comintern ossified.

Several developments, however, prevented the League and the Comintern from playing the role their founders envisaged. On the global level, colonial European empires proved more obdurate and resourceful than either Wilson or Lenin anticipated. Wilson had hoped to sweep aside war-weary Britain and France and conduct a postwar diplomacy under the terms of a new interstate system. But in 1918, just prior to the peace conference, British Prime Minister David Lloyd George and French Premier Georges Clemenceau won smashing electoral victories, while Wilson arrived in Europe having received a major setback in the midterm congressional election. Lloyd George and Clemenceau then isolated and outmaneuvered Wilson at the Versailles conference. They wrangled numerous concessions from him on the terms of the treaty with Germany and on the disposition of colonies and territories seized during the war. In return, they promised to participate in a League of Nations neither of them believed in. Clemenceau was particularly critical of Wilson's attempt to act as above-the-fray arbiter of the peace conference and to impose American standards on European states. "Wilson," he said sarcastically, "has Fourteen Points, but God had only Ten."[29]

Having survived the war as victors, Britain and France were reluctant to relinquish its spoils. The territories and League mandates they acquired from Germany and Turkey swelled the British and French Empires and brought to an all-time high the extent of the world's territory and people under European colonial rule.[30] And having deflected the U.S. attempt to change the status quo, the European colonial empires could resist the calls (by lesser states in the League) for a more equitable world order or for movement toward independence in the newly mandated territories.

Without U.S. participation, moreover, the League backtracked on the principle of self-determination. In 1921, a League commission was asked whether the League should permit a minority to secede from a state, either to join another state or to become independent—the heart of Wilsonian self-determination. After considerable deliberation, the commission replied: "The answer can only be in the negative. To concede to minorities either of language or religion, or to any factions of a population, the right of withdrawing from the community to which they belong, because it is their wish or good pleasure, would be to destroy order and stability within states, to inaugurate anarchy in international life. It would be to uphold a theory incompatible with the very ideas of the state as a territorial and political entity."[31] If Wilson's League could be said to have died by 1921, this could be its epitaph.

Lenin, too, had hoped that the war would do in Western European countries what it had done in Russia—weaken the grip of the monarchy, the bourgeoisie, and the bureaucracy, radicalize the hungry masses, and permit revolutionary socialist movements to seize state power. Socialist movements throughout Europe attempted to revolt after the war. A few, like Béla Kun's Communist regime in Hungary (1919–20), actually took power briefly. But despite their weakened condition, conservative governments in Europe were able to rebuff indigenous insurrections and attack the call for revolution emanating from the Soviet Union. Indeed, the only successful revolution outside Russia took place in Ireland. And it was led not by revolutionary socialists, as Lenin and other socialists might have expected, but by independence-minded nationalists. By 1921, Lenin and the Bolsheviks admitted that the postwar upsurge had failed and that the prospect for revolution in Europe had indefinitely receded.[32]

But postwar global developments did not alone subdue the League and the Comintern. Powerful domestic forces within the United States and the Soviet Union also turned them aside. Just as the great colonial powers were not ready to relinquish control of the interstate system, domestic politicians in the U.S. and the U.S.S.R. were not ready to participate fully in a new, as yet untested, system. In the 1920s, politicians came to power who believed that they should look after their country's own interests first.

In the United States, Warren G. Harding and the Republicans, campaigning on the slogan "A Return to Normalcy," swept back into power in 1920. They handily defeated James M. Cox and his young running mate, Franklin D. Roosevelt, who had supported U.S. entry into the League of Nations. In his inaugural speech, President Harding outlined his views on foreign policy and U.S. participation in global affairs: "I have confidence in our America that requires no council of foreign powers to point the way to American duty. . . . Call it the selfishness of nationality if you will, I think it an inspiration to patriotic devotion—To safeguard America first. . . . To think of America first, to exalt America first."[33] Thus inspired, Harding led a full-scale U.S. retreat from Wilsonian internationalism, the League, and self-determination.

In the Soviet Union, the retreat from Leninist internationalism, the Comintern, and self-determination was led by Joseph Stalin. Stalin succeeded Lenin after his death in 1924 and bested Leon Trotsky in a contest for political power. Stalin was a Soviet-firster; Trotsky a world-revolution-firster. Stalin viewed the Comintern in much the same way that Harding viewed the League; he called the Comintern a *lavotchka*, or grocer's shop, and said, "The Comintern represents nothing. It only exists because of our support."[34] Stalin never believed, as Lenin did, that the Comintern could effectively promote a revolution in Europe that would assist the development of socialism in the Soviet Union. Even before the Comintern was established, Stalin argued, "There is no revolutionary movement in the West. There are no facts; there is only a possibility [of revolution], and with possibilities we cannot reckon."[35] As Lenin's role in the Comintern and Bolshevik Party diminished between 1921 and 1924, Stalin increasingly argued that the Comintern's role was to defend the Soviet Union and its attempt to build socialism in one country. As a result, the Comintern increasingly subordinated the interests of its constituent parties to the foreign policy needs of the Soviet state.[36] And as this occurred, it deemphasized the importance of self-determination, since this concept suggested a measure of independence and autonomy from the Soviet Communist Party. Lenin's idea of national self-determination gave way to the phrase "the right of self-determination of the working masses," which was Stalin's way of circumscribing its meaning.[37] This may well have been the epitaph for Lenin's Comintern.

Wilson's and Lenin's attempts to create a new interstate system based on the idea of self-determination and on global institutions foundered on the rock of global and domestic political realities. As a result of their unexpected resilience in the face of war and their successful obstinacy toward challenges from would-be superpowers, Great Britain and France were able to isolate both the United States and the Soviet Union and deflect, for the next quarter century, the call for self-determination and the creation of a new interstate system. But while European colonial empires and America-first and Soviet-first isolationists remained strong throughout the interwar period, they would not survive the combined assault of a great depression and another world war.

· 4 ·

Dominion and Union

British and French officials did not believe that the interstate system should be radically transformed along Wilsonian or Leninist lines. They did not accept the view that territories and colonies should be granted self-determination and permitted to form independent nation-states. But neither did they stand pat. The impact of the war, U.S. and Soviet challenges to their right to rule over vast colonial empires, and the increasingly impatient demands for independence by indigenous movements forced European colonial empires to reassess their colonial policies and to advance reforms that would alter the look but not the character of the interstate system.

The great and would-be great powers advanced several different kinds of interstate systems during the interwar period. Against the idea of self-determination, the British argued for a system based on "dominion," the French for "union," the Germans for "Reich," and the Japanese for a "Greater East Asia Co-Prosperity Sphere." Each represented an attempt to reform or create an interstate system that would secure or promote the position of their respective states. Each was fundamentally less egalitarian than that proposed by Wilson and Lenin, despite the hierarchical features implicit in the League and Comintern models.

The British and French conceptions were essentially modifications of the pre-World War I balance-of-power system. Both would maintain colonial empires and resist calls for independence and self-determination. The German and Japanese conceptions, though different in some important respects, represented attempts by would-be imperialist states to carve out new empires at a time when overseas territories were no longer free for the taking. Their wartime occupation of huge stretches of territory, however brief, suggests that they sought to develop highly stratified, hierarchical colonial systems that would have none of the egalitarian features found in the U.S. and Soviet interstate systems.

During World War I, it became evident to beleaguered British leaders that some power would have to devolve to constituent members of the empire. Members of the Empire were then graded in a complex hierarchy. At its apex stood the British Crown and the Parliament of the United Kingdom, which consisted of England, Scotland, Wales, and Ireland. Below it in a first tier were arranged the white-settler colonies, or "dominions"—Canada, Newfoundland, New Zealand, Australia, and South Africa—which possessed separate but more or less equal status. A step down was another tier of Crown colonies—India, Burma, Ceylon, Malaysia, Egypt, Nigeria, Hong Kong, and so on—and below that, administered territories and, after the war, mandated territories. The historian Edward Grierson lists four distinct kinds of colonial territory (the dominions were not referred to as colonies): Crown colonies, protectorates, protected states, and mandates, these last being subdivided into "A" class mandates, such as Palestine (which by the terms of the League of Nations charter had to be prepared for early independence), and "B" class mandates, such as Tanganyika (which were of normal colonial status but for the provision that they could not be permanently appropriated by the mandatory power).[1]

This general structure was complicated by vertical fissures into which countries like Ireland fell. Nominally part of the kingdom at the crown of Empire, Ireland was administered like a third-rate colony. In negotiations about its postwar status, British leaders debated whether Ireland should be treated like other white-settler dominions and given home rule, an indication of Ireland's actual inferior status. And territories in the third rank might be treated quite well by the Empire—the inhabitants of Gibraltar and Malta receiving preferential treatment vis-à-vis, say, Burma or Guyana. The structure was further complicated by horizontal faults. The British practiced colonialism— subjecting indigenous peoples to foreign rule—in places like China, which it did not formally colonize or incorporate into its Byzantine hierarchy.[2]

To rally support for Empire during and immediately after the war, and to deflect U.S. criticism of British colonial policy, which threatened to prevent U.S. participation in the war on the Allied side,[3] Lloyd George's government promised devolution, in some form, to a variety of imperial constituencies. For members of the bottom tier, Foreign Minister Arthur J. Balfour in 1917 made two remarkable promises, almost simultaneously. In the first Balfour Declaration, issued on August 20, the government promised to work toward the "gradual development of self-governing institutions with a view to the progressive realisation of responsible government in India as an integral part of the British Empire."[4] In the second Balfour Declaration, announced on November 2, the government promised to "favour the establishment in Palestine of a national home for the Jewish people."[5]

For its first-rank colonies—the white-settler dominions—the British promised greater equality with Britain. Symbolic of this was British insistence that the different dominions plus India, which had contributed so much to the war effort, separately sign the Versailles Peace Treaty and join the League of Nations as individual states. South Africa, New Zealand, and Australia even became mandatory powers in the League.[6] As Lloyd George said, "A diplomatic unity had declared war; a diplomatic multitude proposed to conclude Peace."[7]

The newfound equality for dominion states was prompted in part by a desire to stack the cards in Britain's favor in international forums. Instead of speaking with one voice, the Empire could now speak with several. And Britain upgraded the nominal status of dominion states, calling them Commonwealth nations and dropping the term "dominion" in intra-imperial communications.[8] This upgrading did not place them on an equal status with Britain itself, but it did promote them in relation to the rest of the colonies.

Lloyd George was prepared, perhaps more than any other British leader of the preceding or succeeding generation, to make some form of devolution within the Empire a reality. He even went so far as to use the rhetoric of self-determination. In a speech describing British war aims on January 8, 1918, he declared that "a territorial settlement . . . based on the right of self-determination or the consent of the governed" was one of the fundamental conditions of peace.[9] He did not, however, equate self-determination with the right of secession; in fact, Lloyd George was not particularly sanguine about the prospect of self-determination, despite his adopting its rhetoric. "It fills me with despair," he said of newly liberated nations attending the Versailles conference, "the way in which I have seen small nations, before they have hardly leapt into the light of freedom, beginning to oppress races other than their own. They are more imperialistic than either England or France, certainly than the United States."[10]

On the Irish Question, Lloyd George worked with Balfour and Winston Churchill, members of an interparty coalition on this issue, to negotiate a treaty that granted "dominion home rule" to the newly created Irish Free State. The idea was to establish an Irish parliament and to grant it power to legislate on domestic affairs (home rule), but to keep it within the Empire and retain for Britain its prerogatives on matters of Irish security and trade (dominion). This arrangement, however, was compromised by the partition of Ireland: the North would remain part of the United Kingdom with its own measure of devolved power, while the South would become a dominion (see Chapters 6 and 7). This devolution of power resulted not only in partition but in civil war in the South, and a repudiation of its British architects at the polls—Lloyd George and Churchill were defeated in the 1922 elections. For many, Lloyd George had gone too far on behalf of devolution. Afterward, successive governments retreated from dramatic attempts to devolve power quickly or to make good the promises made to imperial constituencies during the war.[11]

Throughout the interwar period, British administrators advocated dominion, not self-determination. In theory, dominion would equalize relations within the Empire. Balfour articulated the new egalitarian meaning at the 1926 conference on interimperial relations, which adopted his definition as a guide to future relations: "They [the dominions] are autonomous communities within the British Empire, equal in status, in no way subordinate to one another in any aspect of their domestic or external affairs, though united in a common allegiance to the Crown, and freely associated as members of the British Commonwealth of Nations. The British Empire . . . depends on positive ideals. Free institutions are its life-blood. Free cooperation is its instrument, Peace, security and progress are its objects."[12]

But this egalitarian meaning of dominion was quickly qualified. "While equality of status is thus the root principle of our Inter-imperial

Relations," Balfour continued, "the principles of equality appropriate to status *do not universally extend to function*. . . . In the sphere of defense the major share of responsibility rests now and must for some time continue to rest with His Majesty's Government in Great Britain [emphasis added]."[13] Furthermore, dominion's potential for equality extended only to the first-tier, white-settler colonies. The other colonies would move toward dominion, though at a much slower pace. As British colonial minister Malcolm MacDonald said in 1938, "The great purpose of the British Empire is the *gradual* spread of freedom . . . that freedom is a slow evolutionary process. In some parts of the empire, in the Dominions, that evolutionary process has been completed. . . . In others it is necessarily a much slower process. It may take generations, or even *centuries*, for the peoples in some parts of the Colonial Empire to achieve self-government [emphasis added]."[14]

Under dominion, equality was qualified by hierarchy. Balfour could say that "we depend as an empire upon the cooperation of absolutely independent Parliaments" and add that "the British Parliament is supreme over the Parliaments of Canada, of Australasia, or the Cape, or South Africa."[15] The British retained supremacy in matters of defense and intercommonwealth trade. They could, for example, declare war on behalf of the Empire's constituent members. They would not permit "autonomous communities" to secede from the Empire. And they would not extend the self-governing, egalitarian parliamentary franchise to non-white colonies until the British believed them to be fully capable of self-government. In the second- and third-rank colonies, that would not, at the end of World War I, be any time soon.[16] As one British leader said, the argument that "whatever is good in the way of self-government for Canada must be good for India" was a "gross and dangerous sophism." It was like arguing that because a fur coat is needed in the Canadian winter, it is needed in the Deccan.[17]

At bottom, dominion did not represent a significant departure from empire. Under attack for being imperialist, the British moderated imperialist rhetoric with dominion and reference to the new egalitarian character of commonwealth (first-rank) states. Nor did leaders of the British constellation of imperial states, colonies, territories, and mandates agree that its constituent parts take a single form, say, that of a nation-state. Rather, they continued to insist that the Empire's component political units take *different* forms, which suited their degree of political maturity. At no time during the interwar period did

British statesmen advance the idea that a single form be adopted, as Wilson and Lenin had urged. Balfour once remarked that institutions cannot be imported as easily "as you import a new locomotive. . . . Free institutions on the British model or the Dominion model are among the most difficult institutions in the world to manage properly. . . . The notion appears to be that if you leave India alone, India will at one stride join the ranks [of other great, free and self-governing communities] as a natural equal. That is entirely to ignore the teaching of history."[18] The British, moreover, preferred a system composed of heterogeneous units, which could then be managed through balance-of-power diplomacy. British hegemony depended on maintaining this complicated system, which they alone could master. Better to confront the United States, the Soviet Union, Germany, or Japan as a global empire—taking, at different times, one face and then many—than as a single, homogeneous nation-state.

Although the British did not attempt to change substantially the shape of their imperial system or its relation to the interstate system as a whole, they did try to manage demands for devolution and independence in ingenious ways. The Anglo-Irish Treaty was a novel attempt to resolve a long-standing problem. In the second- and third-rank colonies, the British attempted to manage devolution by applying the idea of dominion. But despite prodigious, even monumental efforts, this attempt failed. Independence movements rejected reforms leading to dominion because they viewed it as a poor alternative to independence and self-determination. In India and Palestine, for example, successive British efforts to reform political institutions and move toward dominion home rule, though sometimes inventive, proved unworkable.

After announcing its intention in 1917 to grant "responsible government in India," the government introduced two major reforms: the Montagu-Chelmsford reforms of 1919 and the India Act of 1935. These devolved limited self-government to Indians at the provincial level; the India Act also provided for elections in which Indian political parties could participate. In addition, the British convened roundtables in 1930 and 1943 and issued a mountain of white papers and reports. The massive Simon Report was issued in 1930, and high-level missions, like the Cripps Commission in 1942, were sent to iron out the problems with preceding reforms and to suggest new remedies. During the course of one of the many parliamentary investigations into reform in India, a joint committee of both Houses met for eighteen straight months, held 159 meetings, examined 120 witnesses, and interviewed one of them, Sir Samuel Hoare, for nineteen days, during which time he answered more than seven thousand questions.[19] Not to be outdone by white-paper-issuing commissions, the Indian National Congress in 1928 issued its own white paper, the Nehru Report (named after Motilal Nehru, Jawaharlal's father), which outlined constitutional reforms of its own.

And it all came to nothing.

None of the interwar reforms, determined as they were, granted India a status equal to that of the white-settler dominions, much less independence. The comprehensive 1935 reforms reserved for the British Governor-General control over all matters relating to defense and foreign affairs. He could, and in 1939 did, declare war on India's behalf without consulting any representative Indian body. The reforms also gave the British the right to act unilaterally to maintain domestic peace and order.[20]

It is not surprising that the independence movements rejected these reforms. As Muslim League president Sir Sayed Wazir Khan said of the 1935 reforms, "A constitution is literally being forced on us by the British Parliament which nobody likes, which no one approves of. After several years of Commissions, Reports, Conferences and Committees a monstrosity has been invented. . . . It is anti-democratic. It will strengthen all the most reactionary elements in the country, and instead of helping us develop on progressive lines, it will enchain and crush the forces making for democracy and freedom."[21] And as early as 1926, Churchill recognized that "our rule in India is as it were a sheet of oil spread over and keeping free from storms a vast and profound ocean of humanity."[22] But it would be clear by World War II that there was either too little British oil or too vast an anti-colonial ocean.

An analogous attempt to manage devolution through piecemeal reform failed in Palestine as well. The succession of white papers and commissions that visited Palestine was met with hostility by Zionists and Arabs alike. And the proposals made stimulated anxieties and conflict rather than attenuating them. (The path to devolution in India and Palestine is discussed in greater detail in Chapter 6.)

With the onset of World War II, it became apparent that the attempt to construct dominion through grandiose managerial reforms had failed to change substantially relations within the British Empire or to provide a model of interstate relations that might be grasped as an alternative to the U.S.–Soviet or Axis systems.

Dominion failed because independence movements in Ireland, India, and Palestine rejected it. The Irish refusal to join the Empire in the Second World War, and the Indian National Congress's policy of wartime non-cooperation, provided concrete evidence that dominion as a goal had not taken root in colonial countries near and dear to Britain. Self-determination and independence were simply more attractive; few would settle for dominion when self-determination might be in the offing.

Dominion would also be hard-pressed by German and Japanese challenges to British hegemony. While neither German nor Japanese colonialism was viewed as an attractive alternative to that of Britain, France, or Holland, their initial success exposed the vulnerability of European colonial empires, particularly in Asia, where Allied forces were routed. Britain had claimed its superior position in the Empire because it promised to provide for the defense of subordinate colonies, through balance-of-power diplomacy and, when necessary, by force of arms. Early British reverses in Asia, Africa, and Europe demonstrated that British security guarantees, upon which dominion rested, were hollow. Neither the British Empire, nor the European empires acting in concert, could withstand the Axis assault. Only U.S. and Soviet intervention could stem the onslaught. A broader conception of security, wider than that promised by empire, was seen as necessary. In that regard, too, the U.S.–Soviet conception of an interstate system that could provide common security seemed more attractive to colonial peoples.

Throughout the interwar period, the French rejected both "dominion" and "independence" as a way to shape relations within its Empire or within the interstate system as a whole. Instead, French leaders after World War I promoted the idea of "Greater France," in which "the continental Fatherland and the Frances of overseas are, if not indissolubly merged, at least linked and compose the real force of a Greater France whose security no longer relies on 40 million but on 100 million human beings and which can demand all the nourishment it needs for its life from the whole of a domain twenty times the size of the mother country."[23] During World War II, the French leadership replaced reference to Greater France with the term "union."

The chief proponent of French union was Charles de Gaulle. During the Second World War, de Gaulle sought to reform the Empire in order to preserve it, though he was not prepared to go nearly so far in the direction of equality or self-government as the British had. "We must organize the empire," he said in 1943, "on a larger and more fair basis, a collaboration between the sovereign power [France] and the loyal millions whom it is its duty to guide."[24] Without reforms, de Gaulle feared, France stood to lose its own independence. "For us, in a world like this and with things as they are, to lose the French Union would be a reduction that could cost us our independence."[25]

De Gaulle took a serious interest in colonial reform because it was in the colonies, particularly those in sub-Saharan Africa, that Free French forces took refuge during the war and began to rally opposition to French capitulation and collaboration. In 1944, he organized a conference in Brazzaville, then capital of French Equatorial Africa, where he outlined the idea of union and instituted some modest reforms, such as widening the franchise.[26] This conference, however, rejected any prospect of independence or autonomy. "The aims of the work of civilization accomplished by France in its colonies exclude all idea of autonomy, all possibility of evolution outside of the French bloc of the Empire; the eventual establishment, even in the distant future, of self-government is to be dismissed."[27]

After the war, the French were prepared to promise some nominal equality within the Empire as part of a new union. The preamble to the constitution of the Fourth Republic stated: "France, together with its overseas population, forms a Union founded on the equality of rights and obligations, without distinction of race or religion. . . . Faithful to its traditional mission, France aims to lead the people in its charge to the freedom of administering themselves and conducting their own affairs democratically: avoiding any system of colonization founded on arbitrary principles, it guarantees everyone equal access to public offices and to the individual or collective exercise of rights and liberties proclaimed or confirmed above."[28]

But like dominion, the nominal equality promised by union was qualified and compromised at every turn. Within the union there was an implicit hierarchy, with France at its apex. Members of the union were graded into several categories. As the historian Bruce Marshall notes, "The terms citizen, subject, and national were not synonymous. . . . Rather they described differences in status between those inhabitants of metropolitan France or the overseas areas who are fully subject to French law in civil as well as public matters (*citoyens français*), and those who did not enjoy political or private law protection but were instead subject to local, traditional laws (*sujets*). The term nationals referred to the distinction between foreigners and persons enjoying French nationality regardless of civil status. To further complicate matters, the Constitution of the Fourth Republic uses the term *ressortissants* as a euphemism to avoid speaking directly of natives as 'non-citizens' or 'subjects' who were, nevertheless, French nationals."[29]

Unlike the British Empire, which organized a colonial hierarchy through a variety of administrative structures—dominions, colonies, mandates, territories—the French organized an empire with a single administrative state, which had overseas departments or provinces. The French Empire, which proved more resistant to change in the interwar period than the British, was also more vulnerable when German and Japanese push came to shove. The idea of a French union was compromised by virtue of French humiliation and collaboration in North Africa, in Indochina, and in France itself. Independence movements, particularly those in Algeria (France's Ireland) and Vietnam, found little merit in unrepentant claims for empire under the guise of union with France. The United States and the Soviet Union, which were unimpressed by the Free French war effort, viewed French colonial schemes with distaste. Outside the French Empire, no one viewed union as a way to organize interstate relations in the postwar world.

While the U.S.–Soviet conception of a new, more egalitarian interstate system challenged European colonial empires from the left, nascent Japanese and German systems threatened them from the right. As latecomers to the competition for overseas colonies, the Japanese sought to trespass on territories where colonial claims had already been staked, while Germany tried to create an empire out of already independent nation-states. These would-be great powers briefly advanced extremely hierarchical, imperialistic relations between states, and their early successes during the war demonstrated the seriousness of their challenge. Although their success was brief, the outlines of alternative interstate systems can be discerned from their occupation policies and practices.

The Japanese had gained some colonial concessions as a result of their opportunistic participation on the Allied side during World War I, obtaining German territories in China and tacit recognition of Japanese claims on Korea and Taiwan (Formosa). During the interwar period, Japan invaded China, seizing Manchuria, without prompting interference from Europe or America.

After Japan entered World War II, the size and speed of its advance into American, British, Dutch, and French colonies was breathtaking. In the four months following Pearl Harbor, the Japanese brought some 500 million people into their Empire, which at its peak measured 8,100 by 6,250 miles.[30] In doing so, says the historian Jon Dower, "they became entangled in a web of contradictions: creating new colonial hierarchies while preaching liberation; singing the glories of their unique Imperial way while professing to support a broad and all-embracing Pan-Asianism."[31] Thus, like other twentieth-century colonial systems, the Japanese "Greater East Asia Co-Prosperity Sphere" espoused a nominal equality while imposing a rigid hierarchy. Formally commissioned on August 1, 1940, the Co-Prosperity Sphere was designed "to proclaim and demonstrate the *kodo* [imperial way] throughout the world," according to Japanese Foreign Minister Matsuoka Yosuke. "Viewed from the standpoint of international relations this amounts . . . to enabling all nations and races to find each its proper place in the world."[32]

Although the Japanese ideographs used to describe the Co-Prosperity Sphere could be translated into English as "collectivity of peoples," "racial community," or "racial cooperative body," each of which suggests an egalitarian collectivism, the Japanese assumed that they would be the leading race (*shido minzoku*) and that all other peoples would find that their "proper place in the world" would be a subordinate one, like that of children to their father in a Japanese family.[33] One writer explained: "We the Yamato race are presently spilling our 'blood' to realize our mission in world history of establishing a Greater East Asia Co-Prosperity Sphere. In order to liberate the billion people of Asia, and also to maintain our position of leadership over the Greater East Asia Co-Prosperity Sphere forever, we must plant the 'blood' of the Yamato race in this soil."[34]

In practice, the Japanese constructed a multilevel hierarchy of overseas colonies. In the Philippines and Indochina, where they were able to find willing collaborators, the Japanese left the existing state apparatus more or less intact, although financial and material resources extracted from these countries was now funneled to Japan instead of to the United States or France.[35] In Burma and Indonesia, they promoted regimes in which genuine nationalists, even revolutionary leaders, took part.[36] But they practiced a more malicious colonialism against the Koreans and Chinese, whom they regarded as on the low rung of the imperial hierarchy.[37]

Although the Japanese irrevocably crippled European colonial power in Asia, their attempt to create an empire on a regional and, perhaps, on a global scale foundered on stubborn Chinese resistance on the Asian mainland and American determination to advance on Japan through its Pacific island approaches. Although there was no equivalent of Stalingrad in the war with China, the bulk of Japanese forces were tied down in China, fighting a war they could not win or, for a long time, lose. U.S. forces confronted rather small contingents of Japanese forces in successive Pacific archipelagos and, after destroying Japanese naval and air power, advanced to Japan without ever having met the main Japanese Army in battle.[38] But the European colonial forces in Asia, unlike the Chinese, Americans, Australians, or indigenous independence movements in Indochina and Burma, were never able to mount effective resistance to the Japanese in Southeast Asia.

Less need be said of the Third Reich as an alternative interstate system. German leaders dispensed with egalitarian language to describe the Reich, except when addressing German-speaking peoples in countries outside Germany and Austria. In theory and in practice, Adolf Hitler promoted a highly stratified hierarchy with Germany at the top. The German Empire was centered in Europe (although it did make some headway in North Africa), because the European colonial empires had expropriated German overseas possessions after World War I and foreclosed the prospect of renewed overseas German colonialism.

In previous centuries, European colonial empires had been highly stratified, hierarchical structures that did not pretend to be egalitarian. In certain respects, the Third Reich was a throwback to colonial practice of the sixteenth and seventeenth centuries. But even in those terms, the Germans stretched the limits of hierarchy. European colonial empires as late as the eighteenth and early nineteenth centuries consisted of free, semi-free, and indentured peoples—slaves, and "Indians" or indigenous peoples—which they occasionally massacred but more often left to die of starvation and disease. The elimination of slavery and an increasing toleration of indigenous populations compressed the hierarchies of colonial empires: the range between apex and base was narrowed.

The German Empire, however, attempted to widen the range between top and bottom. At the top, of course, was Germany-Austria. And German racial theories elevated Aryan peoples not only above non-European peoples but above other Europeans as well. Indeed, Nazi theories of racial supremacy embarrassed even British and French colonialists. The German attempt to create an empire aroused the great powers, not so much because they opposed colonialism, or even German colonialism, but because the Germans sought to colonize Europeans. German racism threatened to sweep white Europeans into the same category (or worse) as that of peoples in New Guinea, the Sudan, or Guyana.

Arranged below the Germans in the Nazi hierarchy were the peoples of the occupied territories, under collaborationist governments in Vichy France, Hungary, and Norway.[39] The rest were arranged in descending order, using German supremacist racial theories and practical political and economic considerations as a guide. In addition, the Germans reintroduced forced drafts of labor, resuscitated slavery, and assigned large populations to a below-subsistence existence. Further, they slated millions for extermination. Spanish and Dutch colonialists in the sixteenth and seventeenth centuries had attempted to exterminate some indigenous populations (particularly in the Caribbean, Latin America, and Indonesia), but the Germans applied modern technologies to this task and slaughtered millions of their fellow Europeans. This hierarchy, which elevated the top and depressed the bottom, and the savagery with which it was implemented, was unprecedented in world historical terms.

The mobilization of Allied states and indigenous resistance movements around the world destroyed German and Japanese military power and extinguished their imperial projects. The collapse of these nascent empires, the failure of British and French imperialists to devise workable alternatives to independence and self-determination, and the general crippling effect of the war on European empires would permit the United States and the Soviet Union not only to emerge as superpowers but also to reshape the interstate system along Wilsonian-Leninist lines.

· 5 ·

A New Interstate System

"In the Second World War," Charles de Gaulle once told Richard Nixon, "all the nations of Europe lost. Two were defeated."[1]

World War II not only destroyed German and Japanese would-be empires; it also fatally wrecked the ability of victorious European colonial states to maintain their own empires. Despite Churchill's insistence that he had "not become the King's First Minister in order to preside over the liquidation of the British Empire,"[2] many Britons shared de Gaulle's view. At war's end, *The Times* of London wrote: "We must ponder the means of our escape. We escaped by coalition with 'the numberless millions of the Russian people' and the 'immense superiority of the power used by the United States.' "[3] And one Member of Parliament observed, "We are sitting here today as the representatives of a victorious people, discussing the economic consequences of victory. If a visitor were to come . . . from Mars . . . he might well be pardoned for thinking that he was listening to the representatives of a vanquished people discussing the economic penalties of defeat."[4]

In 1945, France's national income was half what it had been in 1938, and the British found that they had exhausted their financial resources and could not, without immediate American loans, maintain the economy of Britain or of empire.[5] Chancellor of the Exchequer Hugh Dalton warned that unless American aid was quickly forthcoming, the standard of living in Britain would sink below that of an Irish peasant.[6] (This is itself an instructive measure of Ireland's place in the British hierarchy.)

The battering of two world wars and a great depression weakened Britain and France and crippled the interstate system they had shouldered. But while war and depression rolled back Anglo-French power, it advanced the position of the United States and the Soviet Union. In economic terms alone, the war greatly enriched the United States. At its conclusion, Washington held gold reserves of $20 billion, nearly two-thirds of the world's total, and manufactured more than half the world's goods.[7] War mobilized U.S. industry and agriculture in a way that the New Deal had not, and it brought some 10 million people into the work force. In the Soviet Union, the war had destroyed 1,700 towns, leveled 70,000 villages, and left 25 million people homeless. Twenty million died, 600,000 of whom starved to death in the siege of Leningrad.[8] But while war destroyed much of the Soviet Union's infrastructure and productive capacity, it also mobilized its financial, human, and material resources in a way that forced collectivization and successive five-year plans had not.

The isolationist great powers had become, during the war, global superpowers. And together they fashioned a new interstate system that simultaneously promoted the proliferation of independent nation-states and assigned preeminent positions to themselves. The standardization of the system's political units was accompanied by the rise of a new, more informal hierarchy, with the United States as its standard.

The architects of the new system, U.S. President Franklin Roosevelt and Soviet Premier Joseph Stalin, had been lieutenants of Woodrow Wilson and Vladimir Lenin. Although they were to create a new interstate system along Wilsonian-Leninist lines, during the interwar period they had retreated from the internationalist diplomacy of their mentors and adopted America-first and Soviet-first isolationism. Roosevelt, it is true, had campaigned vigorously for ratification of the League of Nations Covenant as the Democratic vice-presidential candidate in 1920. But when he sought the party's presidential nomination in 1932, Roosevelt needed to obtain the support of William Randolph Hearst, the ruler of an extensive newspaper empire. Hearst demanded that candidates for the nomination repudiate Wilson's "visionary policies of intermeddling in European conflicts." And Roosevelt complied. He announced that "the League was not in accord with fundamental American ideals," stating flatly, "I do not favor American participation."[9] For his part, Stalin regarded Lenin's Comintern as a futile institution. His interest in it waned during the interwar years and he convened only two world congresses of the Comintern in the eighteen years between 1925 and its dissolution in 1943.

But surprise attacks, by the Germans in June 1941 and by the Japanese six months later, persuaded Stalin and Roosevelt that a Wilsonian-Leninist approach was necessary to keep the peace. They recognized that no single nation could survive the combined Axis onslaught and they returned to Wilson and Lenin's idea of collective security embodied in international institutions. As they did so, their latent anti-colonialism revived. They began to press for the devolution of power within colonial empires and for the creation of independent nation-states based on the Wilsonian-Leninist principle of self-determination.

Roosevelt argued that "the colonial system means war," and told Churchill, "I can't believe that we can fight a war against fascist slavery, and at the same time not work to free people all over the world from a backward colonial policy."[10] At Big Three summit meetings during the war, Roosevelt and Stalin regularly huddled together to make disparaging remarks about British imperialism. And U.S. policymakers argued that "victory must bring in its train the liberation of all peoples. . . . The age of imperialism has ended."[11]

U.S. and Soviet opinion of French imperialism was even lower. During one summit, Stalin said that France "had no right to retain her former empire" and added that the French ruling class "was rotten to the core."[12] And while Roosevelt told the French in public that their Empire would be returned to them (in order to shore up anti-Nazi resistance), in closed meetings he affirmed that "when we've won the war, I will work with all my might and main to see to it that the United States is not wheedled into the position of accepting any plan that will further France's imperialistic ambitions, or that will aid and abet the British Empire in its imperial ambitions."[13] Secretary of State Cordell Hull went even further: "France has had [Indochina] . . . for nearly one hundred years, and the people are worse off than they were at the beginning. . . . France has milked it for one hundred years. The people of Indochina are entitled to something better than that."[14]

U.S. and Soviet leaders condemned imperialism and championed independence for two reasons. First, they wanted to break up European empires and devolve power to indigenous movements, which could then be expected to provide political support and economic opportunities to the new superpowers. As de Gaulle correctly observed, "Roosevelt expected that the crowd of small nations would assault the position of the colonial powers and assure the United States an enormous political and economic clientele."[15] Second, they sought to transfer European political power to themselves. To accomplish this, they jointly fashioned a new interstate system at a series of great power conferences and summit meetings held during and immediately following the war. Of these meetings, the two at Yalta and Potsdam are the most famous. But there were others. Held in sites scattered around the world (an indication, perhaps, that they would have global import), these summits together laid the groundwork for the new interstate system.

In August 1941, Roosevelt and Churchill met on a ship off the coast of Newfoundland and outlined the Atlantic Charter, a first draft of the postwar system. It was during this summit that Roosevelt first coined the term "United Nations," applying it to the Allies fighting the war. This preliminary outline was then endorsed by twenty-six countries on January 1, 1942, and twenty-one more states signed on as the war progressed.[16]

The Big Three—Roosevelt, Stalin, and Churchill—held their first wartime summit in Teheran from November 28 to December 1, 1943. Roosevelt and Churchill had met with Chiang Kai-shek but not Stalin in Cairo the week before, on November 26, 1943, and all three assembled in Yalta in February 1945. At the first postwar conference, held in July 1945 in Potsdam, Truman replaced Roosevelt, who had died in the interim, and Clement Attlee replaced Churchill, who lost an election midway through the conference. Truman and Attlee were joined by Stalin. Finally, the United Nations, great and small, assembled in San Francisco in June 1945 to sign the UN Charter, which had been hammered out at previous summits and at ministerial conferences such as the one held at Dumbarton Oaks in Washington, D.C., in August 1944.

Another development contributed to this process. In 1943, at Roosevelt's request, Stalin dissolved the Comintern. This cleared the way for the two superpowers to concentrate on the creation of a unified interstate system. Stalin, not firmly committed to an international organization based on political movements, was prepared to concede to Roosevelt a system based on independent states. This move was also a tacit admission that the Soviet Union would accept a subaltern role in the new system vis-à-vis the United States.

The Yalta agreements have often been criticized for unnecessarily conceding to the Soviet Union a sphere of interest in Europe, which resulted in its division between East and West. But every summit contained agreements recognizing the right of the superpowers to dominate certain spheres. The United States insisted on it. These agreements helped differentiate the great powers and also distinguish great states from small. During the various summits, the United States obtained preeminent rights in Japan, China, the Pacific archipelagos, the Middle East (particularly Iran but also Turkey), the Mediterranean (particularly Greece), and Western Europe, in addition to recognition of its existing preeminence in Latin America, accorded to itself by the Monroe Doctrine. In return, the United States recognized the Soviet Union's preeminence in the territories occupied by the Red Army, but nowhere else. And the United States gave European colonial empires only the assurance that it would not actively assist independence movements in their colonies, though it would welcome their secession and independence.

As a document, the UN Charter represents the full expression of Wilson and Lenin's call for common security, creation of independent nation-states, break-up of colonial empires, and secession based on self-determination. The historian Franz Gross summarized its main points as follows: "The first duty of the United Nations was to induce all nations to preserve peace (Preamble of the Charter) and that war was outlawed (Article 2, paragraph 4). Second priority was given to the establishment of human rights, and a third priority to guaranteeing the territorial integrity and political independence of all states, by sanctions or military force (Chapter VII) if necessary. Fourth, steps for the attainment of higher standards of living, social progress, and cultural cooperation were to be promoted (Chapters IX and X). Finally, colonialism was to be eliminated gradually through the institution of self-government on the basis of the paramount interest of the inhabitants."[17] The United States and the Soviet Union proposed amendments to the charter that referred to relations among nations "based on respect for the principle of equal rights and self-determination of peoples."[18] Neither Wilson nor Lenin could have asked for more.

Great and small member states would meet as equals in the United Nations General Assembly. Unlike the League of Nations, the UN did not provide separate membership for colonized territories. The constituent unit would be the independent nation-state. This egalitarianism gave European colonial empires pause. Throughout the war, Churchill tried to confine the egalitarian principles of the Atlantic Charter, and its call for self-determination, to those European states occupied by the Nazis. Roosevelt, however, insisted that it apply around the world.[19] In one outburst at Yalta, Churchill said he would never "consent to forty or fifty nations thrusting interfering fingers into the life's existence of the British Empire," adding, "No one will induce me as long as I am Prime Minister to let any representatives of Great Britain go to a conference where we will be placed in a dock and asked to justify our right to live in a world we have tried to save."[20] But Churchill's fulminations fell on deaf ears. Roosevelt and Stalin, anti-colonialist partners, remained adamant about self-determination applying around the world and insisted that independent nation-states be equal in the new system. Indeed, they both hoped that the new states would "thrust interfering fingers" into British imperial affairs.

If the great powers had stopped there, the United Nations would have been a novel, radical political institution. But the United States and the Soviet Union tempered equality with hierarchy, through a variety of forms. The trustee system differentiated member and nonmember states. Voting privileges differentiated member states. And the Security Council, with veto power for the Big Five (the United States, the Soviet Union, Great Britain, France, and China), as well as the provision for the creation of politico-military caucuses or blocs, which would institutionalize informal spheres of influence, distinguished great states from small.

Like the League, the United Nations created a trustee system for administering territories not yet "ready" for independence. Roosevelt argued that "trusteeship is based on the principle of unselfish service. For a time at least there are many minor children among the peoples of the world who need trustees in their relations with other nations and peoples."[21] This view differed little from colonial European attitudes toward non-European peoples, except that Roosevelt, like Wilson, believed the period of trusteeship should be shorter than that envisaged by the British colonial minister who said that centuries might be needed for some peoples to achieve self-government.

But for Roosevelt, the trusteeship period could still be a rather long time. In an exchange about the future of Korean trusteeship, which was to be divided between the United States and the Soviet Union, Roosevelt proposed that it last twenty to thirty years and Stalin countered that "the shorter the period the better."[22] In any event, some of the territories assigned to the United States were to be held in trustee status for thirty years or more. And when those under trusteeship came of age, the United Nations would make provision for plebiscites to determine their future.[23]

Voting privileges also subtly differentiated states within the United Nations from non-member states outside it. Only independent states could become members and vote. This standard gave the U.S. a considerable advantage, for a large number of the independent states were located in Latin America and could be expected to vote with the United States. Great Britain could count on fewer votes because only Commonwealth states (which by the end of the war had been granted the right to secede so that they might qualify as "independent" states under the UN Charter) could vote in the United Nations. The rest of the colonies, numerous as they were, were combined into one British vote. This is one reason why Britain moved after the war to decolonize many of its possessions—to increase its weight in interstate affairs. Churchill objected to the UN's franchise system, which gave Britain few votes in proportion to the territory it controlled. Yet this was precisely what Roosevelt had in mind. He counted on friendly independent states to provide a working majority for the United States.[24]

The UN franchise also troubled the Soviets, who realized that they would be regularly outvoted in the United Nations given the allocation of voting members in the postwar world. Stalin thus asked Roosevelt to extend the franchise to all fifteen Soviet Republics, which Stalin claimed had the right to secede and should therefore be considered "independent."[25] Roosevelt rejected this particular demand, but agreed to let the Soviet Union have three UN votes—one for the Soviet Union and one each for Byelorussia and the Ukraine—in order to ensure Soviet participation in the United Nations.[26] In return, Stalin offered the United States three votes, which Roosevelt refused because he was confident that it would be unnecessary as well as unseemly. With the votes of independent nation-states stacked behind it, the United States could afford to be generous with the Soviet Union.

But this minor episode illustrates the extent of Soviet inferiority vis-à-vis the United States in the new system.

As the UN's franchise was extended in the postwar years—it now has 159 member states—and the number of socialist, non-aligned and independent-minded states increased, the United States could no longer count on an automatic majority. But Roosevelt made plans for just such an eventuality by insisting on a Security Council, whose five permanent members each had the power to veto General Assembly resolutions. By including nationalist China (then a compliant U.S. ally) as a permanent member, the United States ensured itself a dominant voice within the UN's "senate" or "executive" chamber. The UN Security Council grew out of Roosevelt's belief that great powers should keep the peace. Roosevelt told British Foreign Minister Anthony Eden that the United States, Great Britain, China, and the Soviet Union would play a dominant role in the postwar world, adding that they "would be the powers for many years to come that have to police the world."[27]

This departure from Wilson's conception of the League was designed to secure U.S. Senate approval and the participation of the other great powers. On the necessity of a Security Council with veto rights, the great powers could agree. They disagreed only on which powers should receive a permanent seat and a veto. Churchill complained that Roosevelt's insistence on the extension of a seat to China amounted to the creation of a "faggot vote," which would side with the United States "in any attempt to liquidate the British overseas Empire,"[28] and Stalin grumbled about including France, which he viewed as undeserving, given its wartime role. But in the end, none of the great powers made too much fuss because Security Council majorities would count for nothing if any one permanent member could veto unacceptable resolutions. In the end, the great powers agreed with Stalin that "the large powers must dictate to the small."[29]

At the United Nations' inaugural conference in San Francisco, Senator Arthur Vandenberg and a young assistant secretary of state for Latin American affairs, Nelson Rockefeller, drafted provisions (Article 51) for inclusion into the UN Charter that permitted the creation of politico-military blocs outside the charter but within its principles.[30] Initially drafted to permit the formation of Monroe Doctrine–oriented military alliances in Latin America, Article 51 permitted the United States to organize a series of its own military alliances around the world: NATO, CENTO, SEATO, and ANZUS.[31] The ANZUS alliance, consisting of Australia, New Zealand, and the United States, even excluded Britain from an alliance with its own dominions. One British historian has written that "Britain was deliberately, humiliatingly, excluded."³² The creation of U.S. blocs in turn prompted Soviet imitation: Stalin formed a new Communist International—the Communist Information Bureau—in 1946, and later established the Warsaw Pact as a response to NATO.³³

Another development, which took place outside the United Nations, also contributed to the differentiation of states within the new system. The invention, construction, and use of nuclear weapons by the United States clearly distanced it from other states, including the Soviet Union. This development pushed the United States, already at the apex of the new system, far above it—at least for a time. The simultaneous arrival of the new order and nuclear weapons should not be seen as unrelated developments. For the United States, nuclear weapons would guarantee common security in a way that was never before possible. Nuclear weapons solidified the system in a way that the British Navy never could.

The division of the world among great powers, the differentiation of great and small states and that of states and trust territories, all combined to create a hierarchical interstate system. Unlike the previous system, with its rigid hierarchy composed of heterogeneous political units, the new order consisted of uniform political units that possessed nominal equality with other independent states. Because its superpower architects insisted on independence, based on self-determination, the new system was considerably more egalitarian than the old one. Although it permitted greater internal mobility—independent nation-states such as Germany and Japan could rise within it without causing the kind of frictions that had led, under the old system, to war—the new system was nonetheless dominated by great states, now called superpowers.

Significantly, the United States and the Soviet Union created this system as partners, and then participated in it more as rivals than as enemies. They shared an anti-colonial perspective—a desire to encourage independence movements to secede from colonial empires and form independent nation-states—and agreed to create a new, global interstate system that would provide common security and promote their positions in it. They succeeded despite deeply held ideological, political, economic, and military differences—and despite obdurate resistance from colonial empires.

The egalitarian hierarchy that the United States and the Soviet Union created was not a completely novel structure. Economic systems are frequently based on the same kind of relations. The global monetary system, for example, can also be described as an egalitarian hierarchy. Currency exchange rates for different countries make it possible to translate prices around the world. Equivalent prices enable producers and consumers to determine the value of goods on a world scale. Competition to produce goods for the world market tends to equalize or standardize the price of goods. This is the egalitarian dimension of the monetary system.

But exchange rates can be set on a world scale only if there is a standard unit of measure, a reference point against which the value of different goods in different countries possessing different currencies can be measured. Historically, this role has been played by gold or, more recently, by the U.S. dollar. It is of considerable economic consequence which particular currency becomes the standard, the reference point for others. Because the owners of the standard currency can determine the terms of its sale—by printing more or fewer dollars—they can profit from its use as a monetary standard. The rise of a particular standard currency results in the creation of a monetary hierarchy, with dollars at the apex, deutsche marks and yen in the first tier, and zlotys, pesos, and yuan arranged below them.[34]

In the interstate system, independent states have equal rights to print their own money, to tax their own populace, and to raise their own armies. But they do not possess equal abilities to set the rate of exchange for their currency, to impose tariffs or taxes on others, or to deploy their armies outside their state's territorial boundaries. Some states—great states, superpowers—possess that ability, and some of them more than others. Their ability to do so is the measure of their position in the interstate hierarchy.

Throughout the interwar period, the United States and the Soviet Union used self-determination as a slogan to promote the secession of colonies from European empires. They inscribed this idea in the UN Charter and proclaimed to the world that self-determination was the unreserved, universal right of any nation or people within the interstate system.

In the context of the old system, dominated by colonial empires, this had been an effective slogan. Independence movements around the world rallied to it. But with the emergence of a new political order after World War II, the meaning of self-determination was transformed. What meaning would self-determination have during the devolution of colonial power to indigenous successors, and what meaning would it have after independent states were formed? Which "nations" would have the right to acquire colonial power and form an independent state? Would other "nations" have the same right to self-determination in the new state? And if only "legitimate" nations had the right to self-determination, how would they be identified? These were questions raised by Wilson's Secretary of State, who viewed self-determination as political dynamite.

None of the independence movements that acquired power from colonial empires, whether by force or by treaty, agreed that the right of self-determination should be given to any people within its territory. Yet the colonial precedent having been established, many would take this as their right. In time, the idea of self-determination would collide head-on with the meaning of *swaraj* or *sinparam* or *doc lap*.

And having superseded colonial empires, what meaning would self-determination have for the superpowers? Would they persist in calling for its continuing, universal application? Would they admit it within their own borders or where it hurt their newly found interests as global superpowers? As it turned out, the meaning Wilson and Lenin gave to self-determination would differ from the meaning given to it by Truman and Stalin; Eisenhower, Kennedy, and Khrushchev; Johnson, Nixon, Ford, Carter, and Brezhnev; and Reagan, Bush, and Gorbachev.

As a result, the meaning of self-determination would diverge from the meaning of *swaraj, sinparam*, and *doc lap*. Indigenous independence movements, joined in common purpose with the United States and the Soviet Union in the interwar period, would find themselves diverging from the superpowers after the war. In the short run, this divergence would lead to partition. In the long run it would undermine the interstate system.

·II·

DEVOLUTION
AND
DIVISION

· 6 ·

The British Balancing Act

Even during the most robust phase of British colonialism, when the British Empire spanned the globe, the sun of its authority was already beginning to set over its nearest and oldest colony, Ireland. By the end of World War I, British rule in Ireland had been eclipsed: the partition of the island in 1920 reduced British rule to six northeast counties called Ulster.

A generation later, after World War II, British rule in India and Palestine would be extinguished as well. And, as in Ireland, the devolution of British authority in these countries would result in partition.

In 1900, British officials could not have imagined that the devolution of British power was possible in the colonies. As Lord Salisbury said of the Irish, the inhabitants were no more capable of self-government than were African Hottentots.[1] Nor would they have believed that devolution, should it come, would result in the division of political power between two competing independence movements. But in Ireland, India, and Palestine, that is precisely what happened.

Although partition was not the inevitable consequence of devolution, it emerged time and again as the most practical solution British authorities could devise. When confronted with seemingly intractable

"Troubles" in Ireland, British officials sought to find a solution that would secure devolution on terms favorable to themselves—what they called "dominion"—and minimize the risk of social conflict among the indigenous inhabitants. As it turned out, partition accomplished neither goal. British interests were irreparably damaged, partition altered the course of conflict but did not avert it, and the Troubles, be they in Ireland, India, or Palestine, continued.

British rule in these three countries was troubled by the rise of indigenous independence movements and by U.S. demands that Great Britain relinquish colonial authority in the name of self-determination. British officials demonstrated some capacity to contain these internal and external political forces by advancing various political reforms in Ireland before World War I and in India and Palestine before World War II. But successive world wars simultaneously strengthened the position of the independence movements and the anti-colonial states, while weakening British authority in fundamental ways. World War I forced the pace of devolution in Ireland and introduced the possibility of self-government in India and Palestine for the first time, with World War II accelerating the progress of devolution there.

The awakening of anti-colonial political forces and the rise of movements demanding independence made devolution an issue in colonial Ireland, India, and Palestine. So long as these movements adhered to constitutional reforms and subscribed to "dominion" (as discussed in Chapter 4), the establishment of independent nation-states could be indefinitely postponed. But as elements within these movements grew frustrated with the pace of reform and the structure of devolution, they began to threaten violence.

In Ireland, the slow but steady progress of an Irish Home Rule Bill frustrated both loyalist Protestants and independence-minded Catholics. First introduced in 1886, again in 1893, and for a third time in 1912, this modest bill would have created an all-Irish parliament that could legislate on civil domestic matters. Authority for trade, security, and foreign affairs would be retained by the British Parliament (in which the Irish would continue to have some modest representation). The Protestant Irish minority objected to the bill because Irish Catholics would command a majority in an all-Irish parliament. Without the protection of their conservative allies in the British Parliament, Irish Protestants feared that the Catholic majority would use this new forum to coerce them. They wanted instead to keep Ireland within the British union, where they could ally with British conservatives to preserve their status in Ireland. Their secessionism thus took a curious form: the Protestants threatened to secede from an all-Irish state so that they could maintain their "union" with the colonial overlord, Great Britain. Irish Protestants and their conservative allies had been able to defeat the Home Rule Bills of 1886 and 1893, but when it became clear that some version of the 1912 bill would be approved by a Liberal-dominated British Parliament, Protestants began organizing an armed militia—the 100,000-member Ulster Volunteer Force—and threatened to secede from a devolved Irish state, saying "Ulster will fight" rather than submit to Catholic Irish majority rule. Protestant leader Edward Carson even urged the formation of a provisional government. When, in March 1914, the British government took steps to protect its arsenals in Northern Ireland from possible assault and seizure by Protestant militias, British officers sympathetic to the Protestant cause announced that they would resign rather than suppress an incipient rebellion. The Curragh incident (named for the military base involved) and the threat of violence by the Ulster Volunteers tested British authority on the eve of world war and stimulated the Liberal government's search for a solution to the Irish problem.

The pace of reform, slowed by the alliance of Protestant unionists and British conservatives, and the character of reform, which would devolve to an Irish legislature only limited power over domestic affairs, frustrated independence-minded Catholics. And the growth of a stubborn, armed, Protestant opposition movement to Home Rule undermined the position of Catholic moderates (who would accept dominion Home Rule) and strengthened supporters of Irish independence. Irish republicans responded to the threat of Protestant violence by organizing an armed militia of their own—the Irish Volunteers—in the prewar years.[2] So long as British approval of an Irish Home Rule Bill appeared imminent, as it did from 1912 to 1914, Sinn Fein, the armed, independence-minded wing of the Irish independence movement, was held in check. Sinn Fein did not want to jeopardize the chances for Home Rule, which was then supported by the moderate Catholic majority.

The outbreak of World War I in August 1914 shifted the ground under all the participants. The British government, which had labored to pass a Home Rule Bill that year, suspended it for the duration of the war. And the competing Irish movements adopted new strategies to take advantage of the war, each in its own way. The Protestant minority rallied to the imperial war effort: the Ulster Volunteer Force transformed itself overnight from a group of rebellious secessionists to an embryonic national guard, which then marched off to be mauled in Flanders fields. The Catholic majority, having been denied Home Rule just when it finally appeared within grasp, fulminated against imperialist war. The moderates became stubbornly uncooperative and demanded that the government commit itself to Home Rule as the price for their participation in the British war effort. The militants plotted revolution. The Easter Rebellion of 1916 announced the independence movement's willingness to use force to secure devolution, much as the Curragh incident had demonstrated the Protestant minority's determination to prevent it.

The suspension of the Home Rule Bill, the execution of the Easter Rebellion's leaders, and the attempt to extend conscription to a recalcitrant populace destroyed Catholic support for dominion and strengthened the republicans, who demanded unqualified independence. In the 1918 election, the moderate Irish Parliamentary Party won only six seats at Westminster. Sinn Fein won seventy-three.[3]

After the war, the Irish republicans withdrew from the British Parliament, declared their independence on January 21, 1919, formed a legislature—the Dail—and began waging an irregular war to overthrow continued British rule. British officials sent in arms and enlisted Protestant irregulars—the Black and Tans and the Auxiliaries—to suppress the postwar rebellion.[4] By the fall of 1919, civil war had engulfed the island, continuing until 1920, when the British moved to devolve authority in most, though not all, of the country. Violence and the threat of violence by both loyalist and independence-minded Irish movements had tested British authority and patience. In the end, British officials were persuaded that Irish affairs were too troublesome to manage and that British colonial authority there would have to be surrendered.

Independence movements in India had supported the British war effort during World War I, and as a price for their participation, they extracted a promise that the British would work toward "the gradual development of self-governing institutions with a view to the progressive realization of responsible government in India as an integral part of the British Empire."[5] Postwar reforms, however, failed to advance self-government significantly in the subcontinent. So from 1920 to 1922, the Indian National Congress and the Muslim League joined forces, under Gandhi's leadership, to mount a non-violent protest campaign and to demand an end to British rule in India. Although the *satyagraha*, or non-cooperation campaign, was predominantly peaceful, violence flared around its edges. Gandhi called off the campaign when it became clear that the independence movement could not control the spread of violence. But the point had been made: while the movement did not condone violence, the threat of popular riot and rebellion lay behind it.

British authorities were able to contain the independence movements during the interwar period. The India Act of 1935, like the Irish Home Rule Bill of 1912, was a moderate reform granting a measure of self-government at the local and provincial level. In the short run it assuaged Congress Party moderates, who were swept into low-level government offices by huge electoral majorities. But it antagonized the Muslim League, which found itself unable to place its candidates in office, even in predominantly Moslem regions. Jinnah and League leaders began to worry that in any devolved state, the Moslem minority would be coerced by the Congress majority. Jinnah told the League conference in 1938 that the Congress would "bully you, tyrannize over you and intimidate you." A year later he said that the aim of the Congress was to get Moslems to "submit unconditionally to the Hindu raj. . . . The high command of the Congress is determined, absolutely determined, to crush all other communities and culture in this country and to establish [Hindu] raj."⁶

The outbreak of World War II altered the political landscape. The British viceroy declared war on India's behalf without consulting the independence movements. This unilateral declaration made a mockery of the 1935 reforms and effectively suspended any progress toward self-government as a British military government assumed control over the subcontinent. Frustrated by the abrogation of even modest reform and minimal participation in government, the Indian National Congress refused to support the war effort, withdrew from office, and launched a non-cooperation campaign. Thousands of Congress Party members went to jail.⁷ On July 6, 1942, the Congress, meeting in Bombay, passed a "Quit India" resolution demanding that the British withdraw from India. If the government refused, it would launch an active civil disobedience campaign. Hard-pressed British officials treated this demand as the non-violent equivalent of the

Easter Rebellion and the next day outlawed the Congress, arrested its leaders, and interned them for the duration of the war.[8]

The Muslim League, which had been hostile to British reform before the war, now saw an opportunity to make considerable gains by rallying to support the British war effort. The League rejected a Congress plea to join forces against the British and agreed instead to participate in the wartime government. The divergent attitudes of the two independence movements toward the war sharply divided the Congress and the League. While the Congress withdrew from participation in government and moved into non-violent opposition, the League advanced its case for special political consideration in any future devolution of British power. At its 1940 conference in Lahore, the League resolved that "no constitutional plan would be . . . acceptable unless it is designed on the following basic principle, viz: that geographical contiguous areas . . . in which Moslems are numerically in the majority . . . should be grouped to constitute 'independent states' in which the constituent units shall be autonomous and sovereign."[9] This resolution constituted a demand for a separate Pakistan, an "Ulster" where the Moslem minority might find refuge from the Hindu majority. And in 1943, the League adopted the slogan that summarized its approach to devolution: "Divide and Quit."[10]

The League made considerable gains during the war, but these were threatened at war's end by British promises to move toward undivided devolution and by the Congress's return to public life. The League moved into the opposition after the war and raised the threat of violence as a means to secure devolution on favorable terms. On August 16, 1946, Jinnah announced that the League would engage in "direct action" and would withdraw from government positions. "Never have we in the whole history of the League done anything except by constitutional methods and by constitutionalism," Jinnah said. "But now we are obliged and forced into this position. This day we bid goodbye to constitutional methods."[11] According to a British participant in British–League negotiations prior to this announcement, Jinnah said that "the British government and the Congress each held a pistol in its hand, the one of authority and arms, the other of mass struggle and non-cooperation. 'Today,' he declared, 'we have also forged a pistol and are in the position to use it.' "[12]

The League's threat immediately provoked widespread violence. In Calcutta alone, some 20,000 people were killed or seriously injured in the days that followed.[13] The violence in Calcutta was the Muslim

League's Curragh. It announced to British authorities and the Congress that Moslems would fight unless they could force devolution on favorable terms.

And for its part, the Congress could not promise to restrain the riot and rebellion that pressed against its non-violent front lines from behind.

The wartime and postwar strategies of the independence movements tested British authority in an effort to advance devolution. Unlike the Ulster loyalists, however, the wartime Muslim League loyalists would not settle for continued union with Britain. Like their counterparts in the Congress, they wanted independence—but on their own terms.

During World War I, Arab independence movements had assisted the British in their war against the Ottoman Empire, which ruled much of the Middle East. But these close wartime relations dissolved once the British and French claimed sizable mandates in what is now Lebanon, Syria, Jordan, and Israel, and as the British permitted Jewish emigration into Palestine as a way to fulfill its promise (made in the second Balfour Declaration of 1917) to create a Jewish national home. After the war, Arab Palestinians rioted periodically—in 1920, 1921, and 1929—attacking British authorities and Jewish communities. With the creation of an Arab Independence Party in 1932, which helped organize widespread Christian and Moslem Arab opposition to continued British rule, sporadic rioting gave way to widespread rebellion in 1936. For three years, Arab Palestinians conducted an irregular war in an effort to force the British to devolve political power in Palestine to the Arab Palestinian majority, which would then move to block Zionist land purchases and curtail Jewish immigration.[14]

Although Zionist leaders pressed British authorities to permit Jewish immigration into Palestine, the movement did not directly challenge British rule during the interwar period. As a response to Arab Palestinian riots and revolt, though, they began to organize their own militias, of which the Haganah (Hebrew for "Defense") was the most prominent.[15]

British authorities responded to the 1936 Arab Revolt by commissioning an investigation into its origins. The Peel Commission noted that "Arab nationalism is as intense a force as Jewish [nationalism]. The Arab leaders' demand for national self-government and the shutting down of the Jewish National Home has remained unchanged since 1920. . . . The gulf between the races is thus already wide and will continue to widen if the present Mandate is maintained."[16] The commission urged the partition of Palestine into separate Arab and Zionist states, with strategic and religious areas such as Jerusalem remaining under British rule.[17]

This proposal, like the Irish Home Rule Bill and the 1935 Indian reforms, frustrated the Arab Palestinian movement's hope for a unitary state and majority rule. And it disappointed militant Zionists who saw a two-state solution as a retreat from the Balfour Declaration. Continuing Arab Palestinian hostility—the Arab revolt resumed with renewed vigor after the report was issued—and Zionist criticism forced British authorities to commission another report. The 1939 White Paper on Palestine repealed the Peel Commission recommendations, ruled out partition, rejected the idea of an eventual Jewish state, and restricted Jewish immigration.

The outbreak of World War II did not immediately change the position of contending independence movements. The Arab Palestinian movement opposed participation in the British war effort (in contrast to their support for the British during World War I), and like the majority movements in Ireland and India, the Arab Palestinian movement pressed vigorously for devolution during the war. Some leaders even collaborated with the Axis. Most of the Zionist movement, however, rallied to support the British. Zionist leaders pressed for the creation of a Jewish division in the British Army and many members of the Haganah joined the British armed forces.

By the end of the war, however, radical Zionist militias—the Stern Gang and the Irgun (led by Avraham Stern and Menachem Begin, respectively)—began to use violence to force the British to devolve power to a Jewish state. The assassination in Cairo of British Minister of State Lord Moyne in 1944 by Zionist irregulars marked the beginning of a campaign to oust the British by force. Although the British cabinet that year had again proposed the eventual partition of Palestine, the Moyne assassination put off any move to implement this policy.[18] And after the war, Foreign Secretary Ernest Bevin announced that "Balfour is dead"—that Britain had retreated from its commitment to an independent Jewish state in Palestine.[19] The British retreat from the Balfour Declaration and the impact of the Holocaust in Europe destroyed the moderate Zionist position, which had been sympathetic to British authority in Palestine (much as the Irish Catholic moderate position had been destroyed during World War I). Factions within the Zionist movement would move increasingly into armed confrontation with the British during the postwar years.

In Ireland, India, and Palestine, contending independence movements switched from cooperation to opposition, opposition that included the threat or use of force to achieve their ends. The effect of these oscillating threats was the appearance, to British authorities, of more or less continuous violence. Although the movements did not devise a common strategy—on the contrary, their tactics were based primarily on opposition and opportunism—the effect was a sort of tag-team approach to devolution. First one movement opposed British rule by force, then took a cooperative breather while the other launched an attack.

Independence movement behavior, moreover, fell into another consistent pattern. During the world wars, majority movements—Catholic Irish republicans, the Indian National Congress, and Arab Palestinians—opposed the British war effort and used rebellion and non-cooperation to test British authority. On the other hand, minority movements—Ulster Protestants, Indian Moslems, and Zionists in Palestine—rallied to support the British. The decision to oppose or support British authority during world war would have important consequences once the British moved to devolve power in these colonies.

And while independence movements within the Empire pressed the British to relinquish power, the United States applied pressure from without. U.S. support for self-determination, as a means of encouraging colonial peoples to secede from empire, remained consistent through two world wars. But it was during those wars, not the interwar period, that U.S. leaders actively demanded British devolution. America-first isolationism in the 1920s and 1930s blunted U.S. enthusiasm for self-determination, and British officials were able to deflect halfhearted demands for devolution by the United States and the Soviet Union through their modest attempts to reform the Empire. During the world wars, however, when U.S. leaders could demand a high price for assistance, their demands for devolution sharpened, and British authorities found it more difficult to resist changing their colonial policies.

During World War I, U.S. interest in the devolution of British rule in Ireland was shaped by a large, vocal Irish immigrant constituency in the United States, which paid keen attention to developments in

Ireland and persuaded U.S. political leaders to do the same. Balfour described this influential group as "coming from that part of Ireland which has never loved England."[20] The 1916 Easter Rebellion and the summary execution of its leaders angered Irish-Americans and inflamed anti-British sentiment in the United States, which had not yet entered the war. Lloyd George, then Minister of Munitions, said that if Britain did not defend its response to the rebellion, "the Irish-American vote will go over to the German side, the Americans will break our blockade, and force an ignominious peace on us unless something is done even provisionally to satisfy America."[21] The British ambassador to the United States likewise warned the cabinet that "the situation is much like that of a soda water bottle with the wires cut but the cork unexploded."[22] President Wilson, responding to congressional demands for Irish self-determination, had his ambassador tell Lloyd George that Britain's failure to advance Irish self-government prevented the United States from lending assistance to the British.[23] And Balfour, visiting the United States, cabled the Prime Minister: "The Irish Question is apparently the only difficulty we have to face here, and its settlement would no doubt greatly facilitate the vigorous and lasting cooperation of the U.S. government in the war."[24]

The British responded to U.S. demands by reevaluating the suspension of the Irish Home Rule Bill and convening an Irish convention to negotiate a settlement that would secure Irish and American support for the faltering British war effort. As Lloyd George told Ulster Protestant leader Edward Carson in 1917, "We've got to settle the Irish Question now—in spite of you."[25] Negotiations failed to produce a satisfactory agreement, but U.S. leaders were assuaged by British assurances to devolve power after the war. The United States soon entered the war on Britain's side.

During World War II, the United States did not press Britain specifically to relinquish colonial power, but U.S. officials did express concern about developments in India, where Indian National Congress obstructionism was seen as undermining Britain's ability to resist the Japanese advance through Southeast Asia and Burma,[26] and in Palestine, where British restrictions on Jewish immigration were viewed as denying safe haven for Jews escaping the gathering Holocaust in Europe. Like the anti-British Irish-American community during World War I, a vocal Jewish immigrant constituency in the United States was keenly interested in British colonial policy in the

Middle East. British officials complained about the pressure exerted by this group during and after World War II in much the same terms that Balfour and Lloyd George complained about Irish-Americans during World War I. In both instances, political constituencies in the United States stiffened presidential demands for the devolution of British colonial power.

The Indian independence movements did not possess an immigrant constituency in the United States, but they did not need one as much as the Irish and Zionist movements, for their demands for devolution exerted considerable direct pressure on British authorities.

In an attempt to contain independence movements, many British officials themselves pressed for devolution. Prewar reforms—the Irish Home Rule Bill of 1912, the 1935 Government of India Act, and the 1937 Peel Commission Report—demonstrated that the British were interested in some kind of devolution and were willing to take steps to implement it. But the pace of reform was extremely slow. The Irish Home Rule Bill was passed some twenty-eight years after it was first introduced. The Government of India Act and the Peel Commission proposals came two decades after the 1917 Balfour Declarations promising some form of self-government in India and Palestine. At this leisurely pace, the managers of Britain's colonial Empire would not have fully devolved power until the 1960s.[27]

The world wars quickened the pace of devolution. To secure the assistance of independence movements in its colonies and of the United States during World War I, British authorities issued a series of declarations in 1917 promising to devolve significant power after the war. Nineteen-seventeen was the nadir of the war for the British Empire and its allies: revolution in Russia threatened to take that nation out of the war and unleash German divisions from the eastern front against Britain and France. It is not surprising, then, that British officials moved to promise devolution as the price for political and military assistance. Ireland came first. On May 16, 1917, Lloyd George promised to reopen the question of devolution in Ireland.[28] This was done to rally support in Ireland so that the large British military forces stationed there in the aftermath of the Easter Rebellion could be reduced, so that Irishmen could be recruited to fill European trenches, and so that the Irish Question would not obstruct U.S. intervention on the Allies' behalf. And on August 20 and November 2 came the two Balfour Declarations, first in India and then in Palestine.

Taken together, these steps demonstrated some degree of British willingness to speed the devolution of power in its colonies, but after the war, British officials began to hedge these promises and burden them with qualifications and restrictions. Independence movements would later object to the British retreat from promises made under the duress of war, but Lloyd George, Balfour, and Churchill (then colonial secretary) had crafted their pledges and declarations in ambiguous terms so that they could later qualify them.[29] Still, the British could not renege entirely on their wartime commitments. Although they managed to defer devolution in India and Palestine until after World War II, they could not do so in Ireland, where irregular war broke out in 1919. Churchill admitted that the war had changed almost everything in the modern world but that the deluge of war had not solved—or even altered—the Irish troubles: "As the deluge subsides and the waters fall short we see the dreary steeples of Fermanagh and Tyrone emerging once again. The integrity of their quarrel is one of the few institutions that has been unaltered in the cataclysm which has swept the world."[30] And so the war-weary British, in an attempt to rid themselves of continuing Irish troubles, agreed to devolve power in 1920.

World War II had much the same effect. Then it was the Indian National Congress's turn to obstruct the war. To counter Congress opposition to the war, British Viceroy Lord Linlithgow promised the Muslim League in April 1940 that no postwar devolution plan would be made without the League's consent. Since the League had presented its demand for a separate Islamic state—Pakistan—to the Viceroy just a few days before, Linlithgow's pledge marked a significant departure from the go-slow devolution policies of the interwar period.[31]

But as the war dragged on and the British experienced dramatic military reverses in Southeast Asia, they sought to enlist the Congress's support for the war by offering devolution on more attractive terms. In 1942, Churchill commissioned a mission to India led by Sir Stafford Cripps, who proposed granting dominion status to India after the war.[32] Congress leaders, however, rejected the proposal because it deferred devolution until after the war and because it implied that the creation of a separate Moslem state might be possible. They then announced the beginning of a civil disobedience campaign. Nevertheless, Cripps's proposals more or less committed the British to some kind of devolution after the war.

Churchill was less eager to make wartime promises to independence movements in Palestine. After the Afrika Korps was defeated at El Alamein and the German threat to the Middle East receded in 1942, the British did not need to rally support in Palestine. And internal disturbances there posed less of a problem during most of the war than they did in India. Unlike Ireland and India, the British held Palestine under a League of Nations mandate, which meant that they had promised to relinquish power at some point. The problem for British officials in Palestine, therefore, was not *if* they would devolve power but *when* and *how* to do so.

Reform and war drove a wedge between independence movements in Ireland, India, and Palestine. As the devolution of British power approached, the conflict between competing independence movements sharpened. These movements began, in turn, violently and non-violently to press British authorities to devolve power. As these intramural conflicts sharpened, British officials began to look for ways to disengage quickly, and partition seemed the most expeditious option. In the postwar periods, then, the British would move simultaneously to devolve and divide power.

· 7 ·

"Divide and Quit"

As the British devolved power in Ireland, India, and Palestine, they also divided it.

The British did not always do so. In Burma, Ceylon, and a host of other Asian and African colonies, they relinquished power to indigenous successors in unified states. But in Ireland, India, and Palestine they divided power between competing independence movements and awarded them separate states. They did so for many of the same reasons: to protect minorities, to reward wartime allies, to avert civil war, and to curry political support in Britain.

During debates over the course of devolution, many British politicians expressed a determination to protect minority rights. When arguing against Irish Home Rule, Balfour invoked John Stuart Mill's warning against the "tyranny of the majority" to protest the imposition of Home Rule on the Protestant minority and said that "handing over Ulster to the tender mercies of the rest of Ireland is surely dishonorable as well as idiotic."[1] During his wartime mission to India in 1942, Sir Stafford Cripps told Congress leaders that their suggestion that the Congress form a national government in which its representatives would constitute a majority "would in fact constitute an absolute *dictatorship* of the majority [emphasis added]."[2] And the 1937

Peel Commission in Palestine urged partition because each side feared the other would eventually become a tyrannical majority. Partition, the commissioners argued, would deliver Arabs "from the fear of being 'swamped' by the Jews and from the possibility of ultimate subjection to Jewish rule," while the Jews would be relieved "from the possibility of . . . being subjected in the future to Arab rule."[3] Minority movements echoed this sentiment. One Muslim League leader warned that "when sure of its power, [the Hindu majority] will, in the name of democracy and with the help of British bayonets, make use of it to coerce and crush us, its prey, into complete captivity."[4]

This British concern for minorities grew out of a conservative political tradition, an identification with members of some minority groups in these countries, and a belief that majority and minority groups were irreconcilable. In reaction to the French and American Revolutions, conservative political theorists in nineteenth-century Britain lamented the development of mass-based democratic movements, which they regarded as incapable of responsible government. They argued that the new majoritarian parties would be even more tyrannical than the despotic monarchs they had replaced, and urged the preservation of rule by responsible minorities—men of education, property, and wealth. They consequently opposed the extension of the franchise to citizens who did not hold property or pay taxes, and they sought to prevent the diminution of the House of Lords' role in Parliament. It was only by having reduced the Lords' ability to veto legislation in 1911 that Asquith's Liberal government was able to advance Irish Home Rule legislation in 1912. In supporting the rights of minorities, conservative British politicians also justified their own status as a well-to-do, educated elite.

Liberal British politicians, by contrast, tended to support the extension of the franchise at home and the devolution of what they called "responsible self-government" overseas. Winston Churchill, then a Liberal, lambasted Tory politicians whose defense of minority rights prevented any recognition of majority rule: "Coercion for four-fifths of Ireland is a healthful, exhilarating, salutary exercise but lay a finger upon the Tory fifth—sacrilege, tyranny, murder."[5]

British sympathy for minority groups had an ethnic dimension as well as a philosophical one. Many British authorities felt a kinship with certain minorities in Ireland, India, and Palestine that they did not feel toward majority groups. And this kinship was based on a

shared ethnic-religious identification. British officials tended to identify with Irish Protestants, many of whom had emigrated to Ireland
from England, Scotland, and Wales. They felt less warmly toward
Irish Catholics, whose confessional religion had been routed in England in the sixteenth and seventeenth centuries. In India, the British
found that Islam, though distant from Protestantism, was at least
monotheistic. Pantheistic Hindu religions stood at an even greater
distance from British faiths. And, as it happened, the British felt a
stronger "racial" affinity with Moslems in India, descended from Aryan cultures to the north and west, than with non-Islamic Hindus. Yet
while British officials might identify with Islamic Indians, they did
not transfer this affinity to Moslem Arabs in Palestine. There they
found a greater kinship with Jews—in part because there was a substantial Jewish population in Britain, in part because while Moslems
stood closer to Protestant faiths than Hindus, Jews stood closer still.

British attitudes toward ethnicity and religion were thus based on
a complex hierarchy, one much like the Empire's Byzantine political
structure. This hierarchy was based on relative, not absolute characteristics, so support for Moslem Indians did not necessarily require
support for Moslem Arabs. Insisting on systemwide consistency
would have made it more difficult for the British to manage their
heterogeneous empire by divide-and-rule tactics.

The British use of ethnic-religious characteristics to divide and rule
imperial populations, moreover, tended to make these divisions *seem*
permanent and irreconcilable. As Lloyd George said of Irish Protestants, they were "as alien in blood, in religious faith, in traditions,
in outlook—as alien from the rest of Ireland in this respect as the
inhabitants of [Scotland]."[6]

Although the two Indian movements had demonstrated a capacity
to work together for independence, British reforms were designed to
divide them, preventing the Muslim League and the Congress from
acting in concert against British rule. In 1905, for example, the British
viceroy, Lord Curzon, divided Bengal into two provinces, one with
a Moslem majority and the other with a Hindu majority.[7] The division
of Bengal effectively split the Muslim League from the Congress: the
League saw partition as a chance to gain power in the Islamic province, while the Congress viewed it as an attempt to weaken its power,
prompting it to demand independence for the first time and to organize its first boycott of British goods.[8] (King George V reunited
Bengal in 1911, which of course antagonized the Muslim League and

exacerbated its differences with the Congress.) A year later, Curzon established separate electorates for Moslems and Hindus throughout the subcontinent, which had the same polarizing effect as the partition of Bengal. The British would retain this practice until the reforms of 1935 eliminated separate electorates and created provincial governments to which the Congress could elect majorities, thus antagonizing the Muslim League. Linlithgow's unilateral decision to go to war in 1939 hammered home the wedge between the two independence movements and divided them further.

By the 1940s, the British authorities had come to view the two movements as permanently antagonistic. After having engineered the partition of India in 1947, Lord Mountbatten concluded, "The responsibility for this mad decision [must lie] squarely on Indian shoulders in the eyes of the world, for one day they will bitterly regret the decision they are about to make."[9] In the end, then, Mountbatten blamed partition on Indian divisiveness, which, he failed to note, had largely been a British creation.[10]

British pragmatism also contributed to division as devolution approached. Because devolution occurred after the conclusion of the world wars, the British gave some weight in devolution deliberations to the wartime roles of independence movements. They were inclined to view the claims of cooperative independence movements more favorably than those of obstructionist, uncooperative, or rebellious movements. As discussed in Chapter 6, minority independence movements—the Irish Protestants, Muslim League Indians, and Zionists—had rallied to the British side during the First and Second World Wars, while the majority independence movements—the Irish Catholics, Congress Party Indians, Arab Palestinians—had obstructed the imperial war effort. Minority movements, moreover, supported partition; majority movements opposed it. And as devolution approached, partition was a convenient way for British officials to reward their wartime allies and punish wartime foes.

British officials also hoped that by granting independence and awarding state power to each movement, partition would avert civil war, which threatened from both sides. Minority movements successfully exploited British fears of civil war in the postwar years, demonstrating (particularly in Ireland and Palestine) that they were willing to wage irregular war to achieve devolution on favorable terms. British authorities took the threat of civil war particularly seriously in Ireland because many British officials had actively encouraged it. Before World War I, British Conservatives announced their support for Ulster unionist intransigence. Conservative Party leader Andrew Bonar Law (who would become Prime Minister in 1922) declared in 1912 that "there are things stronger than parliamentary majorities" and that "I can imagine no lengths of resistance to which Ulster can go in which I am not prepared to support them."[11] This kind of incendiary talk prompted Winston Churchill to remark that advocating civil war was a strange way to prevent it.[12]

Domestic political considerations played an important role in the British decision to divide Ireland, India, and Palestine. Conservative politicians sided with Ulster unionists against Home Rule as a means to attack the Liberals, who had won smashing electoral victories in 1906 and 1910. For Conservatives, the Irish Question could be used to undermine the Liberal government's ability to maintain power. As U.S. Ambassador Walter Hines Page explained, "The Conservatives have used Ulster and its army as a club to drive the Liberals out of power: and they have gone to the very brink of civil war. They don't really care about Ulster. I doubt whether they care very much about Home Rule. They'd slip Ireland out to sea without much worry— except their own financial loss. It's the Lloyd George programme that infuriates them, and Ulster and anti-Home Rule are all mere weapons to stop the general Liberal Revolution."[13]

After the war, however, the Conservatives conceded that Home Rule was necessary, the Liberals agreed that some separate provision for Ulster was necessary, and together they agreed to devolve power so that Britain could retain some measure of power—dominion—in Ireland. Lloyd George and the Liberals were willing to concede a separate Ulster because the continuation of war in Ireland was undermining the war-weary public's support for the Liberal government.

Domestic considerations also persuaded British officials to move toward devolution and division in India and Palestine. The Labour government, which had replaced Churchill's wartime coalition government in 1945, wanted to devolve power quickly in India and Palestine so that it could pursue its domestic social agenda, which was hampered by continued administrative and military expenditures in the two colonies. Division promised a way to devolve power more rapidly in India because it eliminated the necessity for negotiating and drafting an intricate, power-sharing constitution or for providing British guarantees during a potentially difficult transition period. And in Palestine, the haste with which the British abandoned their mandate to the United Nations meant that they had not even had time to divide the country before leaving. They left that task to the United Nations.

In their desire to protect minorities, reward allies, prevent war, and maintain domestic support, British officials increased the weight of minority claims. Ulster unionists could claim to represent only one-fifth of the Irish, the Muslim League only one-quarter of the Indians, Zionists one-third to two-fifths of the inhabitants in Palestine. Yet British authorities treated them as having an *equal* claim on power. Without weighing their own concerns in the balance, British authorities would not have extended these minorities the kind of consideration that they refused to extend to other minorities—Catholic unionists in Ireland, Sikhs and princes in India, Christian Arabs in Palestine. Devolution tended to polarize and restrict political definitions. Groups that did not fit into the two great camps, which were increasingly seen as the only legitimate contenders for power, were ignored and their claims shunted aside.

Before World War I, a substantial segment of moderate Irish Catholic opinion had favored Dominion Home Rule. But they were squeezed out of the picture by the suspension of Home Rule at the beginning of the war, by the Easter Rebellion and British repression during the war, and by the irregular war after it. Partition, no matter how carefully drawn, would not give representation to all. Ulster unionists, for example, wanted nine northeastern counties included in a secessionist state. Three of these counties, however, had substantial, but minority, Protestant populations. The dilemma was this: if they were excluded, substantial Protestant populations would be subjected to rule by Catholic majorities, precisely what partition was supposed to prevent; but if they were included, Catholic majorities in these counties would be subject to rule by the statewide Protestant majority, and their inclusion would narrow the numerical majority that Protestants enjoyed. (A six-county state would give the Protestants a substantial majority; a nine-county state would give them a much narrower majority.)

Even pro-Ulster Balfour admitted, "If you have a Hibernia Irredenta within the province of Ulster, you will greatly add to the difficulties of the Ulster parliament; you will reproduce on a small scale all of the trouble which we had at Westminster during the [last] forty years."[14]

But a Catholic minority would be subject to Protestant rule whether the British created a six-county or a nine-county Ulster. De Valera argued that it was impossible to create an Ulster that did not include substantial Catholic minorities, who deserved the same protection that the British wanted to extend to the Protestants: "[Lloyd George] can't take six counties, no, nor four. Why he can't even take Antrim, because it hasn't a complete Ulster representation. He can't take Belfast, because in Belfast there are more nationalists than in the City of Cork. Therefore, Lloyd George can't himself find the boundary of his Ulster. His homogeneous Ulster does not exist."[15]

The same was true in India. Various large minority populations were excluded from a two-part devolution. The Sikhs in the Punjab argued that if Moslems could use religion as the basis for their claim to a separate state, they could too. So did the Pathans on the northwest frontier, the Nagas on the Assam-Burma border, the Adibasi of Bihar and Orissa, the inhabitants of Darjeeling, and the Dravidians in the South.[16] But the British excluded Sikhs from any meaningful role in devolution negotiations, as they did the princes who ruled some 565 states with varying degrees of autonomy, and the untouchables.[17] These groups did not have the socio-political weight, the mass-based political parties, to participate as *equals* in the devolution process.

As in Ireland, where supporters of Ulster wrestled with the six- vs. nine-county question, the Muslim League struggled to define a large, "homogeneous" Moslem state and prevent the creation of what Jinnah called "a moth-eaten Pakistan."[18] But India's problem mirrored Ireland's. If regions with large minority populations were included, Pakistan, like Ulster, would grow in size, but at the same time reducing the power of the newly created majority. This problem would become particularly difficult in Kashmir, which had a Moslem majority but a Hindu ruling prince; the struggle for control of the province would eventually lead to war between the two new countries after devolution and partition.

In Palestine, the British made some attempt to include Christians in their calculations—recommending at various times the neutralization of Jerusalem so that it would be accessible to all faiths—but the interests of Christians and other non-Islamic Arabs and non-Zionist Jewish groups were swept aside by the two main antagonists.

As a result of this British policy to treat the two big contending movements as equals and to drop smaller movements out of the equation altogether, and as a result of their own separate strategies, the independence movements split apart. As devolution approached, minority and majority movements were persuaded, even coerced, to accept partition as a condition of independence.

In Ireland, the decision to accept partition as the price of independence tore Sinn Fein apart. Following World War I, Sinn Fein had conducted an irregular guerrilla war to force the British to relinquish control of the island. British authorities recruited Ulster unionists to suppress the uprising, and after two years of fighting, the British passed legislation providing for the partition of Ireland and for continued British control over trade and defense. However, the 1920 Government of Ireland Bill failed to end the war; in late 1921, the British agreed to direct negotiations with Sinn Fein to end the war and devolve British power.

In the negotiations, the bipartisan British team (which consisted of Lloyd George, Balfour, and Churchill) offered dominion status to Sinn Fein representatives (led by De Valera and Michael Collins) if they would also accept partition and the creation of a separate Ulster. When Sinn Fein representatives refused, the British offered a carrot and brandished a stick. To make partition palatable, the British promised to hold a reunification referendum in the North and South that would determine whether the separate states would be reunited, two years after partition went into effect. But they also said that if Sinn Fein did not immediately accept this offer, they would abrogate the cease-fire, send new troops to Ireland, and crush the rebellion by force.[19]

At this critical juncture, De Valera was absent from the negotiations. Collins, believing that partition would be temporary and that renewed British intervention could be deterred, agreed to accept the British terms. He did not, or could not, consult with De Valera. The decision to accept partition split Sinn Fein. A narrow majority of the Dail—64 to 57—supported partition and dominion, while the large minority, led by De Valera, violently opposed the Anglo-Irish Treaty and took up arms to prevent its implementation.[20] After two more years of irregular internecine war, during which Collins was killed, the majority suppressed minority resistance and De Valera surrendered. The British, meanwhile, reneged on their promise of reunification elections and the countrywide referendum was never held.

At the British-sponsored 1930 Roundtable conference in India, Muslim League leader Dr. Shafa'at Ahmad Khan said, "We have never tried to create an Ulster in India; that has never been our wish."[21] But ten years later, at the League conference in Lahore, Jinnah demanded that such a separate state be provided for Moslems, saying, "It is a dream that Hindus and Moslems can ever evolve a common identity."[22] The 1935 reforms, which had increased the political power of the Congress and diminished that of the League, persuaded Jinnah that the League could not compete with the Congress in a unitary state. During the war, however, the Congress rejected the League's secessionist demand. As Maulana Abul Kalam Azad, a Moslem leader of the Congress, said of Jinnah's decision to push for a separate state, "Whether we like it or not, we have now become an Indian nation, united and indivisible. No fantasy or artificial scheming to separate and divide can break this unity."[23]

Other Congress leaders viewed partition with ambivalence. Gandhi rejected the the two-nations theory advanced by the League, saying, "Hindus and Muslims of India are not two nations. Those whom God has made one, man will never be able to divide."[24] Yet he also borrowed Lenin's argument that self-determination was like the right to divorce: "The Muslims must have the same right of self-determination that the rest of India has. We are at present a joint family. Any member may claim a division."[25] Indeed, he told the 1942 Cripps Mission that "if the vast majority of Muslims regard themselves as a separate nation . . . no power on earth can compel them to think otherwise. And if they want to partition India on that basis, they must have that partition, unless Hindus want to fight against such a division. So far as I can see, such a preparation is silently going on on behalf of both parties. That way lies suicide."[26] Other Congress leaders refused to consider partition at this date (as late as 1946 they refused to negotiate with the League on anything less than a unified government based on majority rule),[27] but they accepted partition as a temporary expedient in 1947. In April 1947, Nehru said that "the Muslim League can have Pakistan if they want to but on the condition that they do not take away other parts of India which do not wish to join Pakistan."[28] The Congress working committee formally accepted partition in principle on May 1, 1947, less than four months before the British relinquished power.[29]

The Congress was persuaded to accept partition in much the same way that Sinn Fein negotiators were. When Lord Mountbatten arrived in India in February 1947, he announced that the British would withdraw in June 1948. But he soon decided to move up the departure date to August 15, 1947, in the hope that this shortened deadline would force the Congress and the League to agree on devolution more quickly. In negotiations with the Irish, the British had imposed a deadline and then threatened to *intervene* if a satisfactory agreement was not reached. In India, they imposed a deadline (of several months rather than days) and threatened to *leave* if negotiations were not concluded. The effect was the same: the Congress was forced to put partition on the bargaining table. To make it easier for the Congress to negotiate on these terms, Mountbatten, like his predecessors, promised to arrange for reunification elections after partition was completed. And like Michael Collins, Nehru decided that "perhaps the best way [to reunify the country] is to go through some kind of partition now."[30]

The rapid devolution of British power, together with the promise of reunification elections down the road, made partition easier for the Congress to accept. As Azad said of partition on June 16, 1947, "The division [of India] is only on the map of the country and not in the hearts of the people, and I am sure it is going to be a short-lived partition."[31]

In Palestine, by contrast, the Zionists moved toward partition as the British retreated from it. When the Peel Commission first advocated partition in 1937, the Twentieth Zionist Congress commended the report but refrained from endorsing partition in principle.[32] The various political factions within the Zionist movement were sharply divided about the British proposal, but after the British retreated from partition in the 1939 White Paper, important segments of the movement began to regard partition as the pragmatic alternative to minority status in a unitary Palestine.

David Ben-Gurion pushed for partition early on. He welcomed the Peel Commission report because it was "the first document since the Mandate which strengthens our moral and political status. . . . It gives us control over the coast of Palestine; large immigration; a Jewish army; systematic colonization under state control."[33] A pragmatist, Ben-Gurion believed (like Jinnah) that by obtaining even a small, "moth-eaten" Palestine, the Zionists could control the means—immigration, colonization, and an army—necessary to build up that state.[34]

Some Zionists, like Vladimir Jabotinsky, opposed this strategy and rejected partition because they wanted to establish a Jewish state over all of mandated Palestine. Others, like Shlomo Kaplansky, opposed it because they believed that a binational settlement with Arab Palestinians was necessary. And some, like Dr. Judah Magnes, opposed it because they believed partition would unfairly advance the Jewish minority at the expense of the Arab majority.[35]

Ben-Gurion began to press for partition during the war. At the 1942 American Zionist Conference, held at the Biltmore Hotel in New York City, Ben-Gurion joined forces with Rabbi Hillel Silver and passed, over Chaim Weizmann's objections, a proposal demanding "that the gates of Palestine be opened [to Jewish immigration]; that the Jewish Agency be vested with the necessary authority for upbuilding the country . . . and that Palestine be established as a Jewish commonwealth integrated in the structure of the new democratic world."[36] The Biltmore program viewed devolution as a process resulting in the creation of a Jewish nation-state that would be a member of the emerging interstate system—the "new democratic world"—then being created by the superpowers and their allies. Although it did not explicitly advance partition (as the 1940 Lahore meeting of the Muslim League did), the Biltmore program was consistent with it, and it was promoted by Ben-Gurion, who favored partition. After the war, on August 5, 1946, Ben-Gurion convinced the Jewish Agency to adopt partition as the official policy of the Zionist movement.[37]

While the Zionist movement adopted the pro-partition strategy of minority movements in Ireland and India, British authorities, uncharacteristically, moved away from it, though they never abandoned it. Devolution in Palestine took a somewhat different course, for a time, than it did in Ireland and India, because the British devolved power not to indigenous successors but to an intermediary—the United Nations. The UN then simultaneously devolved power and advanced partition. Although the devolution process was different in some respects, its result—partition—would be the same. But British officials could disassociate themselves from the outcome in Palestine in a way that was impossible in Ireland and India.

Although the British were sensitive to foreign demands for devolution in Ireland and India, and were particularly alert to American views on Ireland during World War I, they did not invite or permit the United States or any international organization to participate in the devolution of its nearest and dearest colonies. They took a different view of Palestine, inviting participation in the devolution process in part because the territory was a League of Nations mandate (and therefore had a different international standing than Ireland or

India), and in part because it was a costly property—not the kind of colony from which Britain could reap the kind of financial rewards that it had long extracted from Ireland and India.

The British first explored the possibility of U.S. participation after World War II; a joint Anglo-American Committee of Inquiry was sent to Palestine in the spring of 1946. In April this committee (the Morrison-Grady Commission) issued its report, which stated:

> In order to dispose, once and for all, of the *exclusive* claims of Jews and Arabs to Palestine, we regard it as essential that a clear statement of the following principles be made: 1. That Jew shall not dominate Arab and Arab shall not dominate Jew in Palestine. 2. That Palestine shall be neither a Jewish state nor an Arab state. 3. That the form of government ultimately to be established, shall, under international guarantees, fully protect and preserve the interests in the Holy Land of Christendom and of the Moslem and Jewish faiths. Thus Palestine must ultimately become a state which guards the rights of Moslems, Jews and Christians alike; and accords to the inhabitants, as a *whole*, the fullest measure of self-government, consistent with the principles set forth above [emphasis added].[38]

The report also recommended that the British mandate given by the now-defunct League of Nations be converted into a trusteeship of the newly formed United Nations.[39]

The Anglo-American report reiterated the British position expressed in the 1939 White Paper, which had rejected the 1937 Peel Commission's recommendation that Palestine be partitioned. But the recommendations made by the joint committee were themselves rejected by President Truman on October 4, 1946. Truman was persuaded by Zionists that partition would be preferable to a unitary state in which Jews would be a minority.[40]

After the British attempt to enlist U.S. support for its devolution policy in Palestine failed, the Attlee government decided to force the pace of devolution and adopted Winston Churchill's suggestion (of August 1, 1946) that the "one rightful, reasonable, simple and compulsive lever which we held was and is a sincere readiness to lay our mandate at the feet of the United Nations Organization and thereafter evacuate the country."[41] So on February 18, 1947, Britain announced that it would delegate its authority in Palestine to the United Nations.[42]

The timing of the British announcement is significant. On February 18, the Attlee government announced the end of British rule in Palestine. Two days later, on February 20, Lord Mountbatten announced

Britain's departure from India. Like the two Balfour Declarations of 1917, and the reforms of the mid-1930s, the February 1947 announcements synchronized British movements in India and Palestine. Devolution in both countries would proceed according to the same clock.

When he first announced the British decision to depart from India, Mountbatten named a June 1948 devolution date. He subsequently sped up the process and devolved power on August 15, 1947. While Attlee did not at first set a date for British withdrawal from Palestine—he announced the actual date of withdrawal on September 26, 1947, after the UN Commission on Palestine recommended partition—the British actually withdrew on May 15, 1948, thereby keeping close to Mountbatten's original schedule for devolution in India.[43] The synchronicity of developments in India and Palestine undoubtedly contributed to their singular outcome.

Britain's under-the-gun approach to the devolution process in Palestine quickened developments there, as it had in India. The United Nations assembled a multilateral committee in May 1947 to investigate the issues in Palestine. The committee traveled to Palestine and returned with its recommendations on August 31. The majority recommended the partition of Palestine into a Jewish and an Arab state, with Jerusalem assigned to an international trusteeship. The minority report proposed the creation of a single, federal Palestinian government which would consist of two states (states in the American sense of the term, as in North and South Carolina), one Jewish and one Arab.[44] The majority report essentially dusted off the 1937 Peel Commission Report, adopted its tripartite partition, modified its boundaries slightly, and passed along the updated version to the United Nations for ratification.[45]

The UN committee also recommended that the British stay on to supervise partition. The British demurred from this onerous task. According to the minutes of a September 20 cabinet meeting, "The Prime Minister [Attlee] said that in his view there was a close parallel between the position in Palestine and the recent situation in India. He did not think it reasonable to ask the British administration in Palestine to continue in present conditions, and he hoped that salutary results would be produced by a clear announcement that His Majesty's Government intended to relinquish the Mandate and, failing a peaceful settlement, to withdraw the British administration and British forces."[46] On September 26, the British announced that they would terminate unilaterally their mandate in Palestine and withdraw on May 15, 1948.[47]

President Truman endorsed the UN recommendation for partition in October. And on November 29, the United Nations, with U.S. and Soviet support, adopted the committee's recommendation and endorsed the partition of Palestine.[48] The Soviets, the heirs of Lenin, supported partition because they viewed it as a way to end British colonialism and to promote self-determination. Andrei Gromyko, the Soviet delegate to the United Nations, said, "We cannot agree with the assertion which implies that the decision on the Partition of Palestine is aimed against Arabs and Arab countries. It is our deep conviction that this decision corresponds to the fundamental interests of both Arabs and Jews. . . . The Soviet Union supports . . . the aspirations of any state and any people, no matter how small its weight in international affairs, in the struggle against foreign dependence and remnants of colonial oppression."[49]

The day before the British withdrew, Ben-Gurion read a declaration of independence and announced the formation of a Jewish state: Israel. War broke out the following day and continued until a truce was established in the spring of 1949. Separate armistices were signed between February and July of that year.[50]

Unlike majority movements or factions of majority movements in Ireland and India, Arab Palestinians and their allies in neighboring states never viewed partition as an acceptable by-product of devolution. Had the British not delegated authority for devolution to the United Nations and its U.S.–Soviet architects, Arab Palestinians might have been able to forestall partition. But having failed to create a unified, mass-based political party (like Sinn Fein or the Indian National Congress), they relied heavily on neighboring states and the Arab League to act on their behalf; this was not effective.[51] As the venue changed from unilateral British decision making, where the Arabs had some influence, to multilateral UN decision making, where they could exert less pressure and the American-based Zionists could exert more, partition was impossible to deter.

British officials moved toward devolution and partition in Ireland, India, and Palestine at two speeds. For years, they had adopted a slow, plodding, deliberate pace: they formed commissions of inquiry and enacted modest reforms that inched their colonies toward self-government. But after World War I in Ireland and World War II in

India and Palestine, the British discarded reform, set deadlines, and raced toward devolution at breakneck speed. When they abandoned deliberate managerialism and adopted under-the-gun devolution, partition became a more attractive solution to the problems confronting British authorities, primarily because it could be implemented in a hurry. It did not require a continuing British presence, which would be necessary if a more complex, long-term constitutional solution was adopted. And partition seemed advantageous because it was the only solution to which most or all parties could agree. It offered something for everyone, at least in the short run. It promised to retain certain privileges—dominion—for British authorities in Ireland and India, it promised to break up the colonial empire and advance the creation of independent nation-states for the anti-colonial superpowers, and it awarded a measure of state power to the competing independence movements. Politically, partition was the lowest common denominator.

In their rush to partition, however, the British postponed consideration of some important issues. They put aside the decision as to whether partition would be a temporary or a permanent by-product of devolution. British officials told majority parties that partition would be temporary and provided for reunification elections in Ireland and India. But these provisions were not carefully written and did not stipulate any authority to administer them. It was left to now-independent states to determine whether they wanted to hold elections in which they might themselves be abolished. But few states wither away of their own accord. Not surprisingly, neither Northern Ireland nor Pakistan wanted to exercise this provision of the devolution agreement, and neither Ireland nor India could compel them to do so.

The British also deferred the issue of boundaries. In Ireland and India, British officials set up boundary commissions, staffed with political cartographers, to adjudicate disputed territorial claims. But theirs proved an impossible task. The lines they drew satisfied no one. No matter how carefully they might be drawn, boundaries between divided states left too many people on the wrong side. The same ethnic population would be part of a majority or a minority, depending on where the line was drawn. The result was the creation of a territorial basis for powerful irredentist claims.

In Ireland, the British gave Northern Ireland six counties, not the nine counties claimed by Protestants. And when the Hindu maharajah of Kashmir, a predominantly Moslem state lying between India and West Pakistan, joined India, military forces from both countries fought for control of the state. After inconclusive fighting, they divided it between them, a subdivision that neither regarded as permanent.[52]

In Palestine, no boundary commission was established. It was left to Zionist and Arab military forces to draw the lines. When the first Arab-Israeli war ended in 1949, Israel was 21 percent larger than the territory assigned to it by the United Nations' partition plan and possessed 80 percent of the area assigned to Palestine under the League of Nations' mandate.[53]

· 8 ·

Cold War Partition

After World War II, the devolution of military power in Germany, Korea, China, and Vietnam also resulted in partition. Partition in these countries has to be understood in the context of two developments: the creation of a new interstate system and the division of that system into spheres of influence.

The new interstate system created by U.S. and Soviet leaders during and just after the war was based on independent nation-states and was intended to replace the old system based on colonial empires and heterogeneous states. Although U.S. and Soviet officials disagreed about many things in the postwar period (as they did about the devolution of power in European and Asian countries), both superpowers nonetheless remained committed to the breakup of colonial empires and to the consolidation of this new interstate system. The United States and the Soviet Union thus supported the devolution of British power in Palestine and India, as well as devolution throughout Asia and the Middle East. And they remained committed to the United Nations as the institutional expression of the new system.

Even at the nadir of U.S.–Soviet relations in the late 1940s and early 1950s, neither country abandoned the joint effort to create this new interstate system or attempted to construct an alternative to it. The

United States did not retreat to America-first isolationism as it had after World War I, because the new system afforded it considerable economic, political, and military advantages. And the Soviet Union, which might have been expected to retreat to Soviet-first isolationism in response to U.S.–sponsored policy defeats in the United Nations, did not do so. The Soviets' UN Security Council veto helped them to retain their nation's influence in the UN even though they were regularly outvoted by substantial majorities.

Both countries remained committed to the fundamental features of the system they had created as wartime allies throughout the postwar period. Indeed, U.S. officials worried that the Soviet Union might permanently withdraw from the United Nations during the Korean War and start a rival organization, and they were relieved when the Soviets did not.

Despite sharp disagreements and dramatic fluctuations in bilateral relations, the continued participation of both superpowers in the interstate system is *the* central fact of the postwar period. Despite conflicts over the course of devolution in Europe, Asia, and the Middle East, they generally agreed to disagree and frequently found that partition was a practical way to do so. Through partition, they managed to contain their disagreements and avoid a third world war.

The superpowers could agree to disagree because they had provided for a division of the world into spheres of influence when they constructed the new interstate system at Yalta and Potsdam, as well as under the U.S.–sponsored amendments to the United Nations Charter. At the end of the war, these spheres were regional and limited in scope. Neither superpower claimed or recognized spheres of influence extending around the globe.

Although the superpowers recognized each other's right to claim a sphere, these claims were not carefully defined at the wartime summits, a consequence of the fluid character of world war. The superpowers sketched the outline of some spheres and divided between them the responsibility for occupying certain countries—Germany, Austria, Korea, China, and Vietnam—but these partitions were intended to be temporary, to be sorted out after the war was concluded.

The allocation of spheres of influence and the division of particular states was not inconsistent with the creation of a new interstate system. Although nominally egalitarian, the United States and the Soviet Union intended to fashion a system in which they could wield their newfound power. Spheres of influence permitted each to exercise its hegemony over some, though not all, states in the system. And because superpower partition would in each case result in the creation of two more-or-less independent nation-states, the devolution of power in Germany, Korea, China, and Vietnam would not impede the development of the new system. In fact, the creation of multiple states conformed to the principle of self-determination and augmented the weight of nation-states, as opposed to colonial empires, in the interstate system as a whole.

Although U.S. and Soviet officials agreed in general terms to allocate some spheres and to divide some countries, they disagreed as to the particulars of devolution and division. As tensions rose during the course of the Cold War, U.S. and Soviet spheres of influence widened and the division of particular countries deepened. The modest spheres originally claimed by the superpowers expanded dramatically during the decade after World War II, and the temporary division of Germany, Korea, China, and Vietnam was made permanent. (The partition of Austria was undone in 1955 as Austria became a neutral, unified state that was placed outside superpower blocs.)[1]

The globalization of superpower spheres and the hardening of wartime partitions began and ended in Germany. The attempt to define U.S. and Soviet spheres in the heart of Europe led to sharp disagreement, and during the period from 1945 to 1962, Germany was twice divided. In 1948–49 the country was partitioned along lines defined by wartime occupation zones. Then, in 1961–62, Berlin was subdivided and the partition of Germany was set in concrete.

In the interim, the superpowers also participated in the division of Korea, China, and Vietnam on a permanent basis, leading to the expansion of their respective spheres of influence. By the end of this period, the superpowers defined their spheres on a global basis.

In 1944, Stalin told Milovan Djilas, a Yugoslavian Communist leader, "This war is not as in the past. Whoever occupies a territory also imposes on it his own social system" as far "as his army can reach."[2] This did not happen right away. It took time to devolve power in these territories to regimes resembling the superpower occupiers. But in the decade after the war, both the United States and the Soviet Union established states and social systems in their own image in Germany, Korea, China, and Vietnam. The shifting focus of U.S.–Soviet relations, which moved geographically around the world, expanded their leaders' definition of spheres of influence and deepened their interest in the division of these countries as a way to defend these spheres.

To understand the simultaneous expansion of U.S. and Soviet spheres and the division of countries within their spheres, it is necessary to examine the course of devolution and partition in these four countries. Events in Germany contributed to developments in Asia, which in turn contributed to developments in Germany. For the most part, these developments were sequential: they began in Germany, moved to Korea and then China, and returned to Germany by way of Vietnam.

The superpowers agreed to divide Germany, Korea, and Vietnam during the war. Although they gave considerable attention to Germany at wartime summit conferences, they devoted only passing attention to the disposition of Korea and Vietnam. After the war they retreated from their collective decision to divide these countries, but within a few years, they returned to their initial plans.

During the war, all the Allied leaders proposed that Germany be dismembered, though they each had somewhat different ideas about how this might best be accomplished.

Roosevelt argued that "the war-breeding gangs of militarists must be rooted out of Germany if we are to have any real assurance of future peace."[3] To do this he first suggested that latent separatist tendencies be encouraged so that Germans could divide themselves and return to the disassembled condition of German states that had existed prior to 1871. But if that did not occur, he said, "Germany must be divided into several states."[4] Dismemberment, he told British Foreign Secretary Anthony Eden, was the "only wholly satisfactory solution" to the German problem.[5] Roosevelt first suggested Germany be divided into three states, and later five.[6] His successor, Harry Truman, initially agreed with Roosevelt and told Admiral Leahy prior to the Potsdam summit that "the separation of Germany into separate sovereign states would be advantageous to future peace and security."[7] Churchill was of like mind, proposing in 1943 that the southern German states be detached and united with Austria and Hungary in a "Danubian Confederacy."[8]

Stalin, moreover, told Churchill and Roosevelt in November 1943 that they all "preferred" partition and that he endorsed a threefold partition, which would include a North and East German state, a

Rhineland-Ruhr state, and a "Catholic republic" in Bavaria and Würt-temberg.[9] De Gaulle also indicated his preference for "another Peace of Westphalia, which had once set the seal on the division of Germany into petty principalities and vassal states."[10]

After agreeing to partition at the Teheran summit in late November 1943, the superpower leaders deferred the question of how German division and devolution would actually occur. In the meantime, a working group called the European Advisory Commission was formed to allocate responsibilities for the occupation of Germany pending its ultimate disposition. In January 1944, the British proposed a three-part division of occupation zones, under which the Soviets would occupy an eastern zone, the British a northwestern zone, and the Americans a central western and southern zone.[11] After some discussion about the boundaries of each zone, the U.S. and Soviet governments accepted the British proposal in June 1944. (These boundaries were subsequently adjusted to create a French zone in the southwest.) This occupation-zone division of Germany during the war would become the basis for partition after it.

While the superpowers did not agree to the particulars of partition during the war, U.S. officials prepared plans detailing the division and devolution of power in Germany. Two competing proposals emerged. The first, called the "Program to Prevent Germany from Starting World War Three," was drafted by Treasury Secretary Henry Morgenthau and his assistant Harry White. It provided for the annex-ation of parts of Germany to neighboring Denmark, Poland, and France and for the creation of two independent states, one in the south and west and one in the north and east.[12] Partition would be accompanied by deindustrialization—the closing of all mines and the dismantling of "all industrial plants and equipment not destroyed by military action"—which would transform the two Germanys into countries that would be "primarily agricultural and pastoral in character."[13]

Roosevelt initially endorsed the plan and told Morgenthau in Au-gust 1944, "We have got to be tough with Germany and I mean the German people not just the Nazis, we either have to castrate the German people or you have got to treat them in such a manner so they can't just go on reproducing people who want to continue the way they have in the past."[14] But he later backed away from extreme deindustrialization, saying, "No one wants to make Germany a wholly agricultural nation again."[15]

The State Department had rather different plans. They opposed partition and urged that Germany be retained as an economic unit. State Department planners also opposed the deindustrialization scheme because they believed it would make it difficult for the Germans to make reparation payments to the Soviets, reparations that U.S. officials had agreed in principle to deliver. They feared that the Morgenthau plan would repeat the errors of the Versailles settlement, under which the United States had subsidized the Germans so that they could make reparation payments to the Allies. Under the Treasury proposal, the State Department argued, the United States would have to do the same in order for the Germans to meet post-World War II reparation obligations, for only a reconstructed Germany could make reparations.[16] As Secretary of War Henry Stimson told Truman, Morgenthau's punitive partition plan would be a "grave mistake": "Punish her war criminals in full measure. Deprive her permanently of her weapons, her General Staff and perhaps her entire army. Guard her governmental action until the Nazi-educated generation has passed from the stage—admittedly a long job. But do not deprive her of a means of building up ultimately a contented Germany interested in following non-militaristic methods of civilization. . . . It is to the interests of the whole world that [the Germans] should not be driven by stress of hardship into a non-democratic and perhaps predatory habit of life."[17]

The Treasury-State debate over the future of Germany indicates that U.S. planners were of two minds. During the war they favored Morgenthau's punitive plan. After the war, however, they retreated from it and endorsed the State Department's approach to devolution in Germany, which advocated reconstruction. Then during 1947–48, they adopted parts of each. U.S. officials simultaneously advanced partition, which the Treasury Department had urged, and German reconstruction, which the State Department advocated. The result would be the reconstruction of a separate West German state.

The future of Korea was not high on the superpowers' agenda during the war, though it did come up at superpower summits. At the Cairo summit, the Pacific war allies—Roosevelt, Churchill, and Chiang Kai-shek (Stalin was not present because the Soviet Union was not then at war with Japan)—issued a declaration that stated: "The aforesaid three powers, mindful of the enslavement of the people of Korea [by

Japan], are determined that in due course Korea shall become free and independent."[18]

Before power could be devolved to a "free and independent" Korea, however, Roosevelt thought it should pass through a period of four-power superpower trusteeship (under the United States, China, Great Britain, and the Soviet Union), which would last some thirty or forty years. Roosevelt raised the issue of Korea with Stalin at the Teheran and Yalta Conferences, even though the Soviet Union had not yet declared war on Japan, and Stalin endorsed the idea with one qualification: "The shorter the period [of trusteeship] the better."[19]

After the Soviet Union entered the war against Japan in the summer of 1945, two junior U.S. military officers were assigned the task of demarcating U.S. and Soviet occupation zones in Korea. On the night of August 10–11, Colonels C. H. Bonesteel III and Dean Rusk (who would later be Secretary of State under Presidents Kennedy and Johnson) were given thirty minutes to complete the task.[20] They hastily took out a map and drew a line across Korea at the 38th parallel, choosing this latitude because it divided the country roughly in half and placed the Korean capital of Seoul in the U.S. zone.[21] Although Rusk and other U.S. officials worried that the Soviets would not accept this arbitrary division because Soviet troops could have occupied the whole peninsula before U.S. forces could land, Stalin did halt the Soviet advance at the 38th parallel. Truman later recalled that "the 38th parallel . . . was not debated over nor bargained for by either side."[22]

During this process, Roosevelt's idea of a four-power trusteeship was shunted aside. Unlike Germany, where Great Britain and France were given occupation zones, the other two Asian powers—Great Britain and China—were not allocated zones in Korea. But as in Germany, the occupation-zone partition of Korea was supposed to be temporary. After Japan surrendered, the superpowers would devolve power to a unified country. Within a few years of the war's end, however, they would divide the country, along wartime lines, on a permanent basis.

While the United States and the Soviet Union shunted aside their European and Asian allies in Korea, they found a role for them in the postwar occupation of Vietnam.

In 1943 Roosevelt suggested that Vietnam, like Korea and Germany, be made a four-power trusteeship, again under the United States, the

Soviet Union, Great Britain, and China, and that power devolve to an indigenous government after twenty or thirty years.[23] At one point he even offered China a major role in Vietnam, to which Chiang replied, "It's no help to us. We don't want it. They are not Chinese. They would not assimilate into the Chinese people."[24]

Although Roosevelt was opposed to continued French colonialism in Indochina, he suggested after the Yalta summit that the French be permitted to reassume their authority in the area, provided they promise to devolve power to indigenous groups within a short time.[25] Roosevelt took this step because the other allies were either unwilling or unable to assume such responsibility. And after Truman took office, U.S. officials in May 1945 recognized French claims in Indochina.[26] But because the French were then incapable of immediately acting on such claims, the superpowers meeting at Potsdam assigned responsibility to the Chinese and the British for accepting the anticipated Japanese surrender and for occupying Vietnam. British troops were assigned an occupation zone south of the 16th parallel and Nationalist Chinese forces the zone north of that line.[27] Both countries assumed that their occupation responsibilities would be brief and that they would devolve their authority to the French.

In August 1945, however, the superpower disposition of Vietnam was interrupted by Ho Chi Minh, who announced the creation of an independent Vietnamese republic. Despite Ho's pleas, however, the Soviet Union, which had endorsed the Potsdam plan for Vietnam, refused to recognize his new regime.[28] The British and Chinese proceeded to occupy their respective zones. Without superpower recognition, Vietnamese independence was stillborn, and in March 1946, the British and Chinese began to withdraw their forces in favor of the French.

The superpowers would return to the devolution of French rule in Indochina in 1954, when they would again agree to divide the country, this time at the 17th parallel.

The superpowers took a somewhat different view of China during the war. Unlike Korea and Vietnam, China had not been overrun by the Japanese, though Japanese forces controlled much of the country. For the superpowers, the problem was how to devolve power in Japanese-occupied China, not in China as a whole. No formal assignment of Allied occupation zones was made, as in Germany, Korea, and Vietnam. A sort of free-for-all ensued as the United States and the Soviet Union—and Nationalist and Communist Chinese forces—rushed to occupy territories held by the Japanese. The Soviets occupied much of Manchuria and northern China, where the Chinese Communists were strong, and the United States sent the Marines into central and western China to secure these areas for the Nationalists. The superpowers might have agreed to create occupation zones and partition China into North and South, but they did not do so.[29]

U.S. officials persuaded the Soviets to recognize the Nationalist Chinese government and devolve power in the occupied areas to them in return for Chinese territorial concessions to the Soviet Union: leases on some Chinese ports, railway concessions, and the creation of an independent Outer Mongolia.[30] The Soviets then permitted Nationalist troops to enter much of their occupied territories ahead of the Communists. The Soviets and the Nationalists even signed a Treaty of Friendship.[31] As Soviet Foreign Minister Vyacheslav Molotov told U.S. officials at the end of 1945, "It was without question that we all agreed to support Chiang Kai-shek and that the Soviet Union has embodied this in writing [at Potsdam]."[32]

During and immediately after the war, then, the superpowers opposed the partition of China. It would only be in 1950, as a result of developments in Germany and Korea, that they would change their minds.

Wartime agreements may have provided for the *de facto* division of Germany, Korea, and Vietnam, but partition did not become *de jure* until 1948 in Germany and Korea and 1954 in Vietnam. It was not immediately apparent that these countries would be divided. After the war, in fact, U.S. and Soviet officials retreated from partition and promoted unification, albeit on their own terms. After a few years, however, conflicting political and economic needs persuaded both superpowers to advance partition. In Germany and Korea, partition moved forward at the same pace, almost in lockstep.

In Germany, the American and Soviet leadership were of the same mind. Each wanted a unified German economy and a polity that would serve its own interests. The problem was that they had separate interests. The United States wanted to create a German economy that would assist the reconstruction of Western Europe. As policy planner George Kennan said, "To talk about the recovery of Europe and to oppose the recovery of Germany is nonsense. People can have both or they can have neither."[33] Germany would assist European recovery not by paying its reparations in cash or in kind (sending industrial equipment in lieu of cash) but by providing the goods—coal, industrial products—then in short supply throughout Europe, in exchange for foodstuffs, which were scarce in Germany.

The United States also wanted a German government that would resist both a resurgence of indigenous militarism and the importation of Communism. A neutral or neutralizing government would fit U.S. specifications. But the strongest political party in a united Germany would probably have been the Social Democrats, who were seen by the United States as anti-Fascist but not sufficiently anti-Communist, which meant they could not keep a united Germany neutral.[34]

The Soviets wanted the postwar German economy to assist the recovery of the Soviet Union and then that of Eastern Europe. But because they had suffered devastating wartime economic losses, they wanted Germany to make direct contributions to the Soviet Union with very little in exchange. The Soviets first wanted to receive some $10 billion in reparations, which would be paid for by the Germans in industrial equipment or raw materials, followed by the creation of a German economy that could participate in a wider European recovery.[35]

Like the United States, the Soviets also wanted a neutralizing government, one that could resist resurgent militarism. But they believed that a Communist government, or one friendly to the Soviet Union, could best ensure this. They distrusted the Social Democrats as insufficiently anti-Fascist because they had been unable to prevent the rise of Nazi power in the interwar period.

U.S. officials opposed using the German economy to aid Soviet economic recovery, because they believed such a policy would forestall the recovery of the other war-battered European economies. Unless these other European economies recovered quickly, Communist political movements would grow and the United States could find itself subsidizing Germany and Europe—with much of the aid going to the Soviet Union—without laying the basis for long-term recovery. U.S. officials thus began taking unilateral steps to prevent the Soviet Union from extracting reparations from Germany. A U.S. directive in 1947 stated that "an orderly, prosperous Europe requires the economic contribution of a stable and productive Germany" and that reparations "should not permanently limit Germany's industrial capacity."[36] U.S. officials subsequently refused to fulfill superpower reparations agreements. In the fall of 1946, the United States moved to unify the three western occupation zones in Germany into a single economic unit, which excluded the Soviets, and on June 20, 1948, introduced currency reform in the western zone.[37] The German economy was then integrated into the Western European economy, which received generous Marshall Plan assistance.[38]

By issuing a new currency, U.S. officials hoped to eliminate inflation and the black market. At the time, the preferred unit of exchange in the western zones was Lucky Strike cigarettes (one carton equaled 23,000 Reichsmarks or $2,300 U.S.). This system encouraged hoarding of food and consumer goods. According to one U.S. official, the currency reform "transformed the German scene from one day to the next. On June 21, goods reappeared in the stores, money resumed its normal function, and the black and grey markets reverted to a minor role."[39] The Soviets responded to these measures by introducing their own currency two days later and blockading Allied access to Berlin. Throughout the events that followed, the Soviets would match U.S. moves with nearly identical policies of their own.

The growing division of economic life was followed by an increased separation of political life. After the currency reform, U.S. officials instructed the minister-presidents of West German states to convene a constituent assembly and draw up a "Basic Law" that would guide the development of political institutions and the devolution of Allied occupation authority to an indigenous German government.[40] Administrators of the western zones agreed to allow Germans "those governmental responsibilities which are compatible with the minimum requirements of occupation and control and which ultimately enable them to assume full governmental responsibility."[41] According to the U.S. State Department, this meant reconstituting western Germany "as a political entity capable of participating in and contributing to the reconstruction of Europe."[42]

However, the creation of a full-fledged, all-German constitution, which would establish a wholly sovereign state, independent of U.S. and Soviet authority, was deferred. The Basic Law was approved by the constituent assembly in May 1949 and soon ratified by the individual German states and the occupation authorities. Representatives were subsequently elected to the newly created parliament, the Bundestag.[43] During this period, the Soviets responded by establishing a People's Congress in East Germany, which ratified a constitution in March 1949 and established a government in the eastern zone on October 7.[44]

Both the United States and the Soviet Union wanted German re-unification on their own terms, which were defined by their separate economic needs. Failing that, they decided to pursue their separate economic agendas—reconstruction and integration in the West, reparation and integration in the East—in their separate occupation zones. The economic and the political partition of Germany was initiated by a series of unilateral U.S. actions, to which the Soviets responded in kind. Because the United States could not accomplish its economic objectives in the whole of Germany, officials like George Kennan recommended early on (in March 1946) that the United States and its allies "carry to its own logical conclusion the process of *partition* . . . and to endeavor to rescue [the] western zones of Germany by *walling them off* against eastern penetration and integrating them into [the economic and political] pattern of Western Europe [emphasis added]."[45] Kennan later said, "I hope we won't shrink from carrying out that partition rather than giving the Russians the chance to dominate the whole country."[46]

U.S. officials heeded Kennan's prophetic advice. American actions led to partition, though curiously it was the Soviets, not the Americans, who actually built walls. Responding to U.S. initiatives in Germany, the Soviets first blockaded Allied access to Berlin and closed the inter-German border in 1948–49. They finally sealed off West Berlin with concrete barriers in 1961. But it was the Western Allies that had initially called for these walls. As British Foreign Minister Ernest Bevin said in January 1948, the United States and its allies needed "to reinforce the physical barriers which guard our Western civilization."[47]

Partition in Germany led to the expansion of U.S. and Soviet spheres of influence in Europe. As a result of developments in Europe, and in Germany in particular, the United States gradually increased its political, economic, and military commitments to Europe after the war, most notably in 1947, through the Truman Doctrine and the Marshall Plan. Although the United States had increased its political and economic commitments, it was not prepared in 1947 to make a permanent military commitment. But events in early 1948—the Communist-led coup in Czechoslovakia and, more important, the partition of Germany and the subsequent Soviet blockade of Berlin—changed all that. The British asked the United States to consider forming a military alliance to "protect" Western Europe from Communist intervention and to "permit" U.S. intervention on Western Europe's behalf, in much the same way as the Monroe Doctrine enabled the United States to "protect" Latin America from interference by colonial European powers and to "permit" U.S. intervention in the region. That summer, as the United States began its airlift of supplies to West Berlin, U.S. officials began exploratory talks with the Western European states on the creation of a military security organization. By April 1949, U.S. and European diplomats agreed to establish a U.S.-dominated, collective security institution in Europe: the North Atlantic Treaty Organization (NATO).[48]

To secure Senate approval of the NATO Treaty, Secretary of State Dean Acheson insisted that the United States would not rearm Germany. "We are very clear," he told the senators, "that the disarmament and demilitarization of Germany must be complete and absolute."[49] He said that NATO would not be used to prevent internal subversion in Western European states, that U.S. participation in NATO did not imply its acceptance of European colonialism, and that NATO would not be a permanent alliance (the treaty was supposed to remain in effect for only twenty years). And when asked whether substantial numbers of U.S. troops would have to be sent to Europe to fulfill its commitment to the new alliance, Acheson replied, "The answer . . . is a clear and absolute 'no.' "[50]

As it turned out, Acheson was wrong on every count. Germany would be rearmed by the United States and its allies in 1955, an act that prompted the formation of the Warsaw Pact by the Soviet Union. The United States would use NATO and various covert means to prevent anti-NATO political parties from coming to power in allied countries (Article 4 of the treaty permitted use of troops from member states to suppress uprisings within member states).[51] The United States would support French colonialism in Vietnam as a means of securing French participation in NATO, NATO would become a permanent alliance, and the United States would assign a "substantial" number of troops—some 345,000 in 1988—to NATO in Europe.

Together with the Truman Doctrine and the Marshall Plan, NATO increased U.S. commitments to Europe. These commitments "protected" Western Europe from interference by the Soviet Union while simultaneously "permitting" American political, economic, and military intervention in the region. These developments effectively extended the U.S. sphere of influence to include all of Western Europe. As Senator Tom Connally, chairman of the Foreign Relations Committee, said of the NATO Treaty during the Senate debate: "The

Atlantic Pact [NATO Treaty] is but the logical extension of the principle of the Monroe Doctrine."[52]

But when the treaty was ratified by the Senate on July 21, 1949, NATO was not yet the military alliance it would become. It was, in Bevin's words, "a sort of spiritual alliance of the West."[53] It would take developments elsewhere—in Korea, China, and Vietnam—to activate the new Monroe Doctrine in Europe and give substance to the West's spiritual federation.

The Soviet Union, meanwhile, strengthened political and economic ties within its sphere of influence in Eastern Europe and extended its own version of the Monroe Doctrine there. The Soviets agreed to permit the creation of collective security regimes in the UN Charter, which allowed the United States to retain Monroe Doctrine foreign policy in the Americas, because they wanted to establish their own sphere of influence in Eastern Europe after the war, a sphere recognized by Roosevelt and Truman at the wartime and postwar summits.

At the end of World War II, Soviet troops occupied much of Eastern Europe, but they did not immediately devolve power to friendly, indigenous Communist Parties. As the United States was constructing its European sphere of influence under the Truman Doctrine, the Marshall Plan, and the partition of Germany, however, the Soviets organized the Communist Information Bureau (Cominform) in 1947 as its own version of the Truman Doctrine, and in 1949 organized the Council of Mutual Economic Assistance (Comecon) to develop economic and trade relations as its own version of the Marshall Plan.[54]

Moreover, between 1946 and 1949, as the partition of Germany proceeded, the Soviets consolidated their sphere of influence in Eastern Europe, establishing friendly Communist regimes in Bulgaria, Poland, Romania, Czechoslovakia, and Hungary. In 1947, the Soviets also concluded a treaty with Finland that effectively neutralized that nation. Only Yugoslavia successfully resisted incorporation into the Soviet sphere. Marshal Tito broke from the Soviet Union and participation in the Cominform in 1948 and pursued a non-aligned, though socialist, foreign and domestic policy.

The superpower march toward partition in Korea moved in step with developments in Germany, though it did so for different reasons. Whereas economic considerations forced the pace of partition in Germany, political considerations set the tempo in Korea. Whereas partition in Germany led both superpowers to dig in their heels—keeping their occupation armies in place on a permanent basis—they took to their heels in Korea: after separate states were created, both superpowers began withdrawing occupation forces from the peninsula. Although partition in Germany stimulated the expansion of U.S. and Soviet spheres of influence and their respective Monroe Doctrines in Europe, partition in Asia did not. The deployment of military forces in Korea strained U.S. and Soviet military capacity. While Germany and Japan could sustain the presence of occupying armies—with some difficulty—a poor country like Korea could not. Not only were U.S. and Soviet forces in Korea wholly dependent on long, external supply lines, but in contrast to Germany, indigenous Korean movements of the right and left were quite vigorous and equally determined to get rid of superpower occupation.[55]

Neither the United States nor the Soviet Union intended to stay in Korea. They both wanted to devolve power to indigenous successors. The problem was how to manage this devolution so that friendly political parties would play a prominent role in the devolved state. At the end of 1945, the United States and the Soviet Union agreed that the devolution of political power would best be managed by a four-power commission—consisting of the United States, the Soviet Union, Nationalist China, and Great Britain—which would act as trustee for five years. The joint commission would set up a provisional government and assist "the political, economic and social progress of the Korean people, and the development of national independence of Korea."[56]

This plan initially aroused the opposition of all the political parties in the South, though it came to be supported by the leftist parties after a time. When the joint commission met for the first time in early 1946, discussions stalled because neither the United States nor the Soviet Union was prepared to create a unified economy or policy that would put its indigenous allies at a disadvantage.[57] U.S. occupation officials began promoting rightist parties, particularly the party led by Syngman Rhee, and suppressing leftist parties that had led strikes or protests in the South. The Soviets, meanwhile, suppressed non-Communist parties in the North.[58]

The joint commission met again in May 1947 in an attempt to establish political ground rules for the creation of a provisional government composed of parties from the North and South. But the superpowers differed as to which parties would be recognized as legitimate participants in this process. The Soviet delegation argued that rightist parties, which had opposed the trusteeship plan, should not be allowed to participate; U.S. officials argued that leftist parties were overrepresented.[59]

When the second commission meeting failed to produce a satisfactory plan for devolution, U.S. officials asked the United Nations in September 1947 to establish a commission on Korea that would oversee the election of a national assembly, which would then establish a unified government.[60] (Curiously, the U.S. seems to have borrowed the strategy adopted by the British in Palestine in the same year, though there is no conclusive evidence to suggest that U.S. officials consciously imitated the British move.) The UN General Assembly adopted the U.S. proposal over Soviet objections (the Soviet bloc abstained), established a UN Temporary Commission on Korea, and began preparing for "the observance of elections in all Korea, and if that is impossible, *in as much of Korea as is accessible to it* [emphasis added]."[61]

Commission members themselves disagreed sharply over whether they should participate in a partial election that would result in a permanent division of the country, a fear borne out after the Soviets and their allies in the North refused to participate in the U.S.–UN–sponsored election, which was held on May 10, 1948. (This was five days before the UN–sponsored partition of Palestine took place.) This election resulted in an overwhelming majority—190 of 198 seats—for Syngman Rhee's and Kim Song-su's rightist parties. A constituent assembly convened on May 31, adopted a constitution on July 12 (which claimed to represent all of Korea), elected Rhee as its first President on July 20, and inaugurated the Republic of Korea—and the end of U.S. military rule—on August 15.[62] The Soviets thereupon convened a North Korean assembly that ratified its own constitution on September 3 and elected Kim Il Sung as the Premier of the Democratic People's Republic of Korea, which was officially established on September 10 and quickly recognized by the Soviet Union.[63]

Although U.S. and Soviet officials could not agree on how devolution in Korea should be managed—and partition was the solution that provided some satisfaction to each—they recognized that political power should be devolved and superpower occupation forces withdrawn. Viewing the U.S.–Soviet impasse, American occupation commander Lieutenant General John Hodge said, "Under present conditions with no corrective action forthcoming, I would go so far as to recommend we give serious consideration to an agreement with Russia that both the United States and Russia withdraw forces from Korea simultaneously and leave Korea to its own devices and an *inevitable internal upheaval for its self-purification* [emphasis added]."[64]

And this is what was eventually done.

The Soviets announced the withdrawal of their troops from the North by December 31, 1948, and President Truman announced that "every effort should be made to create conditions for the withdrawal of occupation forces" by the same date, though the U.S. troop withdrawal was not completed until March 1949.[65] The U.S. decision to withdraw reflected Pentagon and State Department opinion "that Korea is of little strategic value to the United States and that any commitment to United States' use of military force in Korea would be ill-advised and impracticable in view of the over-all world situation and of our heavy international obligations as compared to our current military strength."[66] One general, when asked by Congress whether there was any strategic disadvantage in not having a toehold like South Korea in Asia, replied, "It would be a very, very minor disadvantage."[67]

Even as the United States and the Soviet Union moved toward partition in Germany and Korea in the years between 1945 and 1948, they abandoned their wartime attempts to shape the political future of China and Vietnam. By 1945, in fact, the superpowers had withdrawn their troops and were prepared to abandon both countries to contesting politico-military forces: Communists and Nationalists in China, Communists and French colonialists in Vietnam.

For all intents and purposes, China and Vietnam (as well as Korea) lay outside the spheres of influence claimed by the United States and the Soviet Union. This would change with the outbreak of the Korean War in 1950. But for a brief period, developments in China and Vietnam would be shaped primarily by local forces.

At the end of World War II in China, both the Soviet Union and the United States recognized the Nationalist government as the legitimate successor to receding Japanese colonialism and agreed that Japanese-held Taiwan (a colony since 1895) would be returned to Chinese authority. Both sought to prevent the Chinese Communists from challenging Nationalist rule. The United States supported Chiang Kai-shek and, curiously, so did the Soviets. As Mao later said of the Soviets, "They [would] not allow China to make revolution.

This was in 1945 when Stalin tried to prevent the Chinese revolution by saying there should not be any civil war and that we must collaborate with Chiang Kai-shek."[68]

The Chinese Communists did not heed this advice and a mammoth civil war broke out. Nationalist forces, which were strong in southern China, moved to occupy northern China, the Communists' stronghold. But Nationalist forces overextended themselves and were cut off and destroyed by Communist troops, which began to advance to the south, routing huge Nationalist armies. In 1948 and 1949, Chiang and his Kuomintang forces fled the mainland to Taiwan, where they dug in for a last stand. Some 400,000 Nationalist forces and many more civilians, some two million in all, swamped the island and imposed military rule on the indigenous inhabitants.[69] One U.S. State Department official said the new rulers displayed a "genius for mismanagement" in Taiwan. Independence movements in Taiwan resisted the reimposition of mainland rule and in February and March of 1947 demonstrated against the new government and demanded reform. The Kuomintang governor massacred 10,000 to 20,000 Taiwanese demonstrators to crush the incipient revolt.[70]

Chinese Communist defiance and Chinese Nationalist negligence alienated their respective superpower allies. The Soviet Union maintained diplomatic recognition of the Nationalists until the very end and was the only foreign power to move its embassy from Nanking to Canton with the retreating Kuomintang.[71] And U.S. officials toyed with the idea of supporting the Taiwanese independence movement's claims for autonomy from both Communist *and* Nationalist rule.[72]

The Soviets finally recognized the Chinese Communist government in October 1949, but relations were cool and negotiations to establish political and economic relations were difficult and protracted.[73] Because the Chinese had made their revolution on their own initiative and with little Soviet assistance, the Soviets feared that China would follow an independent course, perhaps like Tito in Yugoslavia, and would not be easily included in the Soviet sphere in the same way that East Germany was then being incorporated. Communist governments in East Germany and China were both established in October 1949, but the Soviet Union was far more cordial to the former than to the latter.[74]

As the Nationalist government collapsed on the mainland and retreated to Taiwan, the United States prepared to abandon the Nationalists. In 1947, U.S. officials ranked Nationalist China thirteenth on a list of countries considered vital to U.S. security, and a year later it dropped to number 17.[75] On January 5, 1950, just three months after the Communists established a government in Peking, President Truman announced that the United States would no longer interfere in China and that it would not defend Nationalist government claims to Taiwan, placing Taiwan outside the U.S. sphere of influence: "The United States has no predatory design on Formosa or any other Chinese territory. . . . Nor does it have any intention of utilizing its armed forces to interfere in the present situation. The U.S. government will not pursue a course which will lead to involvement in the civil conflict in China."[76]

By 1950, then, the United States and the Soviet Union had both retreated from China and abandoned their attempt to establish compliant client regimes there. China had been split apart, but it was not yet formally divided.

Much as the United States and the Soviet Union detested French colonialism, particularly in Indochina, they nonetheless retreated from their halfhearted attempt during the war to displace the French and establish a trusteeship in the region that would lead eventually to indigenous rule. At Potsdam, the superpowers assigned British troops responsibility for occupying the southern half of Vietnam and Nationalist Chinese troops the northern half. After the Japanese surrender in August, British and Kuomintang forces occupied the country. At the same time, Vietminh insurgents moved into the cities and announced the formation of a Vietnamese republic. However, neither the United States nor the Soviet Union recognized Ho Chi Minh's government, despite Ho's pleas. He told an OSS officer in the summer of 1945, "I have a government that is organized and ready to go. Your statesmen make eloquent speeches about helping those with self-determination. We are self-determined. Why not help us? Am I any different from Nehru, Quezon—even your George Washington? I too want to set my people free."[77]

In December 1945, Ho confessed that Vietnamese independence was stillborn: "Though five months have passed since we declared independence, no foreign countries have recognized us. Though our soldiers have fought gloriously, we are still far from victory. . . . We could ascribe these setbacks to the fact that our regime is young, or make other excuses. But no. Our successes are due to the efforts of our citizens, and our shortcomings are our own fault."[78]

When Chinese forces decided in February 1946 to turn over North Vietnam to the French, the Vietminh were forced to negotiate. And in March they agreed to let French colonial troops return to the North in return for French recognition of the Vietnam republic as a "free state having its own government, parliament, army and finances, *and* forming part of the Indochinese federation and the French Union [emphasis added]."[79]

Although this might seem a step toward independence, it was really a retreat from it. French officials' conception of "union"—their version of imperial reform—effectively subordinated peripheral peoples to metropolitan French control. And once their military forces were built up by the end of 1946, the French launched assaults on the Vietminh throughout the country. They began their counterattack by bombarding the port city of Haiphong, killing some 6,000 people in November 1946.[80] The Vietminh retreated from the cities to the countryside, and the war for independence began. It would not end until 1954.

After a few years, French authorities set about to create an indigenous Vietnamese government led by Bao Dai, the Vietnamese Emperor who had abdicated in 1945 when Ho Chi Minh founded the Vietnam republic, and integrated this government into the French union as its representative in Vietnam.[81] In the agreement establishing the Republic of Vietnam on March 8, 1949, France retained control of Vietnam's foreign policy, finance, and national defense.

U.S. officials, however, were not eager to endorse the reimposition of French colonialism or the creation of a puppet regime. After the Bao Dai government was created, a State Department report recommended neither "full support . . . of French imperialism" nor "unlimited support of militant nationalism" and urged that the United States "should attempt to have the French transfer sovereignty in Indochina to a noncommunist indigenous regime."[82] But by the end of 1949, as the partitions of Germany and Korea hardened and the Communists came to power in China, the United States began to move toward recognizing the Bao Dai regime. Dean Rusk, the former colonel who had drawn occupation zones in Korea and who was now a State Department official, said on October 26, "We must support against aggressive pressure from the outside even states which we regard unfavorably. We must preserve them merely as states. . . . Our first concern is not with the *internal* structure of states but with their safety from aggression [emphasis added]."[83]

While U.S. officials began to lean toward the French in Vietnam, Soviet authorities offered encouragement to the Vietminh. As in China, the Soviets had withheld wholehearted support for an indigenous Communist movement they did not control. They refused to recognize either the Chinese or the Vietnamese Communist Party as a legitimate government throughout the late 1940s, and the civil wars in China and Vietnam proceeded at the initiative of indigenous movements, not at the behest of the Soviets. The Soviets finally recognized the Chinese Communist government in October 1949 (just as Rusk was moving the U.S. toward recognition of Bao Dai), and the day after the French government ratified its pact with Bao Dai in January 1950, the Soviets recognized the Vietminh. The British and U.S. governments then quickly decided to recognize Bao Dai and similar French puppet governments in Laos and Cambodia.[84]

The extension of U.S. and Soviet diplomatic recognition to contending Vietnamese parties did not immediately widen their spheres of influence. Rather, it left the resolution of conflict in Vietnam to indigenous forces that neither superpower controlled. It would not be until after the Korean War that the superpowers would begin to claim spheres of influence in the region, and not until after the collapse of French colonialism in 1954 that they would intervene directly and attempt to devolve French colonial power to indigenous successors as they had done in Germany and Korea.

Whereas in Germany partition stimulated the expansion of U.S. and Soviet spheres of influence and the extension of their respective "Monroe Doctrines," in Asia the partition of 1945 enabled the United States and the Soviet Union to withdraw and limit their involvement—for a time. Secretary of State Dean Acheson described the U.S. withdrawal in a speech to the National Press Club on January 12, 1950. He placed Korea, Taiwan, and Indochina outside the "defensive perimeter" of the United States and said, "So far as the military security of other areas of the Pacific is concerned, it must be clear that no person can guarantee these areas against military attack. . . . Should such an attack occur . . . the initial reliance must be on the people attacked to resist it and then upon the commitments of the entire civilized world under the Charter of the United Nations."[85] Although Soviet officials did not make a corresponding announcement, subsequent events would demonstrate that they too placed Asia outside their defensive perimeter and let their nominal allies fend for themselves. They would not introduce Soviet troops into any of the Asian conflicts that emerged after 1950.

It was in this context that indigenous movements began to assert their independence. In Korea (and also in China and Vietnam), indigenous movements sought to undo *de facto* partition, unify their countries, and conclude conflicts that had been waged since the end of World War II. The attempt to undo superpower partition and reunify a country by force led to the outbreak of war in Korea in June 1950. The Korean War then precipitated a series of sweeping geopolitical developments in Asia and Europe between 1950 and 1955, triggering superpower intervention, solidifying partition, expanding U.S. and Soviet spheres of influence in Asia, and deepening the division of Europe into U.S. and Soviet blocs.

The Korean War was the product of an ongoing conflict between indigenous forces, a conflict that predated the Cold War and the devolution of U.S. and Soviet authority in their respective occupation zones. It thus cannot be said to be a product of the Cold War or an expression of superpower conflict in the peninsula. Rather, having agreed to divide Korea and withdraw, the superpowers left indigenous forces on their own to conclude this contest for power.

The North Koreans started the war by sending troops south across the 38th parallel on June 25, 1950. U.S. officials believed that Stalin directed the North Korean attack and that the North Koreans were merely Soviet surrogates. But according to Nikita Khrushchev, it was North Korean leader Kim Il Sung who proposed the attack; Stalin and Mao Tse-tung merely agreed.[86] After it began, the Soviets did not participate in the war. Indeed, Andrei Gromyko told the Truman Administration that the conflict was "a civil war among Koreans" and the Soviet Union would not intervene in it.[87] When the U.S.–led United Nations army swept into North Korea, the Soviets did not mass troops on the Soviet-Korean border or intervene in the conflict. The Chinese, however, did. According to Huang Hua, a member of the Communist leadership, Stalin initially opposed Chinese intervention because "[Chinese] action would anger the United States, thus triggering World War III."[88] The Soviets did not at first even provide the Chinese with military supplies.

The superpowers may have approved or welcomed Korean attempts to unify the country on their own, but they did not initiate these efforts or themselves start the war. The Koreans had every reason to act on their own. Since 1946, they had been involved in a violent contest for power that had preceded the superpower partition of their country.

Between 1946 and 1950, civil and irregular war in Korea had claimed 100,000 lives.[89] Urban riots and strikes in 1946, a large-scale insurrection on Cheju Island in 1948–49, border clashes at the 38th parallel, and irregular warfare by indigenous Southern guerrillas and infiltrators from the North rocked the southern half of Korea throughout this period. To resolve the ongoing conflict, both Syngman Rhee and Kim Il Sung had vowed to reunify the country by force *before* full-scale conventional war broke out in 1950. As early as 1946, Syngman Rhee had said, "On my returning to Korea I advocated unification . . . so that we could drive the Russians from North Korea. . . . As soon as the time comes, I will instruct you. Then you should be prepared to shed blood."[90] And on December 30, 1949, he reiterated his determination to reunify the country despite superpower partition: "In the coming year, we shall unanimously strive to regain lost territory . . . through our own efforts."[91] During this period, Kim Il Sung expressed a similar desire to use North Korea "as a democratic base for Korean unification."[92] The withdrawal of superpower occupation forces merely cleared the way for the two Korean governments to pursue reunification on their own. As it happened, the North Koreans struck first.

Although indigenous in origin, the Korean War quickly widened. And the war in Korea triggered U.S. intervention not only in that country but in China and Vietnam as well.

With the Soviets absent from the Security Council, the United Nations passed a U.S.–sponsored resolution on June 27 providing for UN participation, and assigned command of U.S. and UN forces to General Douglas MacArthur. When he arrived in Korea to assume his command, MacArthur announced that the 38th parallel was a "barrier [that] must and will be torn down. Nothing shall prevent the ultimate unity of [the Korean] people."[93]

Although sixteen countries contributed soldiers and equipment to the UN forces in Korea, the United States directed the campaigns, made the decision to cross the 38th parallel and occupy the North as a prelude to reunification, contemplated the use of nuclear weapons during the course of the conflict, and conducted negotiations that would conclude the war. As MacArthur said of the U.S. role, "The entire control of my command and everything I did came from our own Chiefs of Staff. Even reports which were normally made by me to the United Nations were subject to censorship by our State and Defense Departments."[94]

On the day the United States obtained UN participation in the Korean War, President Truman ordered the Seventh Fleet into the Taiwan Strait "to prevent any attack on Formosa [by Communist China]. As a corollary of this action, I am calling on the Chinese Government on Formosa to cease all air and sea operations against the mainland. . . . The determination of the future status of Formosa must await the restoration of security in the Pacific, a peace settlement with Japan, or consideration by the United Nations."[95] Truman took this action to prevent the invasion of Taiwan by mainland forces, which were then preparing for a seaborne assault to unify the country under Communist rule. Truman's action would have important consequences for the conduct of war in Korea.[96]

On June 28, Truman ordered that U.S. aid to the French in Vietnam be accelerated; he even began sending military assistance before legislation providing such aid could be drafted and approved by Congress.[97] The Administration announced in July that "the United States does not intend to permit further extension of Communist domination on the Continent of Asia or in the Southeast Asia area."[98]

U.S. actions in Korea, China, and Vietnam began to define and extend the U.S. sphere of influence in Asia, a process that by 1954 would result in the solidification of partition in these three countries. In concrete terms, military intervention in Korea and China, multilateral recognition of the Nationalist government in Taiwan, the creation of new security organizations—ANZUS in 1951 and SEATO in 1954—and the intervention in Vietnam on behalf of the French and, later, its South Vietnamese successor, defined and extended the U.S. sphere.

Until 1950, the United States had argued that Taiwan was part of China and that its reincorporation was a foregone conclusion. This attitude changed with the onset of the Korean War and the imposition of U.S. naval forces between the island and the mainland. But unless the United States could persuade other countries to recognize the Kuomintang government as legitimate, U.S. officials could not permanently prevent the forcible reunification of China. Many countries, including Great Britain, had broken ties with the Nationalists and recognized the Communist government in Peking, and others threatened to do the same. Early in 1950, the U.S. blocked a Soviet attempt to unseat the Kuomintang delegation to the United Nations. But this was a temporary action. Events in Korea, however, enabled the U.S. to defend the Kuomintang in the United Nations, which deepened the partition of China.

At the beginning of the war, North Korean troops drove south and forced U.S.–UN and South Korean forces to retreat to a small enclave near the southern port city of Pusan. In September, MacArthur launched a successful amphibious invasion at Inchon, near the South Korean capital of Seoul (midway up the western side of the peninsula), and North Korean troops withdrew from the South and retreated behind the 38th parallel. In late September, UN forces headed north across the 38th parallel to destroy the North Korean Army and fulfill MacArthur's promise to reunify the country. North Korean forces were driven back to enclaves along the Sino-Korean border, and on November 24, MacArthur launched an "end-the-war offensive" to eliminate North Korean resistance up to the Yalu River, the border with China. Two days later, the Chinese intervened in the war and counterattacked, driving UN forces out of North Korea and, by January 1951, back across the 38th parallel. During 1951, the opposing armies checked each other and the war stalemated. Peace negotiations began in the summer of 1951, but dragged on for two more years until July 27, 1953, when the country was again divided near the 38th parallel. Korea was thus three times divided at the 38th parallel: in 1945, 1948, and 1953.

It is important to note that by blocking the incipient Communist Chinese invasion of Taiwan, the United States made it possible for the Chinese to invade Korea as MacArthur's armies approached the Yalu. Chinese intervention in Korea was made possible only by transferring north the troops preparing to invade Taiwan. By all accounts, this was a difficult decision, since the Communist leadership was more eager to unify China than to unify Korea.[99] It is perhaps ironic that U.S. action at the outset of the Korean War *prevented* the Chinese invasion of Taiwan but *permitted* its invasion of Korea. However, the result in both Korea and Taiwan was the same: U.S. action and Communist China's response led to the deepening of partition not only in Korea but in China as well.

With the outbreak of the Korean War and the imposition of the U.S. Seventh Fleet in the strait in the summer of 1950, the breach between China and Taiwan widened. Toward the end of that war, in 1953, President Eisenhower quietly removed the fleet,[100] but one year later, in the fall of 1954, mainland forces began shelling the islands of Quemoy and Matsu, which were held by the Kuomintang, perhaps in preparation for a renewed invasion attempt on Taiwan. In January 1955, the U.S. Congress gave Eisenhower authority to take steps to defend Taiwan, and he sent the Navy once more into the strait, where it would stay until 1969.[101] During a second Quemoy-Matsu crisis in 1958, when Communist shelling intensified and troops moved into coastal areas near the offshore islands, Eisenhower dispatched an armada—130 warships, including seven of the thirteen U.S. aircraft carriers—into the strait.[102] This naval screen effectively detached Taiwan from China and reconfirmed the division of China into separate states.

The division of China was effected primarily at U.S. initiative; the Soviet Union played only a minor role. During the first Quemoy-Matsu crisis in 1954, the U.S. ambassador to Moscow reported that the Soviet Union was probably not prepared "to run [a] serious risk of involvement in [a] major war over Chinese claims to Formosa."[103] And Eisenhower told his press secretary in 1955, "I have a feeling that the Chinese Communists are acting on their own on this, and that is considerably disturbing to the Russians."[104]

The Soviets did little to support Chinese attempts to reclaim Taiwan or to stop the U.S.–initiated division of China. And as the Soviets and Chinese began to differ on a host of other issues and the split between them widened in the late 1950s and early 1960s, the Soviets adopted their own quiet "two Chinas" policy. In the mid-1960s they even referred to Taiwan as a separate "state" or "country."[105] Nor did the Soviets actively challenge the Taiwanese delegation's claim to represent China in the United Nations or link the recognition of China to other issues at various superpower summits with the United States.

The outbreak of the Korean War also led to an intensification of the ongoing conflict in Vietnam. The French used the Korean War, and the accompanying extension of the U.S. sphere of influence in Asia, to press for increased U.S. support. The French successfully persuaded U.S. officials to discard long-standing reservations about French colonialism and the Bao Dai regime and to increase financial and military aid. By 1954, the United States was paying about one-third of the annual cost of the French war effort.[106] With U.S. political support and financial assistance, the French embarked on a major military campaign to defeat the Vietminh insurgents before the United

States changed its mind. French Premier Georges Bidault feared that U.S. support might evaporate "if peace were reestablished in Korea while the war continued in Indochina."[107]

After the Korean armistice was signed in the summer of 1953, General Henri Navarre, the French military commander in Vietnam, drew up a plan for a decisive military campaign. In November, he parachuted troops into a remote valley in northeastern Vietnam, there to build a fortress that would invite Vietminh attack. Confident that superior French firepower and coordinated air strikes would decimate Vietminh attackers and inflict a decisive defeat on his guerrilla opponents, General Navarre said of his prospects, "Now we can see it clearly—like light at the end of a tunnel."[108] But it would not be the French who found light in a place called Dienbienphu. It would be their Vietminh opponents. There, on May 7, 1954, French colonialism was extinguished. Some 50,000 Vietminh troops overwhelmed the French garrison of 13,000 on the very day that Vietnamese peace talks opened in Geneva.[109]

Despite the Vietminh's victory at Dienbienphu, the representatives of indigenous Vietnamese, Laotian, and Cambodian movements were shunted aside at the peace conference and were pressured to agree to decisions made by the great powers—Great Britain, France, the United States, the Soviet Union, and China. Great Britain had helped to organize the peace conference, and Prime Minister Churchill urged "some form of partition" as a solution.[110] Likewise, French Premier Pierre Mendes France, who had just won election on the promise to withdraw French troops from Indochina, persuaded Chinese Premier and Foreign Minister Chou En-lai to agree to partition, at least on a temporary basis, until reunification elections could be held. The French wanted to divide the country at the 18th parallel: this would give them a majority of the country's land and population even though the Vietminh controlled three-quarters of the country, including large areas in the South. And the French wanted to put off elections until an electoral majority could be built for the regime in the South.

The Vietminh, persuaded that some form of partition was the only settlement the superpowers would accept, proposed a division at the 13th parallel. And they advocated early elections, within six months of a cease-fire, which they were confident they could win.[111] As Eisenhower later remarked, "I have never talked or corresponded with a person knowledgeable in Indochinese affairs who did not agree that had elections been held at the time of the fighting, possibly 80 percent of the population would have voted for the Communist Ho Chi Minh as their leader rather than Chief of State Bao Dai."[112]

Chou En-lai and Soviet Foreign Minister Molotov then mediated the difference, proposing *unequal* concessions by the French and the Vietminh. As Chou told Mendes France, "The two parties should take a few steps toward each other—which doesn't mean that each has to take the same number of steps," adding, "We are here to reestablish peace, not to back the Vietminh."[113] When French and Vietminh negotiators deadlocked, Molotov simply told the participants, "Let's agree on the 17th [parallel]."[114] The French thus had to take only one step to reach agreement with Molotov; the Vietminh took four. And on elections—Mendes France wanted an open timetable while Vietminh representative Pham Van Dong had revised his initial request for elections from within six months to a year or more—Molotov firmly suggested, "Shall we say two years?"[115]

And so it was done. The agreement reached on July 20, 1954, provided for the separation of three states—Vietnam, Laos, and Cambodia—from French Indochina and the partition of one: Vietnam, which would be divided at the 17th parallel pending reunification elections in the North and South in two years.[116] The agreement also prohibited the North Vietnamese from joining a military alliance or establishing foreign military bases on their soil. But it left the door open for South Vietnam to join a military alliance—it would join SEATO later that year—and for the development of a massive U.S. military presence.[117]

The representatives of indigenous movements in Vietnam, however, were frustrated by the course of negotiations at the Geneva conference and by the fact that partition had been drawn by non-Vietnamese hands. South Vietnamese representative Tran Van Do said, "We fought desperately against partition . . . [but it was] absolutely impossible to surmount the hostility of our enemies and the perfidy of false friends. Unusual procedures paralyzed the action of our delegation. All arrangements were signed in privacy. We express deepest sorrow in this total failure of our mission."[118] The Vietminh delegation also expressed frustration at having been denied at the conference table what had been won on the battlefield and having been pressured by its allies to accept an agreement that would forestall the unification of the country.[119] As Ho Chi Minh asked rhetorically,

"Suppose we Vietnamese . . . proposed ourselves for a peacekeeping role in Europe. What would you Europeans think?"[120]

U.S. delegates to the conference took a low profile. Secretary of State John Foster Dulles had initially objected to a conference that included a Chinese Communist delegation and had been unenthusiastic about the British proposal to divide the country, but he agreed to back partition as a way to make the best of a bad situation. He was completely opposed to reunification elections, however, fearing that such a plebiscite would undermine U.S. efforts to replace French colonialism with U.S. assistance and to establish a strong anti-Communist regime in the South. As Dulles told reporters, "At the present time in a country which is politically immature, which has been the scene of civil war and disruption, we would doubt whether the immediate conditions would be conducive to a result which would really reflect the will of the people."[121]

The United States then moved quickly to establish a viable Southern regime, persuading Bao Dai to appoint Ngo Dinh Diem as Prime Minister and then retire to Paris, organizing SEATO to provide collective security for South Vietnam, and supplying military-political advisers and financial assistance to the new government. Between 1955 and 1960, the United States provided nearly $15 billion to the regime in Saigon.[122] And as in South Korea, Diem (with U.S. support) preempted countrywide reunification elections by holding a South-only referendum at the end of 1955, which elected Diem as President of the new "Government of Vietnam."[123]

U.S. officials had also been willing to assist the French and assume greater responsibility in Vietnam, because they wanted to increase French participation in NATO and defend partition in Germany. The war in Vietnam had prevented the French from returning seasoned troops to Europe, and the cost of the war had slowed French postwar economic recovery, considered essential to general European economic development.[124] A U.S. intelligence report in 1952 said that the "financial and manpower drain" of the war in Vietnam "seriously reduce[d] France's ability to meet its NATO obligations and maintain the power position on the continent which is necessary to balance a rearmed Germany."[125]

Moreover, with the outbreak of the Korean War and the commitment of U.S. troops to Asia, the Truman Administration realized that it would need military assistance from other European countries to shore up its NATO defenses. With one-half of the French Army tied down in Vietnam,[126] and the British tied down all over the world, U.S. officials wanted West Germany to provide much needed, skilled military manpower to NATO. As one U.S. analyst observed, "The outbreak of the Korean War . . . brought the German rearmament issue to the forefront of alliance politics."[127] And in September 1950, Secretary of State Acheson proposed the creation of a ten-division West German Army.[128] German Chancellor Konrad Adenauer welcomed this development, because he worried that "Stalin was planning the same procedure for Western Germany as had been used in Korea."[129]

The French, like the Soviets and most other Europeans, opposed West German rearmament. The French had initially agreed to join NATO only on the condition that West Germany be excluded.[130] Therefore, in the early 1950s U.S. officials hoped that if the French could conclude the war in Vietnam on favorable terms and return their troops to Europe, where they could shore up NATO, West German rearmament could be forestalled. And the United States assisted the French with this in mind.

But developments in Asia prevented U.S. hopes from being realized. The French were defeated at Dienbienphu and, after the 1954 Geneva peace conference divided the country at the 17th parallel, they withdrew. The United States then moved in to assist the new South Vietnamese government in France's absence. Because the United States had to expand its military and financial commitments in Vietnam as a result of the French defeat, it was still eager to lessen its responsibilities in Europe, despite the return of French troops. To do this it sought to increase both French and West German military participation in NATO. Thus, while French troops were returned to Europe, they were no longer sufficient, under the new conditions, to eliminate the need for West German rearmament. Moreover, because the United States had taken over for the French in Vietnam, the French could not easily refuse U.S. requests to rearm West Germany, and in December 1954, Mendes France persuaded the French assembly to permit West German rearmament and participation in NATO. The Federal Republic of Germany joined NATO the following May.[131]

The expansion of the U.S. sphere of influence in Europe and Asia was matched, to some extent, by a corresponding extension of the Soviet sphere. Although the Soviets did not respond to the creation of NATO in 1949 by creating their own regional security regime, the

subsequent U.S. insistence on West German rearmament and participation in NATO did provoke this response. On May 14, 1955, just
nine days after West Germany joined NATO, the Soviets organized
the Eastern European states under its control into the Warsaw Pact.
Like NATO, the Warsaw Pact was a common security organization
formed outside the United Nations that would be used to deny Western intervention in Eastern Europe and, at the same time, permit
Soviet intervention there. The pact, in short, was a Soviet version of
the Monroe Doctrine and deepened its sphere of influence in Europe.

The mutual division of Europe into spheres, first begun at wartime
summits, was recognized as a legitimate undertaking by both superpowers. When the Soviet Union exercised its Monroe Doctrine
prerogatives—sometimes called the Khrushchev Doctrine or the
Brezhnev Doctrine—in East Germany in 1953, in Hungary in 1956,
and in Czechoslovakia in 1968, the United States and its Western
European allies did nothing. NATO intervention in the Soviet sphere
would have undermined the prohibition against Soviet intervention
in the U.S. sphere.

But the symmetry between U.S. and Soviet Monroe Doctrines does
not mean they were equal. The Soviets have exercised their "rights"
and intervened in a dramatic fashion in Eastern Europe. The United
States, by contrast, has not had to send its tanks into Paris, London,
or Rome. The Soviets have intervened, and the United States has not,
because the postwar regimes established by the Soviets in Eastern
Europe are weaker—they have less indigenous popular support—
than those in Western Europe.

In Asia, the Soviet sphere of influence expanded as a result of
developments in Korea, China, and Vietnam, but it was not as well
defined or developed as the corresponding U.S. sphere in Asia. Soviet
influence in North Korea, mainland China, and North Vietnam increased during the wars in Korea and Vietnam as various *individual*
military treaties, providing financial and military assistance, were negotiated by these regimes and the Soviet Union. But the Soviets did
not organize an Asian counterpart to ANZUS and SEATO, nor did
their treaties have Monroe Doctrine features: they did not declare
Asian Communist states as within their sphere, which would prevent
U.S. intervention and permit Soviet intervention there.

The Soviets did not intervene in the Korean War, even though two
of its allies were embroiled in the war and even though the conflict
bordered on the Soviet Union. Nor did the Soviets intervene in Viet-

nam. The Soviet "sphere" in Asia was less developed and more dependent on informal relations than on formal political, economic, or military institutions. This sphere was less developed because the indigenous movements were more developed.

By and large, the regimes in North Korea, China, and North Vietnam were far stronger, with far greater indigenous popular support, than those in Eastern Europe, or, for that matter, than their southern and island counterparts. They had won widespread popular support during their long anti-colonial wars, they had had considerable experience at force of arms, and they were determined to secure their independence from colonial empires and superpower states. North Korean, mainland Chinese, and North Vietnamese regimes repeatedly displayed a capacity for independent initiative: the North Koreans initiated a conventional war with neighboring South Korea; the Chinese launched a civil war in 1946 despite Soviet objections, planned to invade Taiwan on their own initiative, and intervened in the Korean conflict on their own; and the North Vietnamese waged an insurrectionary war against French colonialism for four years before the Soviet Union recognized them as a legitimate political entity. Although these Asian movements were influenced by and to some extent dependent on the Soviet Union, they resisted the extension of a Soviet "sphere" in Asia.

The United States, on the other hand, extended its sphere more forcefully in Asia because the indigenous movements and regimes that it supported were weak. In contrast to Europe, where U.S.–supported governments were strong and Soviet-supported states were weak, U.S.–supported regimes in South Korea, Taiwan, and South Vietnam were weak and their Communist rivals strong. The weakness of the regimes in South Korea and Taiwan was made evident by the Korean War, just as the war in Vietnam demonstrated the frailty of Bao Dai's regime. Without U.S. assistance, all three would have been overwhelmed. So while the Soviet Union intervened in Eastern Europe (but not in Asia) to shore up allied regimes, the United States did likewise in Asia (but not in Western Europe).

It is a mistake to attribute all these developments to superpower competition. Many of the conflicts had indigenous origins and predated the emergence of U.S.–Soviet hostility in 1946–47, while several others were between superpowers and indigenous movements: between the Soviet Union and indigenous movements in East Germany, Hungary, Yugoslavia, and Czechoslovakia; between the United States and indigenous movements in Korea, China, and Vietnam. The superpowers regularly described their opponents as agents of the other superpower, justifying intervention as a means to prevent encroachment on their legitimate sphere of influence, but both really intervened to protect weak indigenous allies from strong indigenous opponents. They just did so in different corners of the world: the Soviet Union in Eastern Europe; the United States in East Asia.

The history of devolution and partition differs from one country to the next. But two distinct patterns can be identified: those of British colonies—Ireland, India, and Palestine—and those subject to great or superpower military occupation at the end of World War II—Germany, Korea, China, and Vietnam.

Partition in the British colonies was a unilateral affair. Although indigenous movements played a part, it was a British decision to divide Ireland and India and devolve power to two separate indigenous movements. Other powerful states did not participate in any meaningful way, though they did pressure the British to get rid of their colonies. Even in Palestine, where a great many states participated in partition, they were merely implementing a solution first advanced by the British. Ireland, India, and Palestine were divided along "ethnic" lines and power devolved to movements representing Catholics and Protestants, Hindus and Moslems, Arabs and Jews. These identities, however, were themselves recent social constructions and were defined and developed during the protracted process of devolution in each setting. In this process, the British used the record of indigenous movements in world wars to weigh their claims to power in the devolving states. Partition in the British colonies, furthermore, coincided with the contraction of the British sphere of influence around the world. In Ireland, British authority retreated to an enclave in the northeast. And in India and Palestine, devolution and partition resulted in the complete withdrawal of British influence, bag and baggage.

By contrast, partition in Germany, Korea, China, and Vietnam—states subjected to military occupation after World War II—was a multilateral process. The United States and the Soviet Union were the principal actors, but they did not act alone. Great Britain and France participated in the division of Germany and Vietnam, while China played a role in the later stages of partition in Korea and Vietnam. And the United Nations, representing a host of countries, took part in the partition of Korea. Only in China did the United States exercise nearly unilateral initiative. In other countries, the United States practiced what one diplomat described as "unilateral concerted action,"[132] taking unilateral initiatives that would be supported by an increasingly dense network of allies around the world. The Soviet Union also practiced this kind of diplomacy, though with less success.

Unlike Britain, the United States and the Soviet Union did not attempt to use religious or ethnic characteristics to determine their choice of successors in devolving states. They divided states along ideological lines, not ethnic ones, and devolved power in separate states to indigenous movements that could be characterized as "capitalist" or "Communist." In Germany, the superpowers were able to enlist movements that closely resembled themselves, but they met with less success in Asia, where indigenous capitalist and Communist movements did not always imitate superpower ideology or practice. Movements in Asia were quite capable of taking their own initiative and departing from superpower expectations.

Moreover, while devolution and partition in the British colonies helped contract the British sphere of influence in the world, partition in Europe and Asia contributed to the expansion of U.S. and Soviet spheres. As partition in Germany, Korea, China, and Vietnam deepened, the United States and the Soviet Union expanded their spheres and applied their respective "Monroe Doctrines" to places that lay beyond the perimeters of their power at the end of World War II.

But regardless of whether devolution was a unilateral or a multilateral affair, whether it proceeded along ethnic or ideological lines, or whether it resulted in the contraction or expansion of spheres of influence, the result was the same: permanent partition.

The lines dividing states at the 38th and 17th parallels, in Kashmir or the Negev, were drawn not by indigenous movements but by one or many superpower hands. Partition was supposed to be temporary—the dividers of states typically provided for reunification elections once tempers had cooled. But reunification elections were never held. Partition solidified.

Partition was supposed to permit self-determination, protect residual minorities and superpower interests, and prevent war. But for indigenous movements that had set independence, *swaraj*, *sinparam*, or *doc lap* as their goal, partition would compromise the meaning of self-determination in important ways. And frustration with the limits placed on their independence prompted indigenous movements to reclaim their legacy by force. Ideological movements, no less than ethnic ones, would fight tenaciously for the kind of independence that partition had denied them.

· III ·

THE LEGACY
OF PARTITION

· 9 ·

Citizenship Diminished

Partition transformed the social landscape in unexpected ways. In its aftermath, millions fled their homes, families were divided, and refugees poured across newly created borders. Almost overnight, members of majority populations became minorities. Minorities became majorities.

Once they assumed power, independence movements sought to strengthen their political position and guarantee the rule of the empowered "majority." This effort typically restricted, qualified, or abrogated the meaning of citizenship for minority populations, who found they could not participate as full-fledged members of the polity in divided states. Mahatma Gandhi once said, "One can judge a nation by the way it treats its minorities."[1] By this measure, partition has not fared well.

At the same time, the officials governing devolved states sought to exercise their newfound independence. But sibling states and superpowers, as well as other members of the interstate system, challenged their right to rule and restricted their sovereignty in important ways. International recognition often proved difficult to secure and maintain. Officials in divided states found that they could not participate as equal members in the interstate system. Partition thus proved a

bitter disappointment for movements that had long championed democracy and independence. In the years following partition, citizenship would be compromised, sovereignty abridged, and democracy
impoverished.

As the meaning of citizenship eroded, minority social movements
emerged to reclaim lost rights. When constitutional and legal redress
was blocked, they frequently threatened violence, much as their predecessors had, to achieve self-determination. Where sovereignty was
abridged, state officials sought to reassert their independence—and
when diplomacy failed to establish an unchallenged claim, they frequently turned to war to recover their state's lost sovereignty. The
result in many divided states was that democracy remained unreal-
ized.

The abrogation of citizenship and sovereignty would lead to social
conflict and war within and between divided states. Partition was
supposed to deflect incipient social conflict and deter war. But it did
neither. In the decades that followed partition, such conflict instead
became obdurate and irremediable.

The import and export of huge populations during partition dramatically altered the social landscape, catching state officials unprepared
and creating problems that would be felt for generations. It is difficult
to convey the scale of partition-induced migration or the depth of
feeling that attended this wrenching social transformation. Americans
are an extremely mobile people, moving once in every five years on
average, and they celebrate the fact that they are immigrants—that
they or their ancestors moved to the United States from somewhere
else. But no other country erects monuments celebrating the arrival
of boatloads of immigrants. And no country wishes departing inhabitants well. Most people who leave one country and enter another
are regarded as refugees, a status with negative connotations and
unhappy associations.

In the partitioned states, the scale of migration ranged from modest
to massive. By comparison with the other divided states (and by
comparison with the mass emigration of the nineteenth century),
Ireland's partition-induced migration was relatively small-scale. Some
25,000 Catholics fled Northern Ireland between 1922 and 1924, and
in roughly the same period, 1920 to 1926, 12,000 Protestants left southern Ireland.[2] The larger Catholic migration was due to anti-Catholic
violence in the North, while there was little comparable violence di-

rected at southern Protestants after the Anglo-Irish Treaty was concluded.

Migration on a more considerable scale took place in the ideologically divided states—Korea, China, Vietnam, and Germany. In the years preceding the outbreak of the Korean War, 1.8 million people left the North (and parts of northeastern China) for the South, and another 1.2 million moved South during the course of the war.³ Although estimates vary, it is generally recognized that between 25 and 30 percent of North Korea's population had migrated South by 1953.⁴ Likewise, during the last stages of the civil war between Chinese Communists and Nationalists, about 1.5 million Nationalist troops and refugees from the mainland fled to Taiwan, which at the time had some 8 million indigenous inhabitants.⁵ The heavily armed refugees from the mainland solidified Kuomintang control of the island, and in November 1949, Chiang Kai-shek established Taipei as the seat of the Nationalist government. In Vietnam, as in Korea, 900,000 people, mostly Catholic, left the North for the South.⁶ The execution of many landlords and French collaborators undoubtedly encouraged many to flee.

Although the sibling states in Korea, China, and Vietnam sealed their borders and stopped the flow of migrants soon after partition, migration in Germany continued after partition in 1949, until Berlin was subdivided and the border sealed in 1961. In that period, between 2 and 3 million people, roughly one-sixth of East Germany's population, left for the West.⁷ There was also considerable migration of ethnic Germans from other Eastern European countries into West Germany.⁸ The exodus from East to West, primarily through Berlin, increased in 1953 as a result of the uprising in the East, then remained fairly steady until 1960–61, when it jumped dramatically. In the first eight months of 1961, 155,000 residents of East Germany fled to the West.⁹ This outflow prompted East German and Soviet officials to build the Berlin Wall, which effectively curtailed East German emigration (at least until the recent exodus in 1989).

But it was the partition of India that led to what may have been the largest, swiftest population transfer in history. In the months that followed the August 1947 partition, 17.2 million people crossed the new borders; Moslems and Hindus were uprooted in roughly equal numbers.¹⁰ People fled singly and in huge human caravans that stretched for miles. Lord Mountbatten observed that one refugee column in the Punjab was "drawn up in good marching order along some fifty miles of road."[11] This massive exodus was stimulated by widespread violence throughout the subcontinent. Nearly one million people were killed in the three-month carnage that followed partition.[12] In many places, whole villages were massacred. Refugee columns often passed down the same road, traveling in opposite directions. Such columns met, fought, and killed on the highways in Kashmir, Bengal, and the Punjab.

Neither the departing British administrators nor the newly installed Indian and Pakistani officials were prepared to cope with the flood of refugees or the scale of the violence. Pendrel Moon, a government minister in Bahawalpur, Pakistan, said, "I foresaw, of course, a terrific upheaval . . . but I quite failed to grasp the speed with which disturbances and displacements of population . . . would resolve themselves into a vast movement of mass migration. . . . Punjabis in general were strangely unprepared for what was coming."[13]

The result was chaos. A large-scale war was waged by armies of civilians, many of them neighbors. One non-commissioned officer in Bengal noted, "This country has become a battlefield since the 16th August. One village attacks another village and one community another community. Nobody could sleep for a week. Villages are being destroyed and thousands are being killed or wounded. Smoke-fires are seen everywhere all around my village."[14]

The size and murderousness of the Indo-Pakistani migration was without precedent. In relative terms, however, partition-related migration in Palestine involved fewer people but a much larger percentage of the population, and the violence practiced there was smaller only on a numerical scale.

As a result of the partition in Palestine, a vast population swap took place. The bulk of the Arab Palestinian population was removed and replaced by a Jewish Israeli population, turning the pre-partition Arab majority into a minority. Before partition in 1948, Jews had been the minority in Palestine. Slow, uneven immigration increased the number of Jews from about 11 percent of the population prior to World War I to about 22 percent in 1948.[15] On the eve of partition, Moslem Arab Palestinians made up more than 68 percent of the population and owned 90 percent of the land, and Christian Arab Palestinians composed about 9 percent of the population.[16]

During the war that accompanied partition, between December 1947 and July 1949, most of the Moslem and Christian Arab Palestinian population fled Israeli-held territory. (During the course of the war, the Israelis occupied and claimed territories not awarded to them by the United Nations partition plan. The size of Israel after the 1949 cease-fire was 27 percent larger than the territory allotted it by the United Nations.) Estimates of the number of Arab refugees vary, from 520,000 according to Israeli sources to 900,000 according to Arab sources. UN observers at the time said the real figure was somewhere in between, about 726,000.[17] As a result of partition-induced migration, the Arab population inside Israel dropped to 11 percent. Most fled to Arab-held lands on the West Bank, which was subsequently annexed by Jordan, and to the Gaza Strip, which was under Egyptian control.[18]

In Palestine, as in most of the other divided states, violence and coercion encouraged people to flee. An Israeli Defense Force study of Arab migration between January 1947 and June 1948 found that most Arabs left their homes as a result of (in order of importance): "(1) Direct, hostile Jewish operations against Arab settlements; (2) The effect of our hostile operations on nearby settlements . . . especially the fall of large neighboring cities; and (3) Operations of the [Israeli] dissidents [such as the Irgun and Stern Gang]."[19] Arabs did not leave because they were encouraged to do so by Arab state radio broadcasts. Indeed, according to the Israeli historian Benny Morris, "The Arab Higher Committee decided to impose restrictions and issued threats, punishments and propaganda in the radio and press to *curb* emigration [emphasis added]."[20] The Arabs left because, like most persons in a war zone, they sought to avoid attack.

The Israelis and Arabs, like the Indians and Pakistanis, were surprised by the size of the Arab exodus from the war zone. Arab leaders considered it a temporary problem and believed that the refugee columns would return home after the shooting stopped. Israeli officials, after seeing large Arab cities like Jaffa empty during the fighting, decided to encourage Arabs to leave during the war and then blocked their return. Military assaults on Arab villages, orders to evacuate towns, and psychological campaigns aimed at obtaining an Arab evacuation all encouraged Arab flight. About 350 Arab towns and villages were depopulated during the war, and Israeli demolition teams razed many of them. The majority of these sites were either completely or partly in ruins or uninhabitable. Demolition was so pervasive that Israeli dynamite supplies ran short. This widespread practice was slowed when officials decided that evacuated villages should be kept intact to provide housing for the expected influx of Jewish immigrants.[21]

The Israeli Army then blocked the return of Arab Palestinian refugees, and on June 16, 1948, the Israeli cabinet ratified this policy. Ben-Gurion argued, "I believe we should prevent their return . . . we must prevent their return at all costs."[22] Later that month, the government issued emergency regulations that provided for the seizure of any Arab land or property in an "abandoned area," and transferred the land directly to Jewish settlers or to private Jewish agencies that leased Arab properties to Jews.[23] And in November, while the war was still in progress, the government conducted a census. Any Arab not registered was regarded as an "absentee," which meant they could not claim their "abandoned" property or obtain Israeli citizenship. Refugees who returned to their homes were regarded as "illegal immigrants" and were deported to neighboring states.[24] At war's end, Foreign Ministry Director General Walter Eytan wrote: "The war that was fought in Palestine was bitter and destructive, and it would be doing the refugees a disservice to let them persist in the belief that if they returned, they would find their homes or shops or fields intact. In certain cases, it would be difficult for them even to identify the sites upon which their villages once stood. . . . Generally, it can be said that any Arab house that survived the impact of the war . . . now shelters a Jewish family."[25]

After these Arab Palestinians left Israel, Jewish refugees from around the world immigrated. During the decade that followed partition, nearly one million Jews—half of them from the Middle East and Africa and half from Europe—came to Israel.[26]

The Arab Palestinian population remained a small minority in Israel until 1967. Then, during the Six-Day War, Israeli forces occupied the Gaza Strip and the West Bank, bringing 1.4 million Arab inhabitants under Israeli jurisdiction.[27] Israel annexed East Jerusalem immediately and a portion of the Golan Heights in 1981, but did not formally annex the West Bank or Gaza. By 1984, Arab Palestinians made up 42.5 percent of the total population of Israel and occupied Palestine.[28] Of the 2 million Arab Palestinians there, about one-quarter are considered "citizens" of Israel, though they do not have the same legal standing as Jewish citizens; one-half were treated (until recently) as Jordanian nationals with the status of enemy aliens; and one-quarter were viewed as stateless enemy aliens in Gaza.[29]

In most of the divided states, violence or the threat of violence played a major role in the migrations that accompanied partition. Only Germany was spared the kind of civil and conventional war that punctuated partition in the other divided states. But in its place was the threat of superpower conflict and nuclear annihilation.

Although in many instances refugees left their homes voluntarily, hoping to improve their lot in a state where they could participate as full-fledged citizens, many were also gripped by fear. Fear provided the push, hope the pull. Whether they felt push or pull more strongly, whether their fears and hopes were real or imagined, the experience of partition-related migration was wrenching for millions of people. Moreover, most of the population transfers were sudden, occurring immediately prior to or following partition. Migration across the inter-German border was more protracted than most, but there, as in most divided states, the common border was eventually sealed and the flow of migration staunched for twenty-eight years. The inter-Irish and Indo-Pakistani borders, though, have remained relatively porous. Migration across them continues to this day. But these remain exceptions to the rule; the borders of other divided states present much more formidable barriers, and movement across them is full of risk.

After the great migrations waned and the flood of refugees receded, the social landscape of the divided states emerged transformed. The most important and obvious transformation was that minorities had become majorities and vice versa. Protestants in Ireland, Jews in Palestine, and Moslems in India, minorities all, found themselves rulers of states in which they now commanded majorities. Conversely, Catholics in Northern Ireland, Arab Palestinians in Israel, and Hindus in Pakistan—all members of majority populations in undivided states —discovered that they had each become a minority in their homeland.

In the other divided states, people who had previously expected to rule as a majority over a unified territory found that they could not. And minority political parties found themselves in control of truncated states. In Korea, China, and Vietnam, Communist Parties fully expected to assume state power over a unified country. Without the intervention of the superpowers, they probably would have done so. They could claim, with some justification, to represent the majority of the inhabitants, though the identification of a majority based on political ideology (as opposed to religious belief, ethnic identity, and linguistic practice) is fairly transient, particularly during war. Communists in East Germany could not lay claim to represent a majority of the population, though in the fractured political context of postwar Germany, no single party could make that claim. In any case, Communists and their sympathizers in South Korea, Taiwan, South Vietnam, and West Germany found that they had become unwelcome political minorities. By the same token, non-Communists in North Korea, mainland China, North Vietnam, and East Germany found themselves excluded from participation in government or public life.

If partition was supposed to create states where homogeneous ethnic and secular political groups could exercise self-determination without interference, it was a singular failure. Despite huge population transfers, partition did not result in the creation of homogeneous polities as significant minority populations remained behind. Thus, despite the transfer of 17 million people across the Indo-Pakistani border, as many Moslems remained in India as lived in East and West Pakistan. Despite violence and coercion, many Catholics remained in Northern Ireland, and some Protestants remained in the south. Between 1950 and 1967, Arab Palestinians made up 11 percent of the population in Israel, a proportion which increased to more than 40 percent (of Israeli-held territory) after 1967. And in Korea, China, Vietnam, and Germany, residual minority populations living on the "wrong" side of the border contested majority rule.

Majority rule in the divided states was further complicated by the fact that minority populations retained their links to families, friends, and political allies in neighboring states. Thus, any conflicts between majority and minority populations within a particular state were quickly externalized. Attempts to consolidate majority rule typically provoked protest not only by indigenous minority populations but by populations and officials in neighboring states as well. And such protests were regarded by state officials as unwarranted intrusions into their sovereignty.

Because political relations *within* divided states tended to become the subject of controversy *between* divided states, officials came to regard indigenous protest as synonymous with "foreign" meddling, and they began to treat minority populations as disloyal aliens who owed their allegiance to a foreign power. Ben-Gurion, for example, described the Arab minority in the Jewish state as a potential "Fifth Column,"[30] and Harry Midgley, Minister of Education in Northern Ireland, once said of the Catholic population there, "All the minority are traitors and always have been traitors to the government of Northern Ireland."[31] Because it was seen as inspired or manipulated by outsiders, the indigenous opposition to majority rule was considered illegitimate. As a result, internal conflict was externalized and external conflict internalized. Partition drove a wedge, not only between states, but also within states.

To secure and maintain political power, empowered majorities restricted or qualified the citizenship of minorities, whose "loyalty" to the majority-ruled state was suspect. By enacting laws that restricted minority citizenship, state officials defined "majority" and "minority" in terms of a legalistic analogy. In the law, "minors" are considered incapable of fully exercising their legal rights until they reach the age of "majority." After partition, numerical minorities were assigned the status of minors, a group prevented from participating as equal members of civil society. Unlike children, however, who attain equal rights upon reaching majority, the divided states' minorities were to be treated as minors permanently.[32] Thus, citizenship was divided and civic rights and responsibilities parceled out on an unequal basis. Denied the citizenship given others, minority populations were effectively disenfranchised, their freedom curtailed. As a further affront, state officials frequently awarded automatic citizenship to members of their own ethnic group living in other states, while denying citizenship to some of their own residents. These developments led, in many divided states, to the creation of "civic apartheid," the permanent division of the populace along ethnic or ideological lines.

Such wholesale disenfranchisement has been an ongoing process. During the decades that followed partition, citizenship rights were lost, regained, and lost again. The character and meaning of citizenship for minorities (and for majorities) were frequently altered by changes of government. The history of the divided states is marked by military coups and the imposition of martial law, as well as by the dissolution of military juntas and the installation of civilian government. Because these developments were uneven and differed from country to country, it would be difficult to attempt a single chronological history. Nevertheless, it is possible to describe how certain general rights, usually associated with citizenship, were curtailed in the divided states during the years following partition. In nearly all cases, political officials qualified the right to vote, limited participation in the electoral process, restricted the right to bear arms, imposed military law over civilian populations, and curtailed individual liberties, including the right to exercise religious beliefs or to practice social customs (regarding language, education, marriage, divorce, travel, and property ownership).

Although various "rights" were restricted, they were not restricted vis-à-vis some universally accepted standard. No such standard exists, except perhaps in the abstract. Nor should these rights be understood simply in U.S. constitutional terms. Rather, the electoral, martial, and personal rights—as defined by the divided-state governments themselves—were allocated unequally. And this uneven allocation has generally followed ethnic or ideological lines.

To secure their political power, state officials attempted first to shape and control the electoral process. During partition itself, elections sometimes played a key role in the selection of officials for the devolved states. U.S.–sponsored and UN–supervised elections in South Korea assigned representatives of various political parties to specific offices, as was the case in India and West Germany. But treaty and war served to designate the first generation of governmental officials in divided states, where the superpowers simply turned power over to existing political parties, which then styled themselves "representatives of the people." This was the case in North Korea, North and South Vietnam, Pakistan, East Germany, and Northern Ireland. In China, Taiwan, and Israel, dominant political parties created a government and designated themselves as officials in the devolved state. (In Israel, the UN partition plan had provided for a state in a given territory, but it did not specify the character of the government or identify its rulers.)

Whether they had assumed state power by election, treaty, war, or self-designation, government officials had to decide how their successors would be chosen. Officials in most of the divided states provided for electoral mechanisms, ranging from the truly representative to the unduly restrictive.

In southern Ireland, West Germany, and India, the movements and political parties that took power were relatively strong and the majorities they represented were sizable. Although West Germany and India placed some restrictions on minority participation in the electoral process, opposition parties could exist, significant minority participation in the selection of government officials was permitted, and regularly scheduled elections have been held.

After a period of martial law during the civil war of 1920–22, Irish officials permitted unfettered electoral participation. Eamon De Valera, who had led the opposition to partition and had fought unsuccessfully to prevent its implementation, was eventually permitted to participate in the electoral process. He stood for parliament and served as Prime Minister for many years. Participation by De Valera and his defeated minority party, as well as by Protestants in the south, attests to the relatively unrestricted character of the Irish Republic's electoral system.

West German officials established a parliamentary system dominated by Chancellor Konrad Adenauer's Christian Democrats. During the 1950s and 1960s, opposition parties, including the Socialists, participated in the electoral process, but the Communist Party was harassed and then banned in 1956. The Federal Constitutional Court ruled that the basic elements of any Communist program—their description of wage labor as "exploitation," their rejection of capitalism—was unconstitutional.[33] To some extent, the banning of the Communist Party limited the participation of the Socialist Party, which wanted to avoid being excluded from the electoral process.[34]

Throughout most of the post-partition period, government officials in India conducted regular elections and encouraged widespread participation. Between 1975 and 1977, however, Prime Minister Indira Gandhi (Nehru's daughter) declared a state of emergency and suspended the normal electoral and parliamentary process. Her successor, her son Rajiv, has declared martial law in some Indian states— he did so in 1987 in the Punjab as a result of secessionist Sikh violence—and instituted direct government rule, much as the British did in Northern Ireland following sectarian violence in 1972. Indian politics throughout much of the post-partition period has been dominated by the Nehru–Gandhi family, who have created a kind of informal, hereditary democracy.

Politics in South Korea, Pakistan, Israel, and Northern Ireland have been much more restrictive. In South Korea and Pakistan, electoral systems have been regularly disrupted by military intervention and popular revolt. In Israel and Northern Ireland, state officials have generally adhered to democratic electoral conventions, but participation by minority populations has been formally or informally barred. And in Northern Ireland the electoral process was suspended following the imposition of direct British rule in 1972.

Politics in South Korea have oscillated between civilian and military rule. In the fallout from military coups and popular revolt, the constitution has been overhauled no less than eight times in the last forty years.[35] Syngman Rhee, who took office as a result of U.S.-sponsored elections, attempted to consolidate his hold on power by restricting opposition parties and amending the constitution to preserve his party's power in the assembly and in the executive branch of government. His party strong-armed voters during elections. In 1949 and again in 1952, he had opposition assembly members arrested. In 1952, when his reelection by the assembly was in jeopardy, Rhee arrested forty-five assemblymen and released them only on condition that they vote for amendments that took presidential elections out of the assembly and made them direct, so that he could more easily control them.[36]

Widespread opposition to Rhee's autocratic control of the government and to widespread corruption by its officials prompted a student revolt in 1960. The constitution was rewritten, civil and political rights strengthened, and presidential prerogatives diminished. But a year later, a small group of army officers led by Major General Park Chung Hee staged a coup and established a military junta that dissolved the assembly and banned political parties.[37] Leaders of the coup objected to official corruption and to the chaotic political situation created by the previous constitutional reform. Park ruled until he was assassinated in 1979 during an abortive coup attempt and was succeeded by Lieutenant General Chun Doo Hwan. During the 1970s and early 1980s, the military regime conducted elections, but participation by opposition political parties was carefully circumscribed.[38] Indeed, government agents attempted to abduct opposition leader Kim Dae Jung when he was living abroad, and placed him under house arrest when he returned to Korea in 1987. However, in response to widespread opposition to continued military rule, Chun agreed in 1987 to return the government to civilian rule. In the 1988 elections, General Roh Tae Woo, Chun's chosen lieutenant, emerged the victor when the non-military opposition split between two candidates. Roh has since eased many of the restrictions on political participation imposed by his predecessors.

Like South Korea, Pakistan has also oscillated between civilian and military rule, with the military predominating. During the first decade after partition, an electoral system created by Jinnah and his designated successor Liaquat Ali Khan provided for widespread participation. But in 1958, General Muhammad Ayub Khan led a military coup that toppled the government. As in Korea three years later, the junta claimed the coup was necessary to destroy official corruption. Ayub dissolved the constitution and imposed martial law, but he permitted the electoral process to continue under close military supervision. Ayub restricted participation by opposition parties, particularly those in East Pakistan, where Bengali parties could claim to represent an overall majority. (A majority of the country's population lived in East Pakistan.) Under pressure from Bengali and student protestors in 1969, Ayub devolved power to a military successor, Muhammad Yahya Khan, who reimposed martial law to contain opposition parties but reformed the electoral process and permitted general elections in December 1970 and January 1971. But after the East Pakistani Awami League, which sought to create a more autonomous Bengal, won a majority of seats in the assembly, Yahya refused to convene the assembly and recognize Bengali participation in government. The Awami League responded by declaring its independence and seeking international recognition for Bangladesh. Civil war ensued.[39]

After the civil war resulted in independence for Bangladesh, the discredited military regime returned the government to civilian control and Zulfikar Ali Bhutto became President. But a 1977 coup led by General Muhammad Zia ul-Haq reestablished military rule. Zia arrested, tried, and hanged Bhutto. Since then, political participation has been curbed for majority and minority alike. In a manner typical of the kind of restrictions placed on electoral participation in Pakistan, Zia announced in 1988 that he would hold elections but stipulated that candidates could not affiliate with political parties.[40] Bhutto's daughter, Benazir, emerged as the leader of the opposition to continued military rule in spite of Zia's restrictions. And after Zia was killed in a September 1988 plane crash, Benazir Bhutto won election as Prime Minister in relatively unfettered elections and reestablished civilian rule.

In Israel, a vigorous electoral system has been created in which diverse parties compete for political power and representation in the Knesset, or parliament. Military leaders regularly participate in civilian governments, but they do so as elected officials, not as representatives of a military junta. The Israeli system of selecting government officials, moreover, has not been disrupted in the post-partition period by military coups. But while Jews can participate freely in the electoral process, Arab Palestinians cannot. Arab Palestinian participation is restricted by the Absentee Property Law and, indirectly, by the Law of Return. In the Absentee Property Law, passed in 1950, the Knesset ruled that any person who was away from his home on or after November 29, 1947, would be regarded as an absentee and could not claim property or citizenship in Israel.[41] The great majority of Arab Palestinian refugees, and even a large number of Arab Palestinians who continued to reside in Israel during the bitter war of 1948–49, were denied citizenship and the right to participate in the Israeli electoral process. Children born of Arab Palestinians who *can* claim Israeli citizenship do not automatically become citizens. Arabs who become Israeli citizens can vote, and they usually do so, for the Labor or Communist Parties, but they frequently practice an abstentionist politics—refusing to participate in elections—because they do not have effective representation.[42] Indeed, it is difficult for Arabs to form their own political parties in Israel. One attempt in 1964 to form an Arab Israeli political party—Al-Ard—was blocked by the Supreme Court. Al-Ard had sought "to find a just solution for the Palestinian problem as a whole, and as an indivisible unit . . . [and] work for peace in the Middle East in particular and the world in general."[43] In a ruling that was similar to West Germany's ban on Communist Parties, the Israeli high court ruled that Al-Ard was illegal because its objectives were "utterly destructive of the existence of the state of Israel in general and of its existence within the present frontiers in particular."[44] (Jewish political parties have also been banned for similar reasons. In 1988, the Central Election Committee banned Rabbi Meir Kahane's Kach Party from parliamentary elections because it was "racist" and "undemocratic.")[45]

Arab Palestinian participation in the electoral process is restricted in another, albeit indirect, way. The state provides Jews with electoral rights that Arab Israelis and Arab Palestinians generally cannot possess. The Knesset in 1950 passed the Law of Return, which awards Israeli citizenship to any Jew living anywhere in the world, and grants the right to immigrate freely.[46] During the 1988 parliamentary elections, a number of Jews living in Brooklyn, New York, who were residents and citizens of the United States, flew to Israel and cast ballots for Orthodox religious parties.[47] Arab Palestinians who reside in or are citizens of another country cannot participate in Israeli elections. This right is reserved for Jews alone.

In Northern Ireland, for the first fifty years after partition, a functioning though restrictive electoral system encouraged participation by the Protestant majority while discouraging it by the substantial Catholic minority. Shortly after partition, in 1923, the Protestant-dominated parliament at Stormont abolished proportional representation and began gerrymandering electoral districts.[48] Whereas opposition Catholic parties controlled twenty-five of eighty local councils in the country in 1920, they controlled only two after the 1924 elections. For example, on the Omagh Rural Council, the electorate for which was 61.5 percent Catholic, Catholics had controlled twenty-six of thirty-nine seats in 1920. But after Protestant gerrymandering, Protestant parties controlled twenty-one seats, a majority.[49]

In the decades that followed, the Stormont parliament continued to adjust electoral boundaries to ensure continued Protestant rule. Gerrymandering was most egregious in Londonderry, a city that in 1968 had 14,325 Catholic and 9,235 Protestant voters.[50] By gerrymandering ward boundaries, the Protestant minority managed to obtain a 12-to-8 majority on the council.[51]

Catholic participation in the electoral process was restricted in other ways as well. A 1946 "Representation of the People Bill" denied the right to vote to servants, subtenants, children over twenty-one living at home, and non-taxpaying lodgers.[52] The government gave limited companies the right to appoint votes on their behalf and required loyalty oaths from elected officials. Not surprisingly, the rallying cry of the 1968 Catholic-led civil-rights movement was "one man, one vote," a demand for a return to proportional representation and a widening of the franchise.

In the decades after partition, Catholic political parties participated reluctantly in the electoral process. In the 1930s, when Catholic representatives rose to speak in Stormont, many Protestant ministers and representatives would leave the chamber for the smoke room.[53] Disenfranchised on the stump and humiliated in parliament, Catholic political parties frequently boycotted elections or, if they did participate in elections, absented themselves from parliament for years at a time. At a convention in 1938, for example, Catholic politicians voted not to run a candidate for office because, they said, "we affirm that attendance at the [Stormont] parliament by loyal Irishmen is harmful to the cause of Irish unity since it bolsters up this alien institution and misrepresents the state of Northern opinion."[54] The political conflict between Protestants and Catholics grew increasingly violent in the late 1960s and early 1970s, leading the British to dissolve the Stormont parliament in 1972, imposing direct rule from Westminster.

In the remaining divided states, democratic electoral conventions have rarely been observed. Government representatives in North Korea, China, Taiwan, North Vietnam, South Vietnam, and East Germany were chosen by the single political parties that had assumed power after partition. Instead of creating *electoral* systems to choose government officials, Communist Parties in North Korea, China, North Vietnam, and East Germany practiced what they called "democratic centralism." The collective party leadership assigned party members to positions in the party and in government, and in time the party and the government became more or less synonymous. Although Communist Parties in these states do not permit other political parties to participate in government, they are not wholly unrepresentative. Some of them could, at times, legitimately claim to represent a majority of the population, much as majority parties in Northern Ireland or Israel claim to represent majority opinion. By most accounts, the populations in North Korea, North Vietnam, and China pulled together behind the Communist Parties during the long revolutionary and interstate wars that preceded partition. The Vietminh and the Chinese Communist Party rallied much of the population by their opposition to imperialist rule. And they enjoyed widespread support—though this is hard to quantify—before and after partition. In fact, Communist Parties enjoyed much greater popular support than their erstwhile rivals in South Vietnam and Taiwan. By contrast, the East German Communist Party has not been able to rally the same kind of support, in part because it cannot claim the same kind of wartime record. And neither East German officials nor their Soviet allies put much stock in the electoral process. As Khrushchev said in 1955, when asked why he rejected free elections, "The German people have not yet had time to be educated in the great advantages of Communism."[55] Elections were occasionally held, but they were *pro forma*.

Just as electoral systems played almost no role in selecting government officials in Communist-run states, they also played little or no role in non-Communist Taiwan and South Vietnam. In Taiwan, government officials were "elected," but their election had taken place on the mainland during the civil war of 1947–48. The ruling Kuomintang has never permitted a general election on Taiwan itself, and legislators in the Yuan, or national assembly, are said to represent their original constituencies in, say, Peking or Shanghai. And it is this assembly that selects the President and ratifies changes in the constitution. In 1988, half the legislators were more than eighty years old; some Taiwanese derisively refer to such aged legislators as *zou rou*, or "walking dead."[56] Because, on average, fourteen representatives died every year between 1980 and 1986, the government has held supplementary elections to replace them. These elections began only in 1969, twenty years after the Kuomintang takeover.[57] Until 1974, only a handful of legislators were indigenous Taiwanese (the vast majority of the island's populace), and in 1988 only 73 of 312 representatives were from the island.[58]

Upon succeeding his father as President, Chiang Ching-kuo instituted modest reforms, permitting the formation of an opposition political party in 1977. Many of its leaders were arrested in 1979, but the opposition carried about 25 percent of the vote in supplementary elections in 1980 and 1983.[59] Despite reform, however, elections in the 1980s have been marked by vote buying (the going price in 1986 was said to have been five to ten dollars a vote)[60] and by restrictions on opposition parties, which are prohibited from advertising their campaigns on radio, on TV, or in the newspapers. Most of the island's media, in fact, are owned or controlled by the ruling Kuomintang.[61]

Elections likewise played little or no role in the selection of government officials in South Vietnam. The French-sponsored Emperor Bao Dai designated Ngo Dinh Diem as his successor on the eve of partition in 1954, and although the Geneva accords had provided for general reunification elections in both North and South, Diem announced in February 1956 that his government did not "consider itself bound by their provisions" and refused to hold such elections.[62] The French withdrew the last of their forces in 1956, abdicating their responsibility as the "competent representative authority" for supervising elections in the South.[63]

After surviving several coup attempts, Diem was deposed by a military coup in 1963. A succession of military governments followed until Nguyen Van Thieu was elected President in 1967 and reelected in 1971 as a result of U.S. pressure. But these elections, conducted in the midst of an intense war, were extremely restrictive and could hardly claim to be representative, since large sections of the population were under arms and the opposition—the National Liberation Front (NLF)—boycotted them.

In many divided states, government officials frequently hold rigged or uncompetitive elections. But if they intend to defraud democracy, why bother to hold them at all? Pressure to observe democratic conventions—elections being viewed around the world as one of the most important political conventions—comes from two sources. Before assuming power, the independence movements themselves held congresses, elected delegates, and passed real or symbolic resolutions. Once they assumed power, leaders of these movements could not easily discard these practices without calling into question their legitimacy. Elections also provide opportunities for factions within ruling parties to maneuver for power, even where this process is closed to the population at large. So government leaders frequently hold elections, which they attempt to control, as a response to pressure from within their own ranks and from opposition groups, which demand adherence to global political norms.

The superpowers also pressure state officials to hold elections. The United States, mindful of criticism that it supports dictators, frequently insists that elections be held so that it can claim that the governments of its allies are legitimate. Thus, at various times, it persuaded military leaders in South Korea, South Vietnam, and Pakistan to put their regimes to electoral tests.

Citizenship in the divided states was compromised in other ways as well. To maintain political power, officials in many divided states forcibly disenfranchised the citizenry by monopolizing control of the army and the police, restricting the right of opposition populations to bear arms, deploying irregular police forces and militias to control minority populations, and subjecting the country to martial law and military rule. These measures were commonly introduced to prevent disenfranchised populations from seeking redress and, if they mounted effective political opposition, to crush protest by force.

In South Korea, South Vietnam, and Pakistan, military leaders organized coups, seized power, and established military regimes that ruled for most of the post-partition period. It is worth noting that the initial coups in these three states occurred roughly one decade after partition: Pakistan in 1958, South Korea in 1961, and South Vietnam in 1963. The assertion of military authority after a decade of civilian rule probably attests to the fact that partition created weak political formations in these countries. The leaders of military coups attributed the weakness of civilian authority to corruption—a major complaint of military insurgents in South Korea, South Vietnam, and Pakistan. In these countries and in Taiwan, where the Kuomintang government was installed by the army prior to partition, martial law was imposed much of the time. Under martial law, representative parliaments were dissolved, political parties banned, elections suspended, and the citizenry subjected to arbitrary arrest and prosecution under punitive security laws. Although martial law was occasionally lifted in the other countries, in Taiwan the military government stuck to its guns: the martial law imposed in 1949 would not be lifted for thirty-eight years.

The situation was somewhat different in Israel and Northern Ireland, where martial law existed alongside civilian authority. There, state officials directed martial law provisions against minority populations and subjected them to rule by regular and irregular forces. At the same time, majority populations were provided with arms, were allowed to form irregular militias, and were permitted to remain under civilian jurisdiction.

During the war of partition in Palestine, Israeli forces seized Arab Palestinian villages, disarmed the population, and evicted many of the residents. Those who remained were disarmed and subjected to military laws adapted from British policies.[64] The British had passed an extensive set of laws in 1945 that were designed to curb the activities of Jewish and Arab irregulars. The laws restricted movement, controlled the press and transport, regulated the possession of arms, and gave military commanders vast powers to establish martial law. Military authorities could search, seize, and destroy property, detain and expel persons, impose curfews, and try the inhabitants in military courts.[65] The Israeli government adopted and modified these laws in 1948 so that its military authorities could deploy martial law provisions against non-Jewish populations. Military commanders were given wide discretion to "close" extensive areas of Israel and impose military rule within them. After the Israeli Supreme Court ruled in 1953 that the village of Kafr Bar'am should not be closed by military authorities and that its inhabitants be permitted to return to it, the Israeli Defense Force destroyed the empty village.[66] And the closure of areas has been widely practiced to control the recent *intifada* uprising. Moreover, the Israeli civilian authorities and the courts generally do not challenge the exercise of military authority over non-Jewish minorities.

Israeli military authorities need not disclose which areas are closed and where martial law applies; inhabitants of closed areas may be prosecuted for violating the provisions of martial law even if they do not know that the area is under military control.[67] Areas within Israel can be treated in the same way that military authorities administer the occupied territories on the West Bank and in Gaza. In the occupied territories, Arab and Christian inhabitants are subject to military rule, while Jewish settlers remain under the jurisdiction of civilian authorities.

And while the possession of arms by Arab Palestinians is severely restricted—whole villages have been destroyed and their inhabitants expelled for possessing illegal weapons—Israeli authorities provide arms to much of the Jewish population. For Israeli Jews, guns are ubiquitous, and many Israelis are permitted to carry arms, in public, on a daily basis. Most are members of the armed forces or in the reserves, in which most Jewish men and women are enrolled. But some are settlers or residents of urban and rural kibbutzim who are permitted to carry weapons and use them in self-defense. Although legal restrictions apply to the use of force, the legal definition and social conventions regarding Jewish self-defense are broad, and settlers can use their weapons to intimidate non-Jewish populations with relative impunity.

Officials in Northern Ireland also borrowed martial law provisions from wartime British law and used them to control indigenous minorities. In 1922, they adopted Special Powers legislation that modified the Restoration of Order Act, which the British had used against republican insurgency prior to partition. The Special Powers Act "provided for search, arrest, and detention without warrant; flogging and the death penalty for arms and explosives offenses; and allowed for the total suspension of civil liberties."[68] The act was selectively deployed intermittently against the minority Catholic population until the British reasserted their authority in 1972 and imposed their own version of martial law, the Emergency Powers Act, in 1973.[69] For instance, the government often used the Special Powers Act to intern, or jail indefinitely, people defined as political or military threats.[70] After 1972, British martial law was sometimes used to prosecute Protestant Irish irregulars, but in the main it was directed at Catholic irregulars.

In addition to martial law, government officials in Northern Ireland also deployed Protestant militias and irregulars to maintain Protestant rule. The Ulster Special Constabulary, whose members were drawn from the pre-partition Protestant militia, was established in 1920 as an armed auxiliary to the regular police.[71] And in Northern Ireland, as in Israel, those who possessed the right to bear arms acquired rights that those who did not could not. Irregular police forces and militias used their privileges to extend majority rule over minority civilian populations.

* * *

Besides restricting participation in the selection of government officials and the ability to possess arms on an equal basis, officials in
many of the divided states imposed differential restrictions based on
language, religion, and social custom. Restrictions on these activities
are commonplace throughout the interstate system. Indeed, they are
so common as to be unremarkable. Human rights organizations such
as Amnesty International dutifully catalogue the restrictions imposed
by states on the rights of their citizens, not just in the divided states,
but in countries around the world. But a brief survey of the kinds of
linguistic, religious, and customary restrictions imposed by officials
of divided states illustrates two points. First, restrictions tend to be
differential or unequally applied. They preserve the rights of some at
the expense of others, usually minority populations. Second, their
imposition antagonizes disadvantaged groups, which object to discriminatory practices. As a consequence, issues of linguistics, religion,
and customs frequently foster social conflict within and between divided states.

In some of these states, language poses no social or political problems. The fact that government officials conduct their business in
German in both East and West Germany, where most of the inhabitants speak German, does not present problems, except for non-
German-speaking immigrants (Turkish and Yugoslavian guest workers, for instance). Koreans, North and South, speak Korean; Vietnamese, for the most part, speak Vietnamese.

Where affairs of state are conducted in a language that is not universally spoken, the ability to participate in government and politics
is restricted. China conducts its official business in Mandarin, though
regional dialects proliferate. English is the language of state in India,
though it is not even an indigenous language and the indigenous
population speaks a number of heterogeneous languages and dialects.
The use of standard languages in these countries acts as a *de facto*
restriction on political participation for much of the citizenry, even
though people who speak other languages and dialects are not formally penalized for doing so.

But language is more of a problem in divided states that elevate a
particular language as the official medium of discourse and suppress
others. These countries frequently establish *de jure* restrictions on
political participation by those who speak other languages. The
Kuomintang government in Taiwan, for example, insists on the use

of Mandarin as the language of state, despite the fact that 80 percent of the population speak a different dialect. Indeed, local officials are sometimes brought to task for not conducting official business in Mandarin.[72] Because most residents in Taiwan do not speak Mandarin, their ability to participate as citizens is curtailed.

In Pakistan, Urdu-speaking state officials in the western half of the country attempted soon after partition to make Urdu the official and only language of state. Prime Minister Liaquat Ali Khan insisted, "It is necessary for a nation to have one language and that language can only be Urdu and no other language."[73] But because Urdu was spoken by only 7 percent of the population, and hardly used at all in Bengali-speaking East Pakistan, this policy sparked violent Bengali opposition.[74] When Jinnah traveled to East Pakistan and reaffirmed his support for Urdu, the country's founding father was heckled and shouted down by students at Dacca University, and "angry students tore down his portraits in school and colleges."[75]

Movements opposing Urdu as the official language were organized in 1948, 1950, and 1952.[76] One Bengali leader in the Constituent Assembly complained that the "attitude of the [ruling] Muslim League here was of contempt towards East Bengal, towards its culture, its language, its literature and everything concerning East Bengal. . . . Far from considering East Bengal as an equal partner, the leaders of the Muslim League thought that we were a subject race and they belonged to a race of conquerors."[77] After tumultuous political struggles, the Bengali language was finally given equal status in the constitution in 1956.[78]

Interestingly, after partition in Israel and southern Ireland, government representatives designated as official languages that were not widely spoken by Jews or by Catholics. Hebrew, a language spoken only by biblical scholars and as part of Jewish religious services, was resuscitated and promoted over more widely spoken languages, such as Yiddish, as *the* Jewish language. The adoption of Hebrew helped exclude participation by Arabic speakers. The ascension of Hebrew was followed by steps to suppress other languages in daily life. Road signs were changed from Arabic to Hebrew and villages were renamed. Walter Eytan said that returning Arabs might not find their villages because they had been razed. But within a few years, it was also difficult to locate on a map those villages still standing or to find the way to them on the road.

The effort by Irish officials to revive Gaelic was less successful, but they did make some headway. Political parties adopted Gaelic no-menclature (in 1937 changing the name of the state from Ireland to Eire), a development that restricted political participation by Catholic majority and Protestant minority alike.

Religion has likewise been a divisive force in most of the divided states. State officials have promoted some religions and derogated others, especially in countries ostensibly divided along religious lines—India, Palestine, Ireland. The extension of religious authority and the ascent of particular religions—the "Islamization" of Pakistan, the "Judaization" of Israel, the "Catholicization" of Ireland—have proceeded unevenly. But generally speaking, religious authority has increased over time.

Before partition, members of religious minorities in India, Palestine, and Ireland believed that they could not practice their faiths in a unitary state dominated by adherents of a hostile majoritarian reli-gion. But they turned the tables upon assuming political power. In Pakistan, Israel, and Northern Ireland, government officials promoted their own religion over others, adopted it as the official religion of state, and devolved some governmental responsibilities to religious authorities. This confessionalization of nominally secular states has resulted in the derogation of other religions and has further compro-mised the citizenship of those who profess different faiths.

Although the Muslim League wanted to create a separate state for Indian Moslems, Pakistan was intended to be a *secular* Moslem state. At the Constituent Assembly meeting in Karachi on the eve of in-dependence, Jinnah rejected the idea that the new country should be a confessional state and said, "You are free; you are free to go to your mosques or to any other place of worship in this State of Pakistan. You may belong to any religion or caste or creed—that has nothing to do with the business of the State. . . . We are starting with this fundamental principle that we are all citizens and equal citizens of one State. . . . You will find that in the course of time Hindus would cease to be Hindus and Muslims would cease to be Muslims, not in the religious sense, because that is the personal faith of each individ-ual, but in the political sense as citizens of the State."[79]

But Jinnah's views did not long survive his death in 1948. Some found it disingenuous to create a state based on religious claims and then deny that the state was religious. Others thought that Islam should become the state religion and be used to cement the "nation-ality" of a diverse population that consisted of people with different ethnic identities and separate languages. Religious groups organized in the early 1950s to make Pakistan into an Islamic state that they could control.[80] They forced the government to convene a second Constituent Assembly in 1955, which declared the next year that Islam was to be the state's official religion and that only a Moslem could serve as head of state. Pakistan officially became an "Islamic republic."

Religious authorities, the mullahs, demanded that they be given a role in determining what made the republic "Islamic." And over the years, during the course of revolts and coups that shaped Pakistani politics, government officials have devolved some of their responsibilities to religious authorities and have applied Islamic religious law to all its citizens, regardless of faith. In 1979, for example, the military government decreed that thieves should have their hands cut off and adulterers should be stoned to death in accordance with Islamic law. (The government says it has not applied these laws, in part because doctors have refused to perform amputations.)[81] The government also created a federal Shariat court—Shariat is the body of Islamic law—composed of religious jurists who have been given authority to review Pakistani laws that deal with financial affairs, marriage and divorce, inheritance, and family matters.[82] And in October 1988, Acting President Ghulam Ishaq Khan decreed that *all* Pakistani laws would be subject to Islamic Shariat code.[83]

The Islamization of Pakistan has adversely affected the standing of many of its citizens. Women, certain Moslem sects, and non-Moslems have all lost ground during this process. For example, Pakistani law derogates the testimony of women in court: the testimony of two women is necessary to equal that of one man in financial cases, and four men must testify to obtain the conviction of a man charged with sexual offenses, no matter how many women have given testimony.[84] "Women have always been the greatest sufferers in the enforcement of their rights in this country," Hina Jilani, a feminist activist, said of Islamic laws in Pakistan.[85] And some Moslem sects, such as the Ahmadiya, who believe that Mohammed was not the last prophet, have been denied recognition by the government, which has ruled that they are "non-Moslem." Members of this sect, many of them professionals and scientists, have lost their jobs and have had their property and mosques seized.[86] And non-Moslems have found themselves subject to Moslem religious law, even though they profess different faiths.

The Zionist founders of Israel, like the Islamic founders of Pakistan, were not particularly "religious," even though they argued that Israel would be the state of the Jewish people throughout the world. Like Jinnah, Ben-Gurion and Weizmann believed in a secular state in which all Jews—belonging to Orthodox, Conservative, and Reform denominations alike—could practice their faith. Many Orthodox Jewish sects, however, argued that the attempt to create a state, as opposed to creating an exemplary religious practice, was blasphemous. Some Orthodox Jews refused to accept identity papers, observe Israeli Independence Day, or serve in the army.[87] In their view, the government did not have the right to compel people who observed sacred law to follow secular law. Rabbi Menachem Porush, the leader of an Orthodox political party in Israel, has said that Zionists have "carried two flags, one of nationalism and another of Torah. They are always torn between the two. We have one flag: the Torah."[88]

Israeli government officials have also ceded responsibility for some civil matters to religious authorities, but to a lesser extent than in Pakistan. A Chief Rabbinate and Chief Rabbinical Council decide on the interpretation and application of Jewish law in some civil matters—the certification of food, instruction in the state's religious schools, and matters relating to marriage and divorce.[89] The 1953 Marriage and Divorce Law prohibited civil marriage and assigned jurisdiction over marriage and divorce to Orthodox rabbinical courts.[90] The Orthodox clergy has since extended its jurisdiction, pushing for the right to determine who is a Jew, and therefore who can claim the rights to full Israeli citizenship. Although the Knesset in 1988 narrowly rejected a measure that would have given Orthodox courts the exclusive right to decide who is Jewish under the Law of Return, the courts have been able to narrow the definition over the years.[91] They have thus derogated not only non-Jews but also Conservative and Reform Jews in this process. One Orthodox rabbi justified this development by saying contemptuously, "Reform is a bridge for Jews to take to assimilation."[92]

As in Pakistan, a variety of groups have been disenfranchised in this process, and others threaten to be. Moslem and Christian Arabs in Israel have found it difficult to observe their faiths in a Jewish state. Practicing Jews who are not born of Jewish mothers, some converts to Judaism, and people who cannot produce acceptable documentation of their conversion to Judaism cannot claim the full benefits of Israeli citizenship. One decorated army veteran had his Jewish identity established when he immigrated, but then had it revoked. Because he was no longer "Jewish," he could not marry unless he converted under Orthodox supervision. (Jews are not permitted to marry non-Jews in Israel.) And when called up for military service, he was told by his superiors that if he was killed in battle, he would not be buried in a Jewish cemetery.[93]

Secular Zionists and Reform and Conservative Jews also stand to lose if government authority over civil affairs is further devolved to the Orthodox clergy, who have campaigned for strict observance of the Sabbath and other religious strictures. The November 1988 elections in Israel gave Orthodox religious authorities a potentially decisive role in the formation of a government, and they announced that they would use any power they acquired to expand and enforce Jewish religious law. Secular and non-Orthodox Jews petitioned the leaders of the two major political parties—Likud and Labor—not to allow Orthodox parties into the government. The leader of one Orthodox party, Rabbi Itzak Peretz, responded by attacking non-Orthodox Jews, saying, "They don't have any right to settle in Israel if they are willing to throw away the religious heritage passed on from our ancestors. Israel was given to the Jewish people for one overwhelming reason. That is, to live life as described in the Torah."[94] After failing in an attempt to bring Orthodox parties into a majority coalition, and after the United States agreed to hold talks with the PLO in December 1988, the Likud entered into a coalition government with the Labor Party that excluded Orthodox religious parties.

The two Irish states were also divided along religious lines, but the process of confessionalization has not proceeded quite so far as it has in Pakistan or Israel. After partition, state officials in both states introduced religious instruction into their schools and provided special benefits to majority religious schools. In southern Ireland, the constitution of 1937 recognized "the special position of the Catholic Church," but did not cede civil authority to the Church. Instead, the Dail passed legislation that censored films and books, prohibited divorce, and made the sale of contraceptives and, later, provision of abortions illegal.[95] A 1986 referendum that would have permitted divorce was defeated by a margin of 63 to 37 percent.[96] But even though De Valera had described the south as "a Catholic nation," Catholicism never became the official religion of the republic. As in the North, where Protestantism also occupied a "special position," the Catholic Church in the south remained a *de facto*, not a *de jure*, partner of the state.

In East Asian states and in Germany, however, state officials have encouraged or discouraged religious practices, but they have not tried to elevate particular religions over others, recognize certain faiths as official, or turn government offices or the courts over to religious authorities. While government officials in North Korea, China, North Vietnam, and East Germany actively suppressed religious practices and attempted to establish wholly secular Communist states, their counterparts in South Korea, Taiwan, South Vietnam, and West Germany encouraged religious observances. Although these leaders declared no particular religion official, they did favor those faiths that they practiced themselves. Such favoritism would lead to difficulties for those Asian leaders (Syngman Rhee, Chiang Kai-shek, Ngo Dinh Diem) who practiced "exogenous" Christian faiths shared by only a small minority of their compatriots.

This situation proved particularly troublesome for Diem, who discriminated against South Vietnam's Buddhist population while rewarding Catholics, many of whom had fled the North, with influential posts in the military and in the civilian government, as well as lucrative economic privileges.[97] On May 8, 1963, Catholic South Vietnamese officials banned the flying of Buddhist flags during a march in Hue commemorating the birth of Buddha—this after having permitted Catholics to display papal banners during a march a week earlier. When Buddhists gathered for the march, the army opened fire on the crowd. Nine people were shot or trampled to death.[98] Buddhists then began organizing opposition to Diem throughout the country, and on June 11, Quang Duc, a sixty-six-year-old Buddhist monk, immolated himself on a busy street in Saigon. After the government blamed the Vietnamese Communists for the troubles, more monks burned themselves in protest. Diem's sister-in-law, Madame Nhu, added fuel to the political fire by saying that these self-immolations were a "barbecue." "Let them burn," she said, "and we shall clap our hands."[99] The religious opposition soon ignited a political struggle, setting the stage for a military coup that toppled the Diem regime and murdered Diem and his brother on November 1.

Rhee, Chiang, and West Germany's Konrad Adenauer never attempted to promote their faiths as vigorously as Diem. They encouraged such beliefs as a personal matter, not as a matter of state.

And they did not institutionalize or codify the derogation of other religions as occurred elsewhere.

Government officials in the divided states also split their citizenry through restrictions on property. In some states, property rights were differentiated on the basis of ethnicity; in others, on the basis of class. Both criteria served to establish citizenship distinctions between majority and minority populations. Two examples illustrate this point.

In Israel, state officials used the 1950 Absentee Property Law to "nationalize" or expropriate the property of many Arab Palestinians. Before 1947, Jewish individuals or corporations owned just 10 percent of the land in what would become the state of Israel, but the law reclassified 70 percent of the land in the country as "absentee property."[100] This land then passed into the custody of the state or to parastatal Zionist agencies, which administered it, sometimes leasing it to Jewish settlers and sometimes to Arab Palestinian renters. By 1954, one-third of the Jewish population lived on absentee property.[101] Land owned by Jews or the state cannot be sold or transferred to non-Jews under Israeli law, and absentees cannot claim, use, or profit from the property seized, because they possess no legal standing in Israel. When Israel occupied the West Bank and Gaza during the 1967 war, government officials designated 36 percent of the Jordan valley as absentee property and made it available to Jewish settlers.[102]

Officials in other divided states likewise expropriated land and confiscated property held by minority groups. In both North and South Vietnam, Communist *and* capitalist government officials expropriated property and used class to distinguish between the rights of its citizens to hold and to use land. In the North, as in other Communist Asian states, officials practiced large-scale land reform, distributing land held by "bourgeois" and "feudal" landlords to the rural populace. For a time after partition, officials in North Vietnam defined as a landlord anyone who hired labor, and expropriated their land, transferring nearly 2 million acres to 2,220,000 families.[103] The "bourgeois" minority, many of whom were killed, was barred from buying or selling land or profiting from land worked by others. In South Vietnam, by contrast, Diem's government reclaimed the 5 million acres expropriated from the French and redistributed by the Vietminh during the pre-partition war.[104] And to deprive the Vietminh of its rural support, Diem's regime dispossessed rural inhabitants of their land

and moved them into *agrovilles*, later known as ".
by the Americans, which were administered by
Hundreds of thousands of rural inhabitants lost the.
ancestral graves, and their land as a result of such
relocation projects.

There is another, further dehumanizing, dimension to ..ce practice
of differentiating between the inhabitants of divided states. When
equal citizenship is denied to large groups or classes of people, there
arises a tendency to treat them as a collective, not as individuals. The
group itself is thus held responsible for the actions of its individual
members. State officials regularly mete out collective punishment and
hold individuals liable for actions that they did not themselves commit.

One common form of collective punishment is to make the restrictions imposed on one generation heritable. In Israel, the children of
an Arab Palestinian classified as an absentee are themselves designated as absentees and are thus deprived of citizenship, even if they
were born in Israel.[106] In North Korea, government officials classify
individuals according to their *songbun*, or family class background.
Children of families whose relatives fought against the Japanese receive preferential treatment—bigger housing allotments, larger food
rations—over descendants of families with "bourgeois" class back-
grounds. Landlords, capitalists, rich peasants, collaborators with the
Japanese, and members of religious groups as well as the families of
persons who fled to South Korea are denied access to good schools
and government jobs, and they receive smaller housing allotments
and smaller food rations.[107]

In the divided states it is not always children who are punished
for the sins of their fathers. Sometimes parents are punished for their
children's errant behavior. Israeli Defense Minister Ariel Sharon has
recalled how he found a way to stop Arab Palestinian children from
stoning Israeli soldiers patrolling Gaza in 1973: he instructed his soldiers to meet with parents of Palestinian youths and explain that they
would be held responsible for their children's behavior. If their children were caught throwing stones, Sharon recalled, "well, we took
their father or their older brother. We gave them a canteen full of
water, a piece of bread, a Jordanian dinar and a white flag. We took
them up to the Jordanian police station at the border and marched
them across." Sharon said that after a few dozen parents and siblings

ₑen expelled, "instead of soldiers beating the students, fathers
ₘere beating their own sons and daughters. You could hear the
screams all across Gaza. And the stonings stopped."[108]

Partition drives people apart, not only by creating separate states but
also by dividing people within these states. Partition separates people
from their homes and families and deprives them of their rights.
Minority populations are effectively disenfranchised by state-spon-
sored measures. Electoral participation is curbed, military service
barred, languages and religions derogated by law. The meaning of
citizenship is compromised, stunted, and deformed. The result of this
process is the creation of political systems that divide and disenfranchise citizens, what might be called systems of apartheid.

Those laws and social practices that assign different rights to different groups, which effectively disenfranchise large numbers of individuals and ethnic or secular groups, create systems of apartheid.
And apartheid reinforces and maintains social divisions and unequal
citizenship over time. State officials do not distribute citizenship on
an unequal basis simply to be punitive, though some measures are
clearly retributive, but as part of an effort to create a unified, homogeneous nation-state that can participate equally in the interstate
system. Yet this attempt to create a strong, homogeneous nation-state
(sometimes called "nation building") is a utopian project. Partition
created states where both majorities and minorities could exercise
power over particular geographical areas, but it failed to create homogeneous states, where one group of people could exercise their
power without constraint or complaint.

The attempt to create a state based on a socially and ethnically
homogeneous population is accompanied by measures designed to
strengthen majority rule, and these measures tend to result in the
diminution of rights for minority populations, who resent and resist
them. Indeed, the effort to create a unified nation-state in the divided
states produces only greater division and dissension.

One of the most emblematic features of divided states is the walls
they erect. Some of these walls are concrete, some psychological. They
fortify and cement the political, social, and economic divisions between and within states. The wall erected by the Soviets and East
Germans in Berlin is the most visible, notorious symbol of such division. Construction of the wall began on the night of August 13,
1961, when the Soviets and East Germans decided to stop emigration

to the West from East Berlin and sealed the border between occupation zones in the city. The wall now stands about ten to thirteen feet tall and has a smooth concrete finish and a rounded top, to prevent anyone from grasping it and pulling himself over. The wall completely encircles West Berlin; if straightened, its serpentine route would measure one hundred miles—the distance from New York to Philadelphia.[109]

The wall also has a psychological dimension, which is harder to measure but no less real. This dimension can be gauged by the space the wall occupies in newspapers and in literature. Newspaper stories about it appear every August, on the anniversary of its construction; it has been used as a backdrop for speeches by U.S. Presidents and as a staple setting for spy novels. Peter Schneider, author of *The Wall Jumper*, a collection of fictionalized tales or fables about the wall, describes it as "a concrete symbol of the divided self." He observes: "The dialog between East and West German authors has made it particularly clear that the cement and barbed-wire Wall corresponds to a mental one. . . . It will probably take longer to tear down the Wall in our heads than the one made of concrete."[110]

The wall in Berlin is not the only barrier separating divided states and peoples. There are others. The inter-German border is also heavily fortified, as is the Panmunjom cease-fire line in Korea. The 17th parallel, which divided Vietnam for many years, suggests a neat line on the map, though the actual demarcation line was more tortuously drawn. A sea wall—the Taiwan Strait—divides the two Chinas. The frontiers between India and Pakistan were drawn by military forces. In the disputed Kashmir region, the boundaries have never been fixed, and Himalayan ranges serve as a mountainous wall between opposing forces.

A line on a map, which is sometimes secret, divides Arab and Jew in Palestine. Military authorities can close an area inside Israel proper, "walling" it off and preventing entry and exit. They need not publicly specify where these walls are; one discovers its existence by bumping into it. There is also the "Green Line," another permeable sort of wall separating Israel and its occupied territories, which are also under military jurisdiction.

Informal walls divide people as well. Meron Benvenisti, a former deputy mayor of Jerusalem, recently wrote: "Late one afternoon in March, I was driving to the Hebrew University campus on Mount Scopus. Suddenly, as I was waiting near Damascus Gate for the traffic light to change, I made a decision: Instead of driving directly, as usual, through the Arab section, I turned left, taking the 'Jewish way'— through the safe Jewish neighborhoods. It was at this moment, I realized with astonishment, that I had succumbed to the geography of fear. For the first time in 21 years I allowed my tribal affiliation to determine my psychological space in my own hometown."[111] The walls Benvenisti describes may be hard to locate on a map, but inhabitants of divided cities and divided states know instinctively where they are.

And finally, there is a wall that acts as a symbol of division in Jerusalem: the Wailing Wall. Jews venerate the Wailing Wall because it is the exposed, western part of a foundation on which the Jewish Second Temple was built. (The Romans destroyed the Temple in A.D. 70.) Islamic shrines, including the Dome of the Rock mosque—the site of Mohammed's ascension to heaven—were subsequently built there. Moslems call it Haram al-Sharif, Jews call it the Temple Mount. These piggybacking shrines have been the site of repeated confrontations. Jewish excavations around the wall's foundations have led to Moslem rioting, as did a court decision permitting Jews to pray there. Jewish religious militants have twice plotted (in 1981 and 1984) to dynamite the Dome of the Rock and thereby remove it from sacred Jewish ground.[112]

The same sort of invisible yet tangible walls divide Catholic and Protestant in Northern Ireland. Although there is no single Berlin-style wall in Belfast, there are a series of fifteen-foot-high "peace-keeper" walls that run through the yards, alleys, and streets between Catholic and Protestant neighborhoods. The British and Belfast city planners erected these corrugated-iron barriers to prevent sniper fire and rock-throwing incidents across "the line." Demolished, burned, or boarded-up houses between neighborhoods also serve as barriers, much as unoccupied buildings did in Berlin before they were torn down and replaced by a wall that could be more easily patrolled. When one city planner suggested demolishing a row of abandoned and derelict houses and using the strip as parkland, people on both sides of the proposed park objected, saying it would permit sniping and rock-throwing at the border.[113] In its place, both sides approved a plan for a twenty-foot-high wall trimmed with thorny shrubs. The planner in charge of the project said, "It is a serious plan, but everyone is holding off because no one wants to build it. The cost of construction of a brick wall, coupled with the feeling that you'd be dividing the city off with a Berlin-type wall, is just too much for people *outside* the community to take."[114] A Department of the Environment official agreed: "One argument against putting up a permanent wall is that it is far easier to put them up than it is to take them down. By and large, it looks like we have built a psychological barrier, and it's the psychological barrier which is hard to take away."[115]

Psychological barriers are more difficult to describe, though one writer discovered a set of rules that enables one to identify religious divisions in Northern Ireland: "In Belfast . . . the most segregated city in the North, one can quickly determine a man's religion just by asking him where he lives or what school he went to. Often one can tell from a person's name what church he or she holds dear: anyone named Sean, Seamus, Kieran, Patrick, Damien, Eamonn, Malachy, Theresa, Bernadette, Deirdre, Finnoula, or Colette is Catholic. William, Sammy, Ian, Hope, Joy, and Grace are all Protestant."[116] Residents of Belfast are provided with a whole series of clues to identify "the other." Once identified, a psychological wall can quickly be erected. As in Benvenisti's Jerusalem, the walls individuals carry around in their heads can be deployed in an instant and guide their behavior as surely as a series of traffic diverters.

Walls between states, within states, and within individuals divide people from each other, and from themselves. The construction of such barriers results in what might be called "schizophrenic states." In psychological terms, schizophrenia refers to psychotic reactions characterized by the withdrawal from reality with highly variable accompanying affective behavioral and intellectual disturbances. In the divided states, partition and its consequences have created conditions from which people recoil. States refuse to recognize sibling states, majorities disenfranchise minorities, and individuals discriminate against their neighbors. The refusal to recognize the sovereignty and citizenship of other states and of minority peoples represents a withdrawal from reality. The denial of political reality leads to governmental and individual behavior that tends to deepen social divisions and to exacerbate social conflict within and between states.

· 10 ·

Sovereignty Denied

In the years following partition, disenfranchised groups within the divided states began to resist the derogation of their rights and the restrictions on their citizenship imposed by state officials and dominant social groups. A second generation of independence movements soon emerged to reassert the rights of disenfranchised groups and to bid for state power of their own.

Some of these movements—the Irish Republican Army in Northern Ireland, the National Liberation Front in South Vietnam—were the direct descendants of pre-partition independence movements. Others—the Palestine Liberation Organization and the Awami League in East Pakistan—were offshoots of previously existing movements. They retained some organizational connection with the older movements but drew their leadership from different sources and relied on new political and social constituencies. And some—rebellious students in South Korea, indigenous islanders in Taiwan, and workers in East Germany—sprang up spontaneously, autonomously. By and large these were short-lived political movements.

Second-generation movements, like their direct and indirect predecessors, drew on both parochial and cosmopolitan ideologies. The National Liberation Front in South Vietnam appealed simultaneously to rural Vietnamese farmers and to college students in France and the United States. Nguyen Van Thieu (not the same man who would later become President of South Vietnam), a member of the NLF's central committee during Diem's rule, recalls that, at home, "we did not stress that we were fighting for *freedom* [a cosmopolitan idea]—that would come later. . . . Big words are just so much hot air. What matters most is the land."[1] The NLF thus stressed parochial land reform in the countryside. But it stressed "self-determination," a term filled with "hot air," abroad. Students in the United States took up this cosmopolitan slogan in the late 1960s, chanting "Ho Ho Ho Chi Minh, the NLF is gonna win" at anti-war demonstrations.

The NLF and the Awami League in East Pakistan, both of which succeeded in seizing state power, organized indigenous inhabitants and appealed successfully to sympathetic communities in neighboring states and to superpower states, which assisted their efforts to become independent. The NLF obtained support from people in Cambodia and Laos and also from the Soviet Union and China; the Awami League from populations in India and its ally the Soviet Union. The South Korean student movement in the early 1960s was also successful; it managed to overthrow Syngman Rhee's government and helped establish a more democratic government in the early 1960s, for a short period of time. These students, like college students elsewhere, stand at the intellectual crossroads of cosmopolitan ideologies: scientific, legal, political, social, and economic. They are, to paraphrase Thieu, enamored of "big words."

Movements such as the PLO and the IRA have not been as successful in terms of achieving state power, but they too have combined cosmopolitan and parochial appeals to organize indigenous support and gain credibility abroad. By contrast, those movements that rely primarily on parochial appeals—Sikhs in India, Pathans in Pakistan —labor in comparative obscurity. Because they are relatively isolated and unconnected with wider cosmopolitan ideologies or movements and do not avail themselves of the kind of political and financial assistance that a cosmopolitan approach can provide, they are also relatively unsuccessful.

Second-generation movements, whether cosmopolitan or parochial or both, share a common desire for independence. In the post-partition context, however, independence acquired a new meaning. Before partition, independence movements had sought to secede from colonial empires and acquire state power in a single, devolved territory. But after partition, when devolution resulted in the creation of two states, independence took on two possible meanings. For the NLF in South Vietnam and the IRA in Northern Ireland, independence meant the *reunification* of two separate states. They believed that independence could be realized only in a single, united nation-state in which the overall majority would rule. South Korean students in the early 1960s and late 1980s demanded democratization and reunification with the North as a means of promoting Korean independence. Other movements, such as the Awami League in East Pakistan and the Sikhs in India, defined independence as *secession*, the further division of a divided state and the creation of a new nation-state in which they could exercise majority rule on their own terms.

Some movements argue for reunification as a means of achieving their independence, but they practice a form of separatism. Reunification has long been the ostensible goal of the Kuomintang in Taiwan, but the party clings to *de facto* separatism to survive and has made no real attempt to reunify China. The indigenous Taiwanese are more consistent. When they have asserted demands for independence, they have urged the creation of a separate Taiwanese state that is free from both mainland Communist and Kuomintang rule.

Until 1988, the PLO rejected the UN–sponsored partition of Palestine and argued that Palestinians would secure their independence in a unified, secular Palestine. Arab Palestinians would make up a majority in such a unified state, and some Jews would be permitted to remain as a minority. But in November 1988, in the wake of the Arab Palestinian uprising in the Israeli-occupied territories (the *intifada*), the PLO redefined its goals and demanded the creation of a separate, independent Palestinian state along lines suggested by the United Nations in 1947. So while they have long urged reunification, the PLO has moved toward a separatist definition of independence.

Post-partition independence movements sought to realize their goals by various means. Student movements in South Korea, Buddhists in South Vietnam, the Awami League in East Pakistan, Arab Palestinians in Israel, East German workers, and Catholic civil-rights activists in Northern Ireland all attempted to redress their grievances by legal means. They used elections, protest marches, and demonstrations to press for independence. But when "civil" means failed or were subjected to attack by military and paramilitary forces (often resulting in the deaths of non-violent protesters), civil protest gave way to martial resistance. Whether by choice or necessity, the NLF, the Awami League, Sikhs in India, Pathans in Pakistan, the PLO, and the IRA all organized irregular, guerrilla forces to resist the derogation of their rights and to press for state power and independence.

Naturally, government officials and military leaders and representatives of dominant communities viewed the development of second-generation independence movements with alarm. Moreover, the development of civil and martial resistance to partition and discrimination created a backlash in the majority populations. To a large extent, the coups that established military regimes or the imposition of martial law in many of the divided states (South Korea, Taiwan, South Vietnam, Pakistan, Israel, East Germany, and Northern Ireland) were a direct response to the challenge presented by the resistance of indigenous minority groups. In tightening control over subject populations, the dominant communities and state officials further derogated their political and legal standing.

Second-generation independence movements are viewed with alarm by state officials because they advocate ideas like self-determination that challenge the rule of dominant groups, and because they draw support from sympathetic populations in neighboring states. When Communists in South Vietnam enlisted the support of Communists living in the North, when Catholics in Northern Ireland appealed to their compatriots in the south and in the United States for assistance, the social conflict within divided states became externalized. Instead of confronting a mere indigenous insurrection, state officials also faced the prospect of foreign intervention. And the prospect of such intervention in their internal affairs triggered a visceral reaction in officials bent on maintaining their own sovereignty. Thus Indian officials denounce Pakistan for supporting Sikh insurgency while Pakistani officials accuse India of assisting Bengali separatism. The foreign or cosmopolitan dimension of second-generation independence movements thus represents a far more serious challenge to state officials. Leaders of independence movements understand this and seek to broaden or "internationalize" their struggle. The dramatic airplane hijackings of the 1970s and 1980s are symptomatic of efforts to publicize independence movements on a global scale.

Just as the meaning of citizenship was compromised by post-partition developments in the divided states, the meaning of sovereignty has also been abridged. And just as the derogation of citizenship led to political and social conflict within and between divided states, the derogation of sovereignty has contributed to conflict between divided states and their superpower allies.

Although partition was supposed to result in the creation of separate but sovereign nation-states that could participate as equals in the interstate system, state officials have discovered that partition crippled their sovereignty from the outset and would handicap their efforts to conduct normal diplomatic relations with other states. For the independence movements that assumed state power, this development was extremely disillusioning. Frustrated officials sought to remove the restrictions imposed on them by partition, sibling states, and superpower states and to recover their sovereignty by force. Whereas the derogation of citizenship created second-generation independence movements that sought to take state power by force, the derogation of sovereignty made state officials willing to use force to undo the limitations imposed on their power.

As noted in Chapter 5, the United States and the Soviet Union together created an interstate system that was theoretically egalitarian but in practice hierarchical. No state would be allowed to exercise its independence without restraint, and some would be permitted greater power in the system than others. Nation-states could enact laws, levy taxes, and raise armies, but they could not easily pass laws that offended superpower propriety, levy taxes that expropriated foreign property, or deploy armies against foreign countries without risking sanction by the superpowers and the other members of the interstate system. The superpowers could act with greater freedom than smaller and weaker states, but even at the height of its power, neither the United States nor the Soviet Union could act with disregard for the other or its allies.

When governmental power was devolved, officials in the divided states expected to acquire the kind of sovereignty enjoyed by most other, non-superpower states. Being realists, few expected that they would obtain the freedom of action enjoyed by the superpowers (China is the notable exception). Eamon De Valera, for instance, did not expect that Ireland would be able to act as Great Britain did in international affairs. But officials did expect to enjoy the sovereign rights accorded to lesser states and to be treated as equals in the diplomatic protocols. They soon found, however, that these rights were difficult to obtain because partition had diminished their standing, because the divided states themselves took actions that resulted in the diminution of sovereignty, and because other states obstructed their rights.

Except in Palestine, where a separate Israeli state was created and some of the land assigned to an Arab Palestinian state devolved to Jordan, and in Ireland, where Northern Ireland became a semi-autonomous province of Great Britain, partition resulted in the creation of two new states. From the outset, the status of these states was ambiguous. Because many partition agreements—in Korea, Vietnam, India, and Ireland—provided for reunification elections within a few years, it was unclear whether the states created would be temporary or permanent members of the interstate system. It was also unclear how much territory each state could legitimately claim as its own. Such ambiguity about the status of the divided states arose because they were anomalies in a system based on permanent nation-states with coherent populations and definitive borders. The divided states themselves reinforced this ambiguity by making claims inconsistent with the accepted behavior of separate, sovereign states. The constitutions of many of the divided states, for example, claimed territories not assigned to them and derogated the sovereignty of sibling states, which resulted in the derogation of sovereignty for both.

The preamble of the 1960 constitution of North Vietnam began: "Viet-Nam is a single entity from Lang-Son [on the northern border with China] to Camau [the southernmost tip of the country]."[2] The 1956 South Vietnamese constitution made the same claim, asserting jurisdiction over all of Vietnam, not just half of it. Article 1 read: "Viet-Nam is an independent, unified, territorial indivisible republic."[3] Similar repudiations of partition appear in the constitutions of the Irish Republic, North Korea, South Korea, China, and Taiwan; in Germany, the two states for many years considered each other's claim illegitimate. The Basic Law, West Germany's *de facto* constitution, treats itself as provisional; according to Article 146, "This Basic Law shall cease to be in force on the day on which a constitution adopted by a free decision of the German people [East and West] comes into force."[4]

India and Pakistan recognize each other's existence, but dispute large territories in the Kashmir and in areas that have changed hands as a result of three wars. And in Israel, government officials have refused to recognize the PLO's claims for a Palestinian state, while

PLO officials have not recognized an Israeli claim to any particular territory.

The unwillingness of government officials to accept assigned territories and their determination to claim territories held by others violates the principles upon which sovereignty in the interstate system is based. As the historian Immanuel Wallerstein has noted, "What is conceptually impermissible in the modern state-system was an explicit recognition of permanent overlapping jurisdictions. Sovereignty as a concept was based on the Aristotelian law of the excluded middle."[5] Overlapping territorial claims have prompted objections by sibling states, which view these claims as a direct attempt to infringe their own sovereignty, and have antagonized other states, which doubt the commitment of these states to act as responsible members of the interstate system.

The divided states have also tried to limit the sovereignty of sibling states by insisting that recognition of one state *precluded* recognition of the other. In 1955, the West German government adopted the Hallstein Doctrine, which made either-or recognition the government's official policy. The government refused to maintain diplomatic relations with any country that established relations with East Germany. When non-aligned Yugoslavia did so, the West German government described the move as "an unfriendly act" and severed its existing relations with Yugoslavia.[6] (Curiously, the West Germans did not apply this doctrine to the Soviet Union, which established and recognized East Germany, because they could not get rid of residual Soviet occupation authority without first signing a peace treaty with the Soviets, a treaty that partition had deferred.) The East German government reciprocated in 1967, promulgating the Ulbricht Doctrine, which threatened sanctions against countries that made contacts with West Germany.[7] The two Germanys finally abandoned their either-or recognition policies in 1969; mutual recognition came four years later.[8] It was only after they abandoned their exclusionary recognition policies that they were admitted to the United Nations.

But while the Hallstein approach enables one state to derogate the sovereignty of another, its effect is to derogate the rights of both. In 1957, the Soviets tried to obtain UN membership for North and South Vietnam and North and South Korea, but U.S. officials led the fight against admission into the General Assembly and the proposal was defeated.[9] Like West Germany, the United States preferred that only one state—its ally—be admitted and recognized. Failing that, U.S.

officials preferred that neither be recognized. This was the downside of Hallstein Doctrines everywhere. And as the West Germans discovered, some countries even used the Hallstein Doctrine to extract economic concessions from them by threatening to recognize East Germany.

Such developments have made it difficult for states to secure and maintain recognition in the interstate system. The controversy over admitting a delegation from mainland China or Taiwan into the United Nations illustrates the problematic nature of sovereignty for divided states. While the Soviets and Americans locked horns over this issue for more than twenty years, the governments in mainland China and Taiwan also attached considerable importance to this question. Aside from the practical difficulties that result from non-recognition—it is more difficult to obtain foreign aid and participate in international organizations such as the International Monetary Fund, the World Health Organization, and the Olympics—it undermines one's position in a conflict. When the Soviets absented themselves from the United Nations just prior to the Korean War (which they had done to protest the U.S. refusal to admit China), U.S. representatives were able to persuade the United Nations to commit troops to the conflict and to condemn China's entrance into the war as the illegal act of an aggressor. With some reason, then, the relatively isolated Kuomintang government in Taiwan now fears the same kind of treatment. Should they become embroiled in a conflict with China, the Nationalists might find it difficult to obtain outside assistance without access to the United Nations.[10]

The sovereignty of divided states is also abridged by the actions of other states, particularly the superpowers. After helping to engineer partition, the superpower states continued to take an active interest in the internal and external affairs of these countries. Frequently this interest has been expressed through military intervention and diplomatic meddling, which has infringed the divided states' ability to exercise their full sovereignty.

In Germany, for instance, both superpowers have reserved their rights as occupation authorities. They do not permit either state to conduct a fully independent foreign and military policy. Forty-five years after World War II, the superpowers maintain control over even relatively minor matters. When East German leader Erich Honecker made plans in the early 1980s to visit West Germany and meet with officials there, the Soviets repeatedly canceled his trips, a humiliating experience for a head of state.[11] Likewise, after a group of NATO jets crashed into a large crowd during an air show at a U.S. base in West Germany, killing sixty-five spectators, West German Defense Minister Rupert Scholz's decision to ban acrobatic flying touched off a controversy because he did not have the authority to dictate such prohibitions to the United States and NATO. After the incident, *Stern* magazine editorialized, "The time has come to ask the question of who really governs this country. Almost half a century after the end of the war, West Germany continues to be a nation with only limited sovereignty."[12]

In South Korea, as in West Germany, the United States maintains control of the armed forces, which were placed under United Nations command during the Korean War. In 1960, "Koreans cheered U.S. Ambassador Walter McConaughy's automobile, with its U.S. flags flying, as he proceeded slowly down a main avenue in Seoul" to tell Syngman Rhee that it was time to step down.[13] When the South Korean government sent South Korean troops to crush the 1979 uprising in the city of Kwangju, they first had to obtain permission from the U.S. commander to redeploy their troops. And when President Chun Doo Hwan faced massive demonstrations protesting his attempt to designate a successor without elections, U.S. diplomats in 1987 told Chun to reconsider his decision. He did. A year later, elections were held to choose a successor, and Roh Tae Woo, the commander of the forces that had crushed the Kwangju rebellion, was elected President. The United States played a similar role in South Vietnam, where for twenty years it chose political leaders, sanctioned coups, and controlled, directly or indirectly, the country's foreign and military policy.

U.S. aid is an important lever in its relations with many divided states. A 1957 report of the Senate Foreign Relations Committee concluded: "Technical Assistance is not something to be done, as a Government enterprise, for its own sake or for the sake of others. The U.S. Government is not a charitable institution, nor is it an appropriate outlet for the charitable spirit of the American people. . . . Technical Assistance is only one of a number of instruments available to the United States to carry out its foreign policy and promote its national interests abroad."[14] Recipients of U.S. aid thus found that aid gave U.S. officials a hand in shaping their foreign and military policy. Since divided states are typically immersed in conflict with their neighbors and desperately seek military assistance, they often surrender a great deal of control over their foreign and domestic policy to obtain U.S. assistance, which can make them vulnerable to attacks by domestic opponents.

Prior to partition, Jinnah announced that Pakistan would pursue a non-aligned foreign policy. But after the first Indo-Pakistani war, General Ayub in 1953 negotiated with the United States to obtain military aid. Pakistan was then quickly enrolled in the U.S. sphere of influence. U.S. officials first urged Pakistan to join an alliance with Turkey in April 1954 to form a bulwark against Soviet expansion and, later that year, to join CENTO to "contain Chinese aggression."[15] In 1955, the U.S. persuaded Pakistan to sign the Baghdad Pact with Britain, Iran, Iraq, and Turkey to forestall radical nationalist revolution in the Middle East. Naturally, these developments made it difficult for Pakistan to conduct the kind of independent, non-aligned foreign policy foreseen by Jinnah. The domestic consequences of this were quickly felt in 1956, when Egyptian President Gamal Abdel Nasser expropriated the Suez Canal from the British and French, a move extremely popular among Moslems and nationalists throughout the Middle East and South Asia. But because of its treaty commitments, Pakistan backed the anti-Islamic British, while neighboring India backed Moslem Egypt. Demonstrations against the Pakistani government's policy broke out across the country, and opponents of the government's pro-Western foreign policy formed a political party that would subsequently make considerable trouble for the government.[16]

This does not mean that Pakistan's foreign and military policy was wholly controlled by its superpower ally. Like other divided states, Pakistan could and did take unilateral foreign policy initiatives. State officials in Pakistan three times initiated wars with India in the post-partition period, a fact that attests to their capacity and determination to use military force to exercise their sovereignty. But while Pakistan could begin these wars, it could not conclude them on its own terms, which suggests that even its capacity to wage war was restricted in important ways.

Israeli state officials also found that while they enjoyed the capacity to conduct wars on their own initiative, they could not always conclude them on their own terms. During the first three Arab-Israeli wars—in 1948–49, 1956, and 1967—the Israelis seized the initiative and quickly crushed Arab military opposition. But military victory did not force Israel's opponents to sue for peace, to sign treaties recognizing Israel's territorial claims, or to agree to restrict the size and character of their armies. The only time Israel was able to conclude a favorable peace was five years after the largely unfavorable 1973 war (which had been launched at Egyptian initiative). And even then, the United States had pressured Israel and Egypt to sign the Camp David accords. Israel had not been able to conclude its other wars on favorable terms because in each case the United States, Israel's foremost ally and economic benefactor, insisted that the Israelis limit their military and political objectives and agree to cease-fires that preserved intact their neighbors' armies and governments. U.S. officials restricted Israeli action in part because they wanted to prevent the Soviet Union from intervening on behalf of threatened Arab states and in part because the United States itself wanted to preserve the integrity of certain Arab states, which were important political and economic allies.

The United States has also intervened in Israeli domestic affairs, though not as vigorously as in other divided states. U.S. officials have been reluctant to use massive economic and military aid to Israel as a means of forcing changes in Israeli policy and have not attempted to overthrow or push aside the civilian government, as they have done in some of the other divided states. During the recent Arab Palestinian uprising in the Israeli-occupied territories, however, U.S. officials have condemned the shooting of demonstrators by Israeli forces and have refused to veto a UN Security Council resolution condemning Israel.[17] But while the United States places fewer restrictions on Israel's sovereignty than on some of the other divided states, it abridges, in some way, the sovereign rights of all.

The Soviet Union does much the same thing. It has intervened militarily in East Germany and uses economic and military aid to shape the foreign and military policy of its allies. Ironically, though, the Soviet Union is less effective than the United States at restricting the sovereignty of its divided-state allies. This may at first seem counterintuitive: one would expect the Soviets to exercise greater control over states ruled by like-minded Communist Parties than the United States could over states ruled by democratic, nationalist parties or military regimes. But while the Soviet Union *does* influence directly the domestic, foreign, and military policy of East Germany, it has not been able to establish such influence in Asia because China has been able to forge a relatively independent foreign and domestic policy there. China's ability to assert its sovereignty has provided an example for other divided states to obtain greater rights. In the U.S. sphere of influence, no state (except perhaps France) has been able to obtain the rights vis-à-vis the United States that China has been able to exercise with respect to the Soviet Union.

Government officials in China were able to initiate and conclude several wars—the 1947–49 civil war, the Korean War, the war with India in 1962, and a conflict with the Soviet Union itself in 1969–70 —on their own terms. The assertion of China's independence from Soviet policy dictates led in the late 1950s to a split between the two countries, making it possible for North Korea and North Vietnam to assert their own, though more modest, rights by playing the Soviets and the Chinese against each other. The Sino-Soviet split thus gave smaller divided states greater room in which to maneuver.

During the 1950s, North Korea maintained close ties with both countries, avoided taking sides in the Sino-Soviet disputes, and adopted a policy of studied neutrality in 1961. As the Sino-Soviet dispute sharpened, the Soviet Union practiced its own *de facto* version of the either-or Hallstein Doctrine and withdrew all aid from North Korea because the North Koreans refused to break with China. North Korean officials then sided with China, though they continued to press for Soviet and Chinese aid and insisted on North Korean independence. Tensions between China and North Korea rose during the Chinese Cultural Revolution (1965–69), when Red Guards attacked North Korean Premier Kim Il Sung as a "fat revisionist" and the "Khrushchev of Korea."[18]

Although they were offended by Chinese behavior during the Cultural Revolution, the North Koreans were also offended by the Brezhnev Doctrine, under which the Soviets claimed they had a right to invade Czechoslovakia "to preserve socialism" in 1968. (North Korea, like Czechoslovakia, borders the Soviet Union.) So in the 1970s, they returned to their neutralist position, attempting to keep both China and the Soviet Union at arm's length, and pursuing independent contacts with non-aligned and Third World countries.[19]

The North Vietnamese maintained more consistent relations with the Soviet Union and developed more antagonistic relations with China than the North Koreans, but they too preserved a great deal of autonomy during their long war with France, the United States, and various South Vietnamese regimes. North Vietnam was able to conduct a relatively independent foreign and military policy, initiate and conclude the war on its own terms, play the Soviets and Chinese against each other, and keep some distance from both for the duration of the war. But after the war's conclusion in 1975, the Chinese attempted to assert greater control over the Vietnamese: they initiated a border war with Vietnam in 1979, but were rebuffed; and they sided with the ousted Khmer Rouge after the Vietnamese invaded Cambodia in 1978. Although the Chinese have not been able to bring Vietnamese policy into line with their own, they have in recent years succeeded in confining Vietnamese initiatives and preventing Vietnam from concluding the war in Cambodia on its own terms.

Still, the Vietnamese Communists, like the North Koreans and the Chinese, have exercised control over domestic and foreign policy that Communist regimes in Eastern Europe cannot. For the most part, they have also been able to exercise greater control than their sibling-state counterparts. South Korea and South Vietnam ceded control over their armed forces to the United States and Taiwan was beholden to U.S. naval forces for its very survival. None of these states was able to launch any wars of its own, and the regimes in South Korea and South Vietnam survived only with massive U.S. assistance. By contrast, China, North Korea, and Vietnam maintained effective control over state power (the Soviets did not attempt to organize coups to topple them) and over their armed forces, deploying them effectively and independently throughout this period.

However, the greater sovereignty enjoyed by Communist divided states in Asia did not mean that the superpowers failed to restrict their sovereignty in important ways. It was the superpowers, after all, that prevented the North Koreans and the Chinese from reuniting their countries in the post-partition period and delayed, at great cost, the reunification of Vietnam. Superpower activity also prevented these states from gaining admission to the United Nations and exercising the rights enjoyed by full-fledged members of the interstate system; the abridgment of these rights continues to be a source of frustration and anger for government officials in these states.

India has charted a middle course and has thereby found greater freedom to conduct its foreign and domestic policy than Pakistan and most other divided states. By playing off the U.S.–Soviet and Sino-Soviet disputes, Indian officials have been able to acquire control of their domestic and foreign policy, but the desire of Indian state officials to conduct a non-aligned foreign policy has been frustrated by superpower alignments on issues affecting India and Pakistan.[20] India has reluctantly aligned itself with the Soviet Union, in large part because the United States (and later China) has found Pakistan a useful ally. India has been able to conclude one war with Pakistan on its own terms (1971), but was unable to do so in its previous wars with Pakistan (1947–49, 1965) or with China (1962).

Ireland is the only partitioned country that has not been affected by superpower rivalry. After shaking off the last British restrictions on its sovereignty in 1949, the Irish Republic acquired sovereign rights enjoyed by most members of the interstate system. In Northern Ireland, by contrast, local officials enjoyed considerable autonomy, though not sovereignty (they remained part of Great Britain), for many years. But when they were unable to contain civil and martial Catholic protest and Protestant reaction in the early 1970s, they found their autonomy quickly abridged by British authorities. In 1972, the British dissolved the provincial parliament and took over direct responsibility for civilian and military administration. This legal coup from above severely restricted the autonomy that Protestant officials and political parties had come to expect, and the derogation of Protestant autonomy in Northern Ireland has only deepened since then. The British have raised the prospect of reunification with the south by holding a reunification referendum, which was defeated in 1973 by 57 percent of the electorate,[21] and by permitting southern Irish officials to consult on laws pertaining to the North.

The British recently took a symbolic step that speaks volumes about the derogation of sovereign rights in Northern Ireland and in other divided states. In 1985, the British repealed a thirty-two-year-old Flags and Emblems Law, which had made it illegal for residents to display the tricolored flag of the Irish Republic. Protestant groups had long marched through Catholic neighborhoods beating drums, singing marching songs, and waving the Union Jack as a means of asserting their domination. This law and Protestant practice had angered Catholics, and the British repealed the measure to reduce tension. But Protestants viewed the British move as further evidence that their rights were being abridged and that allowing the tricolor to be raised meant that the Union Jack was symbolically lowered. Ulster Defense Association leader John McMichael defended the old law, saying, "Symbols are most important to people not involved in the niceties of Governments."[22]

Officials in many of the divided states regulate or ban the display of flags representing sibling states or sometimes even the wearing of colors represented on their flags. China submitted an official protest to the Soviet Union after a Soviet magazine appeared with the Kuomintang flag printed on its cover. The Chinese took this as a back-door attempt by the Soviets to recognize Taiwan and to derogate the mainland's sovereignty.

The use of flags and emblems by state officials and citizens is full of meaning. A country's flag, its currency, and its stamps are used to assert sovereign rights and to make claims about the character of its inhabitants. U.S. currency, for instance, is full of totemic symbols (the eye above the pyramid), slogans ("In God We Trust," "*Annuit Coeptis*"), representations of founding fathers, and endorsements by contemporary officials. This is no less true in the divided states. Flags, currency, and stamps are used as the coin of sovereignty. (Traditionally, British gold coins impressed with the monarch's image have been called "sovereigns.")

Officials in some of the divided states also use stamps to complain of partition. The West Germans, for example, have issued a stamp commemorating the 1948–49 Berlin Airlift. The stamp features a tall, arching concrete hurdle, displays the flags of the occupying countries that assisted in the relief of West Berlin—the United States, Great Britain, and France (a usage that also hints at the derogated sovereignty of West Germany)—and notes "*Luftbrücke Berlin*" and the dates 1948–49 to remind contemporary Germans of past events. Not to be outdone, the East German government has issued a stamp commemorating the twenty-fifth anniversary of the *Antifaschistischer Schutzwall* (Anti-Fascist Bulwark), elsewhere known as the Berlin Wall. It depicts the Brandenburg Gate, not the pedestrian cement barrier that encircles West Berlin, in the background and a smiling woman handing red carnations to three smiling, heavily armed soldiers in the foreground.

But it is a South Korean stamp that perhaps best expresses official frustration with partition and the derogation of sovereignty. The red and blue stamp depicts an outline map of the Korean peninsula. A heavy link chain stretches across the 38th parallel, but it is severed midway by a flaming, Olympic-like torch held by three muscular fists and arms. The dramatic imagery is plain: the torch of freedom, held by South Korean "arms," will cut the chain that both divides and enslaves the country.[23]

Just as the disenfranchisement of "minority" populations has created resistance by indigenous movements, the derogation of sovereign rights within the interstate system has stimulated official determination to remove those obstacles that constrain independence. And like second-generation independence movements, which take up arms to assert their rights as citizens, government officials frequently use force of arms to claim their rights as sovereign states. The derogation of citizenship prompts indigenous independence movements to make civil war; the derogation of sovereignty compels government officials to wage interstate war. Each alone is combustible. Together they are explosive.

· 11 ·

States of War

In a speech at the University of Virginia in early 1947, George Kennan said of the Soviets, "I sometimes think they have created something more powerful than themselves . . . that they have sown their dragon's teeth and now they find themselves, willy-nilly, for better or for worse, the masters and the servants of the weird and terrifying warriors who have grown up in their pasture."[1] Forty years later, Kennan's prophetic warning applies not only to Soviet Communism but to the partition policies of all the great and superpower states. Partition prepared the ground for the development of "weird and terrifying warriors" who would wage destructive irregular and conventional wars in the divided states and in neighboring countries.

It is commonplace today to describe irregular warriors—pajama-clad cadre of the Vietnamese National Liberation Front, sword-carrying Sikh secessionists, scarf-wearing Palestinian militia, and ski-masked IRA gunmen—as "terrorists." This term, however, does not adequately describe their social origins, contemporary politics, or future goals. As Christopher Hitchens notes, "terrorist," as it is commonly defined—"one who uses violence for political ends" —is vague. The term's meaning theoretically could "cover any state, party, movement or system not explicitly committed to pacifism or [be] simply a synonym for 'swarthy opponent of U.S. foreign policy.' "[2]

Despite the inherent inexactitude in labeling the irregular forces in the divided states as terrorists, they may certainly be described as "weird and terrifying." It would be difficult, for instance, to describe the Khmer Rouge in Cambodia except as both weird and terrifying. Its national anthem, "Glorious April 17," named for the day in 1975 when the Khmer Rouge seized the Cambodian capital, celebrates a sanguine identity:

> Bright red blood that covers the towns
>   and plains of Kampuchea, our motherland
> Sublime blood of workers and peasants
> Sublime blood of revolutionary men and women fighters
> The blood changing into unrelenting hatred.[3]

It is hard to imagine a tune that could carry this stanza.

The movements that wage irregular wars are not, of course, the only weird and terrifying warriors in the divided states. Government officials who massacre peaceful demonstrators, who adopt "Iron Fist" policies (which include breaking the hands of rock-throwing demonstrators), who subject minority populations to military and paramilitary rule, or who launch surprise attacks on neighboring states might also be described in this fashion.

The superpowers have come to regard some of their own allies in the divided states as weird and terrifying. Soviet Premier Nikita Khrushchev was appalled at Mao Tse-tung's belief that nuclear war was like conventional conflict. "War is war," Mao told Khrushchev. "The years will pass and we'll get to work producing more babies than ever before." Or, "If worse came to worst and half of mankind died, the other half would remain while imperialism would be razed to the ground."[4] Khrushchev believed that Mao's views revealed him as one who might take catastrophic risks. In 1959, he warned China's leaders not to "test the stability of the capitalist system by employing armed force" and accused China of being "keen on war like a bellicose cock."[5] Across the Taiwan Strait, U.S. officials believed that Chiang Kai-shek was an unreliable ally who might start a war he couldn't finish. In 1950, for example, Kuomintang officials expressed the hope that a third world war would give them the opportunity to recover the mainland, and they urged a widening of the Korean War to provoke such a global war.

Allies like Mao and Chiang, who were willing to take potentially catastrophic risks regardless of the consequences, might justifiably be seen as weird and terrifying by U.S. and Soviet officials. But sometimes the shoe was on the other foot: during the course of conflicts in the divided states, U.S. and Soviet leaders many times terrified officials there by threatening to use nuclear weapons. During a 1955 crisis in the Taiwan Strait, Eisenhower said he might use "new and powerful weapons" to prevent "armed aggression" by the Chinese and claimed that tactical nuclear weapons could be used without massacring civilians.[6] From the Chinese perspective, U.S. officials— who had once used nuclear weapons to destroy heavily populated cities in Japan and who now threatened to use them in another densely populated country—might also be regarded as weird and terrifying. Conflicts in the divided states tend to unleash forces and produce consequences that the participants do not intend, fail to anticipate, and often cannot control. Indeed, the distinction between irregular, conventional, and nuclear war easily blurs.

Kennan was prophetic in another respect. Partition and the derogation of citizenship and sovereignty would make great and superpower states "the masters *and* the servants" of other movements and states. Great and superpower states might have mastered these countries during the process of devolution and division, but they could not easily control the developments that followed. Movements and officials in the divided states frequently took matters into their own hands and initiated wars without the consent or approval of their superpower allies, frequently forcing the superpowers to intervene militarily on their behalf. Both the United States and the Soviet Union have often found themselves acting at the behest of allies who have initiated civil and conventional wars for their own reasons, serving their own interests.

Partition, displacement, and the derogation of citizenship and sovereignty in the divided states prepared the ground for the emergence of irregular, conventional, and nuclear warriors. To understand these conflicts and their consequences, which have had a dramatic impact on both divided and superpower states, it is useful to distinguish the three forms that such conflict takes. Although violence occurs across a continuum that makes it difficult to draw sharp distinctions between irregular, conventional, and nuclear war, the actors involved—independence movements, divided states, and superpowers—tend to specialize in particular forms of war.

Displaced and disenfranchised peoples in many of the divided states have adopted irregular war as a means to achieve their secessionist or reunificationist ends. Historically, irregular war has taken many forms: assassination, bombing, booby-trapping, hostage-taking, sabotage, arms-gathering assaults on military posts and police stations, rebellion, insurrection, civil war, revolution. These practices are "irregular" because their adherents are not in the employ of a state and because they challenge both civilian and military authority. There are no established rules of engagement (such as the Geneva conventions), and the practitioners do not usually wear uniforms identifying themselves as soldiers distinguished from the civilian population at large. Various forms of mufti—pajamas, burnooses, ski masks, camouflage fatigues, baseball caps—have become identified with some irregulars by the popular press, but these accoutrements are typically donned to *conceal* the wearer's identity.

Depending on the circumstances, political movements also blur the distinction between irregular and legal means of achieving their ends. In Northern Ireland, for instance, the Catholic reunificationist movement supports the IRA irregulars, but it also runs candidates for elected office through legal political parties. The decision to participate in or abstain from provincial elections has frequently split the movement. In 1969, the Provisional IRA, or "Provos," split from the main body of the IRA over this issue, rejecting the majority decision to participate in elections and pressing ahead with its own paramilitary campaign.[7] Most resistance movements, however, practice an abstentionist politics, though they may also maintain legal front organizations. The PLO supports armed irregulars and unarmed civilian protest in the Israeli-occupied territories, but it actively discourages Palestinian participation in government positions that are filled by Israeli appointment or by Israeli-supervised elections. And in South Vietnam, the NLF did not participate in U.S.–sponsored elections during the 1960s or 1970s.

Straddling the border of legality, the movements that conduct irregular wars make it difficult for state officials to use force against them. By threatening civilian as well as military personnel, these movements can spread out a state's defenses, making it easier for small irregular forces to attack successfully. By concealing their identity, submerging themselves in the civilian population, movements make it more difficult for state officials to use force against them. The state risks attacking the "wrong" people, which can alienate them and encourage them to support the insurgents. And by maintaining a legal presence, movements can act as legitimate participants in the political process. Attempts to suppress legal participation, moreover, often arouse the opposition of other legal parties and organizations who fear that their own, non-revolutionary activity will be jeopardized by the state.

To be effective, movements that wage irregular wars must be able to develop mass-based organizations that will support and protect the clandestine forces, while maintaining discipline among the irregular soldiers. Without disciplined troops who are able to distinguish friend from foe, irregular forces can easily lose popular support. Movements must also obtain and maintain support from *external* sources, from sympathetic populations and state officials in neighboring states. It is much easier for state officials to isolate and destroy irregular forces if they do not receive money, arms, and diplomatic support from abroad.

In the divided states, conditions generally permit movements to obtain indigenous support, maintain discipline, and secure outside assistance. The disenfranchisement of indigenous minorities tends to create communities that are willing to support legal and clandestine resistance to majority rule. But sometimes it takes a dramatic turn of events to energize these communities. In Northern Ireland, for example, the Catholic minority refused to support or assist IRA bombing campaigns in the late 1930s or in the late 1950s and early 1960s. These campaigns were consequently ineffective and most of the irregulars were captured. But after Protestant irregulars and the Royal Ulster Constabulary attacked peaceful mass demonstrations and Catholic neighborhoods in 1968–69, the Catholic population threw its support behind the irregular forces. A significant percentage has maintained its support to this day. In Israel, the Arab Palestinian population was generally unsupportive of irregular *fedayeen* attacks until after the 1967 Arab-Israeli war and the Israeli occupation of the West Bank and Gaza. And even then, its support was muted. It was only in the late 1980s, after Israel's unsuccessful war in Lebanon, that the indigenous population demonstrated widespread support for the PLO, its irregular forces, and the creation of a separate Palestinian state.

First-generation movements that conducted irregular war to win independence in devolved states have provided a model of discipline for second-generation movements. There is no copyright on the methods of irregular war. Its practice has been freely copied by groups professing very different ideologies: capitalist or Communist, ethnic or secular, secessionist or reunificationist. So, for instance, the PLO's conduct of its irregular campaigns owes as much to Zionist irregulars—Menachem Begin's Irgun, the Stern Gang—as it does to Arab irregulars like the Green Hand Gang that operated during the British mandate period.

To be successful, movements that practice irregular war must conduct themselves in a manner that does not alienate their supporters. This means that the violence they employ must be selective, not random. Context is important. The press often describes the incidents that accompany irregular war as indiscriminate acts of violence and terror. The bombing of Irish pubs, car bomb attacks in crowded markets, the massacre of passengers traveling on buses, trains, or planes are usually considered indiscriminate because they are attacks on civilians. But on closer inspection, these attacks are usually more selective. The IRA bombs Protestant pubs, Christian irregulars in Lebanon attack markets in Moslem districts, and in one case, Sikh militants separated Sikh from Hindu before slaughtering the Hindu passengers on a bus in the Punjab. Irregular forces attempt to distinguish between friend and foe and convey these distinctions to their supporters and their enemies. This is why the ubiquitous claiming of responsibility for acts of violence is so important to irregular movements. These claims are part of an ongoing political effort to demonstrate that their use of violence is selective rather than indiscriminate. If violence is seen by potential supporters as random, irregulars will be treated as thugs, hoodlums, or madmen. In this context, an irregular movement's "discipline" is measured by its ability to employ violence selectively and to persuade its supporters that discriminate violence is a legitimate, necessary, and effective means of self-defense. This, however, is very difficult to do, for inevitably friends as well as foes are killed.

The successful conduct of irregular war also depends heavily on a movement's ability to obtain external support. Because partition led to massive migration across newly created borders, minority populations found they could rely on sympathetic populations and officials in neighboring states to provide financial, military, and political assistance. IRA representatives from Northern Ireland raise money from

Catholics in Ireland and the United States and use this money to purchase arms,[8] while the Irish Republic pressures the British to eliminate discriminatory measures against Northern Catholics, to restore human rights, and to end martial law. Likewise, the PLO subsisted for many years on the support of Arab Palestinian populations and sympathetic state officials in Egypt, Jordan, Syria, and Lebanon before wearing out its welcome in each of these states. Sikhs in India rely on Sikh neighbors in Pakistan and depend on state officials there to treat their activities—raising money and acquiring arms—with a wink and a nod. Without the financial, military, and political assistance from external supporters, many movements that conduct irregular war would be more easily isolated and destroyed.

Some movements are more successful than others at indigenous organization, discipline, and external support. In the post-partition period, however, only two movements that have waged irregular war have been ultimately successful. The NLF in Vietnam was the only successful reunificationist movement, and the Mukti Bahini, the armed wing of the Awami League in East Pakistan, was the only successful secessionist movement. Of the two, the NLF demonstrated a greater capacity to enlist popular support; to wage an effective, disciplined irregular war; to secure the support of sympathetic populations in neighboring states (North Vietnam, Laos, Cambodia) and around the world (even, to some extent, in the United States); and to survive a protracted and determined effort by officials in South Vietnam and the United States to crush it. As Douglas Pike, a Rand Corporation analyst, said of the NLF: "If the essence of the Chinese revolution was strategy and the essence of the Viet Minh was spirit, the essence of the third generation revolutionary guerrilla warfare in South Vietnam was organization. . . . The National Liberation Front was a Sputnik in the political sphere of the Cold War."[9] The Mukti Bahini was not as well organized as the NLF, but it was equally successful because it received Indian Army intervention on its behalf.

Movements that conduct irregular war are extremely difficult to defeat once they can develop internal and external support. The South Vietnamese found it impossible to defeat the NLF, even with massive U.S. assistance. The Israelis have never been able to subdue the PLO; they have succeeded only in chasing it from one country to the next, in 1970 from Jordan and in 1982 from Lebanon. And the British have found it impossible to defeat the IRA so long as it obtains support from sympathetic populations in and outside Northern Ireland. As a result, irregular war has become an obdurate feature of conflict in many of the divided states.

Moreover, because movements actively seek to drag outside people and states into war, irregular war frequently contributes to the outbreak of conventional war. In the five years preceding the outbreak of the Korean War, North Korea had supported the irregular guerrilla movement and civilian uprisings in the South; South Korean troops had also made forays across the 38th parallel to attack guerrilla bases in the North.[10] The irregular war increased tensions, contributed to attempts by both sides to build up conventional armies, and spurred South Korean officials to advocate war as a way to eliminate North Korean support for irregulars in the South. And when North Korean conventional troops marched across the 38th parallel in 1950, they evidently believed that their invasion would trigger a popular uprising and assist the beleaguered irregular forces that remained in the South.

The irregular war in Vietnam, which began in 1956–60 as a result of Diem's efforts to destroy the residual Vietminh infrastructure, contributed to the U.S. decision to send military advisers and then conventional troops to assist the South Vietnamese. The U.S. escalation in 1964–65, quadrupling the number of U.S. troops, led in turn to the introduction of North Vietnamese regulars.[11] These developments contributed to large-scale conventional interstate war, with Cambodia and Laos eventually drawn into the conflict.

During the 1947 partition of India, civilian uprisings and irregular war resulted in the deployment of conventional troops and war between Pakistan and India. Although the general outline of partition was determined by the British, the particulars were not nailed down. Ruling princes possessed nominal authority over as much as one-third of the subcontinent as a result of separate treaties made with British administrators in the eighteenth and nineteenth centuries, and while the partition agreement did not automatically assign these states to either India or Pakistan, the independence movements in both countries made it clear that they would not permit princes to retain any autonomous authority within the devolved states. For instance, the Moslem ruler of Hyderabad (a large central state with a predominantly Hindu population) tried to establish authority separate from the Indian government that would be joined with the British Commonwealth. When demonstrations broke out protesting this move, Indian troops entered the principality and forced the ruler to surrender all his authority to the newly created central government.[12] But it was in Kashmir, a predominantly Moslem province in the northwest that is wedged between India and Pakistan, where the outbreak of popular revolt and irregular war provoked conventional conflict.

The Hindu maharajah of Kashmir favored joining India after partition; the 80 percent Moslem majority preferred Pakistan. Armed rebellion broke out in late 1947 and was suppressed by provincial forces loyal to the maharajah. Moslem tribesmen, with the approval of the Pakistani government, then invaded Kashmir to support Moslem insurgency and to force the maharajah to devolve power to Pakistan. As these irregular forces advanced on the Kashmiri capital, the maharajah appealed to India for military assistance. Indian officials agreed to send troops provided the maharajah agreed to devolve his power to India. The irregular war soon developed into a wider, interstate war as Pakistani troops joined the fighting to assist the Moslem irregulars. It was not until January 1, 1949, after fourteen months of war, that a UN cease-fire took effect, along with the *de facto* division of Kashmir between India and Pakistan.[13] In short order, this division created the geographical basis for revanchist claims and further conflicts. India and Pakistan would clash again over Kashmir in 1965 and 1971.

Irregular war in Palestine, which broke out sporadically between 1945 and 1947 and intensified prior to the devolution of British power, contributed to the outbreak of conventional interstate war in 1948, when Arab states joined the fighting. In this regard, the first Arab-Israeli war most closely resembles the Korean conflict, where protracted irregular warfare prior to partition escalated into a wider conventional war.

In Northern Ireland, irregular war did not lead to conventional war, but it did lead to the introduction of British troops into the province in 1969. The deployment of British conventional forces into Northern Ireland resembles the Indian government's intervention in the princely states, which possessed some autonomy though not sovereignty vis-à-vis the central government. In Northern Ireland, as in Hyderabad, the introduction of central government regulars did not provoke a wider interstate conflict with neighboring states, even though the military intervention supported the ethnic majority against minority claims.

Irregular indigenous war and conventional interstate war have a reciprocating effect, making it difficult to establish whether they are "civil" or "international" conflicts. The interstate system is structured so that "aggression" is condemned and punished while "self-defense" is thought legitimate and supported, but this distinction is largely irrelevant in divided-state conflicts. Because partition results in a problematic definition of states, borders, and relations, it is difficult and usually meaningless to try to determine who violated whose frontiers first.

In the post-partition period, large-scale, conventional, interstate war has erupted between most of the divided states. The conflicts in Korea, Vietnam, and India have claimed more lives—civilian and military—than any other war since 1945.[14] And conventional war in India and Palestine has broken out repeatedly. India and Pakistan have waged three major wars; Israel and its Arab neighbors have fought five times, once in every decade since partition. Meanwhile, conventional interstate war has not broken out between China and Taiwan, between East and West Germany, or between Northern Ireland and the Irish Republic. Conflict between these states has taken other forms.

Government officials wage war to resolve social and political problems that were created by partition. By waging a successful war, government officials hope to suppress indigenous insurgencies, remove external threats, settle refugees, define permanent borders, undo the result of previous wars, or improve their standing in the interstate system. But whatever the proximate cause of conventional war between divided states, almost all their wars are initiated by officials in the divided states, not by great and superpower states.

Although great and superpower states helped create conditions that led to war, they did not license their allies to wage war on their behalf. Partition was supposed to *reduce* conflict between indigenous movements. It did not. Instead, the conflicts between indigenous movements, which were contained within single states prior to partition, developed into interstate conflicts to be settled by large armies.

Government officials in the divided states do not wage war at their allies' request, nor do they agree to be surrogates for Cold War superpower conflicts. They initiate war because they have their own scores to settle. Sometimes they receive superpower permission to do so, as the North Koreans evidently did prior to their 1950 invasion of the South, but for the most part they wage war unilaterally. Of the ten major conventional wars in the divided states since partition—the Korean War, the Vietnam War, three Indo-Pakistani wars, and five Arab-Israeli wars—only one was initiated by officials outside the region: the 1956 Suez or second Arab-Israeli war.

After Egyptian President Nasser nationalized the Suez Canal in 1956, the French and British asked the Israelis to precipitate a war with Egypt that could be used as a pretext for French and British military intervention. The French and British would then send troops into Egypt and seize the canal to "protect" it from the Israeli advance. The Israelis agreed to act as a great power surrogate because they hoped to achieve military objectives of their own: to reopen the Straits of Tiran, which the Egyptians had closed to Israeli shipping, and to drive the Egyptian Army from the Sinai and thus create an expansive buffer between Israel and its most powerful Arab opponent.[15] But the great powers failed to obtain U.S. approval; when they put their plan into operation, the U.S. condemned it and forced the French, British, and Israelis to halt their largely successful military campaign and withdraw from territory gained. This experience discouraged the Israelis from playing a surrogate role in the future; they conducted three subsequent wars on their own initiative. (The 1956 war proved to be a rehearsal for the Israelis' 1967 campaign in the Sinai, except that in 1967 they conquered the peninsula on their own.) The Israelis did not seek or secure superpower approval for their conduct in subsequent wars and frequently concealed their moves from their allies as well as from their opponents.

Officials in divided states are not inclined to act as superpower surrogates, because they must live with the consequences of war. The nine other major conventional wars were started by government officials in the divided states. Once under way, however, each of these wars prompted superpower intervention, though the character of such involvement varied widely. In Korea and Vietnam, the United States committed large numbers of troops to the fighting and conducted massive aerial and naval campaigns against their opponents. Although the Soviets did not introduce troops into these conflicts (apart from some advisers), they did provide significant material and financial assistance.

The superpowers have been less inclined to introduce troops into the Israeli-Arab conflicts, though they both have supplied advisers, technicians, and large amounts of military and financial assistance. The United States has sent small troop contingents to serve as partisan "peacekeeping" forces, either in combination with UN forces or on their own, as they did during the 1982 war in Lebanon. The Soviets placed more than 20,000 military personnel in Egypt to provide air defense against Israel between 1967 and 1973.[16]

Superpower intervention in the three Indo-Pakistani wars, however, has been even less tangible. Both superpowers have tried to mediate between the parties and to bring these wars to a speedy conclusion, primarily through their role as permanent members of the UN Security Council. They have also provided advanced military assistance to their respective allies—the United States to Pakistan, the Soviet Union to India. (During the 1971 war, the United States used a formidable display of naval power in an unsuccessful attempt to conclude the war on terms favorable to its ally.) The fact that the Indo-Pakistani wars are far removed from U.S. and Soviet power bases in Europe, Asia, and the Americas, and the fact that neither superpower played a role in the subcontinental partition, helps to explain why their intervention in these conflicts has been less pronounced. (Much the same is true of Ireland; neither superpower has intervened in post-partition conflicts there.)

Although government officials in the divided states can start conventional wars, they cannot finish them. And while the superpowers don't start them, they can stop them, at least for a time. The North Korean invasion in 1950, which initially routed South Korean forces, ground to a halt after U.S. and UN forces joined the war. And the U.S.–UN advance in the North, which nearly reached the Chinese and Soviet borders, failed to retake the North after China intervened on North Korea's behalf. Intervention by U.S.–UN and Chinese forces thus prevented Korean armies from conducting war on their own terms. And the war ended essentially where it began, with armies drawn up on either side of a demilitarized zone near the the 38th parallel. Likewise, when war has broken out between India and Pakistan or between Israel and its neighbors, the superpowers have immediately called for an end to the conflict. The participants conduct military blitzkriegs in part to capitalize on the element of surprise and in part to achieve military objectives before superpower cease-fires take hold.

Partition also forged alliances between indigenous regimes and superpower states, and grouped divided states into collective security regimes organized by the United States and the Soviet Union. Because both parties to conventional war have superpower allies, an attack by one will trigger superpower intervention on behalf of the other. And intervention by one superpower prompts intervention by the other. But while this chain of events, of action and reaction, tends to widen the conflict and turn regional conflicts into global superpower contests, conventional wars in the divided states have never resulted in the introduction of troops by *both* superpowers or direct military conflict between them. Given the fact that their allies have ten times gone to war, it is remarkable that U.S. and Soviet troops have not met in battle.

Regional conventional wars in the divided states have not escalated into direct superpower confrontation because the superpowers have acted to stop or limit them in important ways. Soon after war breaks out, the superpowers begin calling for a cease-fire. After the outbreak of the 1956 Suez war, for instance, President Eisenhower told Secretary of State Dulles to send a scathing message to Israeli Prime Minister Ben-Gurion: "You'll tell 'em, goddamn it, we're going to apply sanctions, we're going to the United Nations, we're going to do everything that there is so we can stop this thing."[17] And at the United Nations, U.S. officials introduced a resolution calling for a cease-fire and the withdrawal of Israeli forces from the Sinai, and called on UN members—including Great Britain and France—to refrain from the use of force and to participate in an embargo against Israel until it withdrew from the Sinai.[18] The Soviet Union, Egypt's ally, threatened to intervene on its behalf and joined the United States in a UN resolution calling for an immediate cease-fire and the withdrawal of Israeli, French, and British forces.

The effect of these U.S. and Soviet actions was to impose a cease-fire before French and British troops could wrest the Suez Canal from Egyptian control. In subsequent Arab-Israeli wars, superpower intervention has brought the fighting to a halt before one side could completely destroy its opponents. As Stephen Kaplan has noted, "Within hours of the [1973] Arab attack, Soviet representatives began asking Egypt and Syria (the Soviet Union's own allies) to halt their offensive. Although Cairo and Damascus would not do this, Moscow continued to press for a cease-fire, thus antagonizing President Sadat and straining Soviet-Egyptian relations."[19]

The superpowers also acted quickly to halt the fighting in the Indo-Pakistani wars. During the second war, in 1965, the United States and the Soviet Union "joined forces in the UN security council to press for a cease-fire, while the United States cut off all military assistance to both parties during the conflict, a step that proved far more damaging to [its ally] Pakistan than to India, as [Pakistan] was almost wholly dependent on U.S. military assistance."[20] And Soviet mediation of the conflict resulted in the Tashkent Declaration, an armistice that ended hostilities.[21]

When the superpowers did not take action to stop conventional wars, they still attempted to limit and confine them in important ways. This was true even in Korea and Vietnam, where the United States participated directly in intense, large-scale wars.

The outbreak of war in Korea triggered massive U.S. military intervention on behalf of its South Korean ally. The introduction of U.S. ground troops and naval and air forces naturally intensified and widened the war, yet the Korean conflict remained "limited," as both the Soviet Union and the United States took steps to contain the fighting to the peninsula. The Soviet Union helped contain the fighting by not reintroducing the troops that had been withdrawn from Korea prior to the outbreak of war. And although the United Nations took a partisan role in the conflict, the Soviet Union did not withdraw from the United Nations (calling instead for a return to the status quo ante), nor did it create a new crisis in Berlin, attack Yugoslavia, or invade Iran during the war.[22] The United States, in turn, did not accept Chiang Kai-shek's offer to send troops to Korea, because it would have antagonized the Chinese and possibly widened the war even further. After U.S. forces failed to reunify the country on their own terms, U.S. officials scaled back their military and political objectives. As Dean Acheson told Ernest Bevin in 1951, "Our purposes in Korea remain the same, namely to resist aggression, to *localize* hostilities, and to wind up the Korean problem on a satisfactory U.N. basis and in such a way as *not* to commit U.S. forces in large numbers indefinitely in that operation [emphasis added]."[23]

As in Korea, U.S. military intervention in Vietnam greatly intensified the war, and helped spread the conflict to Laos and Cambodia. But the great and superpower states, including the United States, also took steps to limit the war's scope. During the course of the war in Vietnam, U.S. officials did not request UN intervention; they did not send the navy into the Taiwan Strait, as they had in Korea (in fact, they withdrew residual U.S. naval forces from the strait in 1969); they did not conduct an Inchon-type landing on the North Vietnamese coast; and they did not cross the Demilitarized Zone at the 17th parallel in an attempt to overrun the North. The United States never challenged North Vietnam's right to exist as a sovereign state or tried to reunify the country on U.S. terms. After the bulk of the U.S. forces were withdrawn in 1973, following the armistice that recognized the 1954 partition as the status quo, U.S. officials did not attempt to reintroduce troops that had been withdrawn (as they had done in Korea in 1950) or renew the air war when North Vietnamese and NLF forces overran the South and captured Saigon in 1975.

The Soviets provided military assistance and financial aid to their North Vietnamese allies. The provision of antiaircraft weapons, planes, and missiles made a significant contribution to the North's war effort—much as the subsequent provision of U.S. antiaircraft weapons would greatly assist Afghan rebels during their war against the Soviets two decades later.[24] But the Soviets did not send troops to participate in the war or challenge the United States elsewhere in the world. Quite the contrary. In the late 1960s and early 1970s, the Soviets sought to reduce tensions in U.S.–Soviet relations by pursuing détente, even while the war in Vietnam raged.

The Chinese also acted to confine the war. They did not send troops to assist their ally, as they had done in Korea, or take the opportunity to threaten an invasion of Taiwan, even after U.S. naval forces had quietly been withdrawn from the strait. Indeed, the Chinese opening to the United States, and President Nixon's visit to Beijing in 1972, occurred during the latter stages of the war in Vietnam.

These developments effectively limited the war and also constrained North Vietnamese officials, who may have preferred a wider war that would involve their allies. North Vietnamese General Vo Nguyen Giap claims that the Chinese collaborated with the Soviet Union to limit the conflict throughout much of the war: "The Chinese government told the United States that if the latter did not threaten or touch China, then China would do nothing to prevent the [U.S.] attacks [on Vietnam]. It was really like telling the United States that it could bomb Vietnam at will, as long as there was no threat to the Chinese border. . . . We felt that we had been stabbed in the back."[25]

The superpowers have consistently acted to limit conventional wars in the divided states for a variety of reasons: to punish or dissuade minor states from waging war on their own initiative; to defend their spheres of influence, which emerged out of the partition process; to avoid direct confrontation, which despite occasional talk of containment and Cold War neither superpower actively seeks; and to protect the general integrity of the interstate system, which they jointly developed and which is undermined by regional wars. As a consequence, it is very difficult for government officials in the divided states to conduct decisive military campaigns or to wage conclusive wars. The World War II concept of "total victory," which results in the "unconditional surrender" of opposing forces, has proved elusive. With the exception of Vietnam, where the North Vietnamese were able to defeat their opponents and reunify the country on their own terms, none of the major conventional wars has been conclusive. Even where military campaigns have inflicted decisive defeats on enemy forces, they have been inconclusive over the long term. Israeli forces have twice conquered the Sinai and many times destroyed Arab armies wholesale, but neither the 1956 nor the 1967 campaigns brought their enemies to terms. It was only after the Egyptians managed a partially successful attack on Israeli forces during the 1973 Yom Kippur War that a partial settlement—the Camp David accords—could be reached. (Camp David marked an agreement between only two of the Middle East's many combatants.) The blitzkrieg campaigns launched by North Koreans, Indians, Pakistanis, Israelis, and Arabs have all failed to achieve decisive results.

Because conventional wars are indecisive, because they cannot or are not permitted to resolve the issues that gave rise to them, they simply provide the pretext for subsequent wars. Successful efforts to limit conventional wars stop the fighting inconclusively, making the recurrence of armed conflict more likely. This is why conventional war, like irregular war, is an obdurate and seemingly irremediable expression of conflict in the divided states.

Ever since they were first developed in 1945, nuclear weapons have been used to achieve political ends. Nations have frequently threatened to use them during the course of conflict in the divided states, with profound consequences for the superpowers and the divided states alike.

It is a commonplace to say that nuclear weapons have been "used" only on two occasions: when the United States exploded atomic bombs over Hiroshima and Nagasaki on the sixth and ninth of August 1945. This use of nuclear weapons was explicit, dramatic, catastrophic. Hundreds of thousands lost their lives in an instant. Many thousands more died from the bombs' lingering effects.

But it is important to recognize that nuclear weapons have been "used" in a variety of other ways as well. States have used the explosion of nuclear weapons at remote desert or island test sites to demonstrate their capacity to develop and perfect complex nuclear weapons technologies. The expansion of nuclear arsenals and the development of tactical and strategic delivery systems have been used to reduce great and superpower states' reliance on conventional military forces. States that possess nuclear weapons have threatened to attack others with them as a way to compel non-nuclear states to change their behavior. And nuclear weapons have been used to deter other nuclear states from using their own arsenals. As Daniel Ellsberg points out, states can use nuclear weapons without firing them: "When you point a gun at someone's head in a confrontation, you are using the gun, whether or not you pull the trigger."[26] In the eyes of the law, a gun is "used" when it is brandished during the commission of a crime. In the same way, nuclear weapons can be used without being exploded over populated cities.

Although the use of nuclear weapons to destroy cities is rare, the practice of using nuclear weapons to compel states to change their behavior is fairly common. According to the Brookings Institution, the United States has issued nuclear threats on some twenty occasions since it destroyed Hiroshima and Nagasaki.[27] (It is hard to be exact about the number because few of these threats were publicly announced.) Some threats were conveyed through third parties, some were deliberately ambiguous, and some were made in rapid succession, which makes them difficult to distinguish. And some of these threats became known only years later, which means that the number may be greater yet. Certainly U.S. officials considered using nuclear weapons—and drew up contingency plans for doing so—more often than they actually used them to make threats. But whatever the exact number, a general pattern of partition-related threats can be discerned.

Although U.S. officials used nuclear weapons to threaten Yugoslavia, Uruguay, Guatemala, Lebanon, and Jordan in the late 1940s and 1950s, and threatened to use nuclear weapons against the Soviet Union during the Cuban Missile Crisis of 1962, the majority of U.S. threats have been directed at or motivated by events in the divided states. The United States threatened East Germany and the Soviet Union several times during the conflicts over Berlin, repeatedly threatened the North Koreans and their Chinese allies during the Korean War, threatened the Chinese in separate conflicts over Taiwan, issued a number of nuclear threats against the North Vietnamese during the later stages of the Vietnam War, used naval nuclear forces to threaten India during the third Indo-Pakistani war, and issued threats against

Arab states and the Soviet Union during various Arab-Israeli conflicts.[28]

The use of nuclear weapons by the United States against opponents in the divided states may seem surprising. But nuclear weapons were first developed with the intention of dropping them on Germany or Japan, and U.S. officials sought to continue to wield them to achieve political goals in conflicts that emerged around the world.[29] In various ways these officials attempted to make plain to others their determination to use nuclear weapons. Secretary of State George Marshall said in 1948, after the U.S.–Soviet confrontation over Berlin had begun, "The Soviets are beginning to realize for the first time that the United States would really use the atomic bomb against them in the event of war."[30]

U.S. Presidents have tended to be more prudent than their advisers regarding the use of nuclear weapons. Truman did not heed Churchill's or MacArthur's advice to employ them widely, nor did he accept the proposal of General Leslie Groves (the director of the Manhattan Project), who advised destroying the atomic-bomb-manufacturing capacity of other countries—particularly the Soviet Union—before they developed nuclear weapons.[31] Nevertheless, by 1953, having already threatened its opponents with nuclear weapons, the United States adopted their use as official U.S. policy: "In the event of hostilities, the United States will consider nuclear weapons to be as available for use as other munitions."[32] Since then, U.S. officials have adopted this policy in their conduct of military diplomacy. As conventional wars and other conflicts in the divided states prompted a U.S. response, nuclear threats often served to move these conflicts toward an outcome favorable to the United States and its allies.

The use of nuclear weapons since Hiroshima and Nagasaki has been constrained in one important way. Nuclear weapons are rarely used by U.S. officials to threaten states that possess nuclear weapons of their own. Typically, U.S. officials threaten *non*-nuclear opponents.[33] The United States threatened the Soviets during the first Berlin crisis in 1948, but this was before the Soviets acquired nuclear weapons. After the Soviets acquired the bomb, U.S. threats increasingly took the form of a standing threat to use nuclear weapons in the event of direct conflict with the Soviet Union, as was the case during subsequent Berlin, Middle East, and Cuban crises. And at least until the 1970s, U.S. nuclear threats against the Soviet Union have to be understood in the context of decisive nuclear superiority,

In 1953, the United States possessed some 1,600 operational nuclear weapons; the Soviets had less than 100.[34] Nine years later, during the Cuban Missile Crisis, Defense Secretary Robert McNamara reported that the U.S. had a 17 to 1 advantage.[35]

More telling is the pattern of U.S. threats in Asia and the Middle East. When U.S. officials threatened North Korea and China during the Korean War, and later threatened China separately during the Quemoy and Matsu crises, neither country possessed nuclear weapons. (The Chinese did not develop nuclear weapons until 1963.) And when the United States threatened North Korea in 1968 and North Vietnam in 1969–72, it was careful not to threaten China or the Soviet Union directly. The United States threatened India in 1971, two years before that country acquired nuclear weapons. And in the Middle East, U.S. threats were typically directed at Arab states that did not themselves possess nuclear weapons. This kind of behavior is not surprising; it is obviously less risky to threaten a non-nuclear opponent than a nuclear one.

The Soviet Union exploded its first atomic bomb in August 1949.[36] Since then, Soviet officials, like their U.S. counterparts, have used nuclear weapons to threaten others, though they have done so less frequently. Soviet officials used nuclear weapons for the first time during the 1956 Suez war, when they threatened Great Britain, France, and Israel. They simultaneously asked Eisenhower to approve joint U.S.–Soviet military action to halt the fighting, and requested that the UN Security Council adopt a resolution calling for the dispatch of UN forces to assist Egypt.[37]

In this instance, Soviet threats were directed at two non-nuclear states (France and Israel) and one country with only a rudimentary nuclear force (Britain). Soviet threats were made only after U.S. officials had condemned their erstwhile allies' attack, were *not* directed at the United States, and were accompanied by a proposal for joint U.S.–Soviet measures to end the fighting. And while the Soviets threatened the British and French with "rocket attacks," they did not mobilize their strategic nuclear forces, as the United States frequently did when issuing its nuclear threats.

The Soviets subsequently threatened to use nuclear weapons against Israel during the 1973 Yom Kippur War, on behalf of its Egyptian and Syrian allies. As in 1956, Soviet nuclear threats were made to stop the fighting, and they were accompanied by proposals for joint superpower action to impose a cease-fire.

While the Soviets made vague nuclear threats on China's behalf when it was threatened by the United States in 1958, the Soviets themselves used nuclear weapons to threaten China several times during 1969 and 1970.[38] It is significant that while the Chinese had some nuclear weapons, they possessed only relatively short-range missiles, and they could not yet count on support from a superpower ally to deter Soviet long-range threats.[39]

More recently, in 1986, the Soviets conveyed ambiguous threats to Pakistan.[40] The Soviets may also have conveyed other secret threats, but the best available source suggests that they used nuclear threats on five or six occasions during the postwar period, about one-third as often as the United States.[41] Soviet threats have not been accompanied by large-scale military moves or dramatic deployments, such as the movement of nuclear-capable forces to the point of regional conflict—as in the U.S. deployment of B-29s to Europe and Asia during the Berlin crisis and the Korean War, or the deployment of naval nuclear forces off the coast of Taiwan or India.[42] The Soviets have not put their nuclear forces on full-scale alert, as U.S. officials regularly have. This does not mean that Soviet threats are less real, only that the U.S.S.R. is perhaps more cautious on nuclear matters.

Soviet threats in divided-state conflicts have been much like U.S. threats in two important respects: first, they have been typically made against non-nuclear opponents (France and Israel in 1956) or nuclear states that possess only rudimentary nuclear capability (Great Britain in 1956, China in 1969, Pakistan in 1986). Second, where U.S. and Soviet nuclear threats have been exchanged, they have usually threatened third parties—Israel or China, for example—not the opposing superpower.[43]

Although the superpowers have at different times promised to deter any nuclear threat made against their allies who participate with them in a collective security organization, they have not always done so. As a result, the credibility of superpower nuclear guarantees has been seriously eroded. Superpower allies have discovered through bitter experience that the United States and the Soviet Union will not necessarily wage nuclear war on their behalf.

Soviet allies in Asia discovered that Soviet officials would not act to deter U.S. nuclear threats during the conflicts in Korea, China, and Vietnam in the 1950s and 1960s. For example, when U.S. forces crossed the 38th parallel into North Korea, the Soviets did not intervene. When China entered the war, the Soviets did not invoke the

Sino-Soviet Treaty, which was a mutual defense agreement, nor did they send troops to join the fighting. And when Presidents Truman and Eisenhower threatened North Korea and China with nuclear weapons, the Soviets did not counter these threats with warnings of their own, even though the Soviets possessed nuclear weapons and its allies did not.

When China was threatened by the United States during the first Quemoy-Matsu crisis in 1954–55, the Soviet Union did not extend nuclear guarantees to China or deter U.S. threats, despite the fact that the Sino-Soviet Treaty contained an implied Soviet pledge to provide China with a nuclear umbrella.[44] U.S. threats demonstrated to the Chinese that they could not rely on the Soviets to protect them. In 1963, Chinese Foreign Minister Chen Yi said of Soviet nuclear guarantees, "How can any one nation say that they will defend another—these promises are easy to make, but they are worth nothing. Soviet protection is worth nothing to us."[45]

The North Vietnamese discovered much the same thing about nuclear-armed allies during their war with the United States. Neither the Soviet Union nor China sent troops to assist the North Vietnamese, as China had done during the Korean War—though the United States did not invade North Vietnam as it had North Korea. And neither moved to deter the U.S. nuclear threats made between 1969 and 1972.

After reviewing Soviet behavior toward its Asian allies, a Brookings Institution report concluded: "In the Korean War, the Quemoy-Matsu missile crises, the Vietnam War and the Sino-Vietnamese conflict, Moscow was more concerned about avoiding conflict with the United States and China than it was about protecting the sovereignty and security of its allies, who, if they may not have expected the Soviet Union to go to war on their behalf, did seem to expect the Kremlin to do more than it did."[46]

In 1956, U.S. allies—Great Britain, France, and Israel—discovered what Soviet allies were learning: that their superpower ally would not necessarily act to deter nuclear threats. The Suez crisis signaled U.S. unwillingness to support its allies, particularly when they initiated war without U.S. approval. This lesson had a profound effect on each of the three U.S. allies. In the year after Suez, the British greatly increased spending for their rudimentary nuclear forces. In a 1957 parliamentary debate, Denis Healey called the expanded program a "virility symbol to compensate for the exposure of . . . military impotence at Suez."⁴⁷ The French historian Bertrand Goldschmidt likewise observed that, in Paris, "the [Guy] Mollet government, which with the Israelis had prepared the Suez operation in utmost secrecy, felt the affront it had just suffered. Its previous hostility toward atomic weapons was transformed overnight into a determined and positive interest in national nuclear armament."⁴⁸ Charles de Gaulle subsequently pursued the development of an independent French nuclear arsenal.

The Israelis were also troubled by U.S. behavior. Yaacov Herzog, Ben-Gurion's principal political adviser, wrote that Ben-Gurion was "entirely unprepared for the vehemence of President Eisenhower's backing of the General Assembly's call for immediate and unconditional Israeli withdrawal. *What the U.S. did then was to remove Israel's —as well as Britain's and France's—protective shield against possible retaliation, leaving them all exposed* [emphasis added]."⁴⁹ Like the French, the Israelis became determined not to rely solely on their superpower ally. This episode fueled their resolution to acquire nuclear weapons of their own. And with French assistance, they eventually did. The *force de frappe*, or independent nuclear force, became the common French and Israeli response to superpower behavior during the 1956 Suez war.

For a number of reasons, the superpowers have not always sought to deter each other's nuclear threats. In seeking to limit conflicts that erupt in the divided states and in using nuclear threats to confine these conflicts and conclude them on favorable terms, they hope to preserve the integrity of the interstate system, which was designed to mitigate against the globalization of regional war. The whole notion of common security through the United Nations was promoted by the superpowers to prevent the escalation of Balkan-type conflicts into world war. The superpowers have thus been unwilling to risk global nuclear war on behalf of the "Serbias" of the world. And for this reason, they try to avoid direct superpower confrontation over regional conflicts. The *de facto* rule seems to be that troops from one superpower may intervene in divided-state conflicts, but not both. In addition, the superpowers are also unwilling to risk global nuclear war on behalf of allies who start their own wars, preferring to let these countries assume the risks attendant upon their actions.

In recent years, then, the superpowers have quietly folded up the nuclear umbrellas they once extended over their allies around the world. Although U.S. and Soviet officials continue to insist that they will use nuclear weapons to guarantee their allies' security, they have in practice demonstrated an unwillingness to do so. Even some U.S. officials and commentators have questioned the reliability and durability of the U.S. nuclear umbrella. In 1979, former Secretary of State Henry Kissinger told a group of Europeans, "Our European allies should not keep asking us to multiply strategic [nuclear] assurances that we cannot possibly mean, or if we do mean, we should not want to execute, because if we execute, we risk the destruction of civilization." He added that it was "absurd in the 1980s to base the strategy of the West on the credibility of the threat of mutual suicide."[50]

This has not been lost on the superpowers' allies. Based on their experience with nuclear threats and with the disappearance of superpower deterrence at crucial times, some of the divided states have decided not to rely on superpower guarantees but to develop nuclear weapons of their own.

In 1962, President John Kennedy said, "We do not believe in a series of national deterrents. We believe that the NATO deterrent, to which the United States has committed itself so heavily, provides adequate protection. Once you begin, nation after nation, beginning to develop its own deterrent, or rather feeling it's necessary as an element of its independence to develop its own deterrence, it seems to me you are moving into an increasingly dangerous situation."[51] Yet this is precisely what has happened. The *force de frappe* has been the generic response; nuclear proliferation has been the result.

For the officials in these states, the acquisition of nuclear weapons has been a difficult process, requiring enormous human and material resources and a determination to proceed whatever the financial or political cost. As Pakistani leader Zulfikar Ali Bhutto is reputed to have said, "If India gets the bomb, we will eat leaves and grass to do the same."

China was the first of the divided states to possess this kind of determination. As early as 1951, Chinese officials argued that "only when we ourselves have the atomic bomb, and are fully prepared, is it possible for the frenzied warmongers to listen to our just and reasonable proposals."[52] But the decision to initiate a nuclear weapons program came after the Korean War, during the first Quemoy-Matsu crisis, when the Chinese were faced with both the U.S.–Taiwan treaty and increased American threats to use nuclear weapons against them.[53]

When they tested their first atomic bomb on October 16, 1964, Chinese officials announced that the weapons would not be used to launch a first strike but would instead be "for defense and for protecting the Chinese people from U.S. threats to launch a nuclear war." When the Chinese had developed long-range delivery systems, the Americans would "not be so haughty, their policy of nuclear blackmail and nuclear threats [would] not be so effective."[54] Mao was even more blunt. He said he hoped the nuclear program would "boost our courage and scare others."[55]

Initially the Chinese relied heavily on Soviet assistance, but as the Sino-Soviet split widened in the late 1950s, the Chinese pursued the project on their own. However, the social and economic cost of developing technically sophisticated weapons in a poor country was enormous. In the decade that the Chinese took to develop nuclear weapons, the government was struggling to recover from the costly Korean War, to feed its population, and to break free from the grip of poverty and backward industrial development. Yet despite these obstacles, Chinese leaders remained determined. As Foreign Minister Chen Yi said in 1961, the third straight year that harvests failed, the strategic nuclear weapons should continue "even if the Chinese had to pawn their trousers for the purpose."[56]

Lacking a sophisticated industrial infrastructure, the Chinese used rudimentary, seat-of-the-pants methods to build the bomb. Thousands of peasants combed the countryside for uranium ore, which they dug up by hand. One official sent to collect the mined radioactive ore found it stored in stalls at a village market. "What a place it was!" the cadre recalled. "Yellow-cake . . . was piled at random and could be seen everywhere."[57] The head of the group developing the detonator for the bomb mixed high explosives in used army buckets over an open fire on the test range in Donghuayuan. And when the bomb was transferred to the test site, "two purplish-red long sofas" were used to cushion it.[58]

China's ability to develop nuclear weapons under these circumstances was, in the parlance of the day, a Great Leap Forward. The Chinese managed to build a bomb because they were determined to do so and because they obtained enough information from U.S.– and Soviet-trained Chinese scientists to figure out the best way to do it on the cheap. As Premier Chou En-lai had said during the program, "Spend less, get more."[59]

Mao may have had the United States in mind when he said that the Chinese bomb would "boost our courage and scare others." But it was another country that received a fright. India had just fought a brief, unsuccessful war with China over disputed boundaries in the Himalayas in 1962. The detonation of a Chinese bomb in 1964 had a profound impact on Indian officials. Within a few days, Homi Bhabha, the head of India's atomic power program, said the only defense against nuclear attack "appears to be the capability and threat of retaliation,"[60] and one hundred members of parliament petitioned the government to develop nuclear weapons.[61]

Prime Minister Lal Bahadur Shastri, who had succeeded Nehru a few months earlier, initially opposed nuclear weapons. But as pressure mounted, he agreed to support their development for "peaceful" purposes, such as excavating and tunneling.[62] Supporters of nuclear weapons development, like the diplomat Sisir Gupta, argued that "China may subject a non-nuclear India to periodic blackmail, weaken its spirit of resistance and self-confidence and thus without a war achieve its major political and military objectives in Asia."[63] The decision to work toward the development of an Indian bomb was taken despite British assurances that they would provide a British nuclear umbrella for India.

During the 1960s, the Indian nuclear program developed slowly, though pushed along by fear of Chinese weapons. Indian officials, however, remained ambivalent about the program and did not rush to develop nuclear weapons, even though the Chinese tested a hydrogen bomb in 1967. The impetus to develop nuclear weapons received a second push during the third Indo-Pakistani war, in 1971. President Nixon's decision to send nuclear-capable naval forces into the Bay of Bengal to warn India against intervention in East Pakistan/Bangladesh, and to prevent India from pursuing an all-out war against West Pakistan, spurred Indian efforts to acquire nuclear weapons. The decision to proceed with the manufacture and testing of a bomb was made in early 1972 (following the cessation of hostilities with Pakistan), and two years later, on May 18, 1974, the Indians detonated their first atomic bomb, which they described as a "peaceful nuclear explosion."[64]

As with China, India's ostensible reason for developing nuclear weapons was to deter threats by the superpowers, but its program frightened not the nuclear-capable powers but a non-nuclear neighbor—Pakistan. Pakistani Prime Minister Zulfikar Ali Bhutto did not accept the Indians' assertion that theirs was a "peaceful explosion." Pakistan, which had been divided in half by the secession of Bangladesh in 1971, now confronted a sibling state that possessed superior conventional and nuclear forces. Although Pakistan had signed a 1955 mutual security treaty with the United States, it did not enjoy nuclear protection against India from the U.S., the Chinese, or the British.[65] During Pakistan's war with India, the United States may have threatened India with nuclear weapons, but it had also slapped an arms embargo on Pakistan.[66]

The initial Pakistani decision to develop nuclear weapons came in 1972, when Prime Minister Bhutto announced his determination to do so at a secret meeting with Pakistan's top nuclear scientists.[67] The subsequent Indian test spurred Pakistani efforts. With assistance from the French and the Chinese, Pakistani officials pressed ahead with their own program.[68] In 1986, Dr. Abdul Quadir Khan, head of the Pakistani project, explained Pakistani thinking in a manner reminiscent of earlier Indian and Chinese proponents of weapons development: "If India openly starts a weapons programme, the deep-rooted Pakistani fears of India, especially after its active role in the dismemberment of Pakistan in 1971, would put tremendous pressure on Pakistan to take appropriate measures to avoid a nuclear Munich at India's hands in the event of an actual conflict, which many Pakistanis think very real."[69]

And a year later, Dr. Khan told an Indian journalist, "What the CIA has been saying about our possessing the bomb is correct. . . . They told us that Pakistan could never produce the bomb . . . now they know we had done it."[70] Pakistani President Zia confirmed this in March 1987: "You can virtually write today that Pakistan can build a bomb whenever it wishes. . . . Pakistan has the capability of building the bomb."[71]

Unlike China or India, Pakistan has never exploded a nuclear bomb. It prefers to retain some ambiguity about its capability and to avoid the risk of censure—and the cutoff of U.S. aid—that an explosion would provoke. But new "flash X-ray" technology makes it possible to test a nuclear weapon without actually exploding it.[72] In his 1987 speech, Zia attempted to play down Pakistani development, saying that U.S. officials should not be unduly alarmed by Pakistan's "tiddly-widdly nuclear program."[73]

But other countries do not view the acquisition of nuclear weapons as a "tiddly-widdly" development. Indian Prime Minister Rajiv Gandhi told parliament, "If Pakistan gets a weapon, India will have to think very seriously about its own option."[74] U.S. officials also considered cutting off aid to Pakistan after Zia's announcement, but they were reluctant to do so while Pakistan was assisting insurgents fighting the Soviets in Afghanistan.[75]

Other countries were also reluctant to view Pakistan's nuclear program as unimportant. The Soviet Union warned that it could not be indifferent to such developments. And Israel viewed the matter with some concern, especially since Pakistani leaders referred to their weapon as an "Islamic Bomb."[76] Thus, like India and China before it, Pakistan antagonized countries that it had not intended to threaten when it decided to acquire nuclear weapons.

During this period, Israel also responded to nuclear threats by pursuing nuclear weaponry of its own. The French helped Israel build its first nuclear research reactor and provided important technical and material assistance, including weapons-grade plutonium.[77] Although Israeli progress was slow, by 1975 Israeli President Ephraim Katzir admitted that Israel had developed the capability of building nuclear weapons, and the CIA concluded that Israel had already done so.[78] According to U.S. analysts, Israel had more than ten weapons in 1975 and between 100 and 200 a decade later.[79] Like the Pakistanis, Israeli officials have kept their program under wraps, have not conducted a public test, and have adopted a deliberately ambiguous nuclear policy: "Israel will not be the first country to introduce nuclear weapons into the Middle East." As one Israeli military analyst argues, "Deliberate ambiguity maximizes our deterrence."[80]

The superpowers have not been happy with these developments and have tried to limit the spread of nuclear weapons. The 1968 Nuclear Non-Proliferation Treaty, which the superpowers negotiated and signed, attempted to limit the spread of nuclear technology by regulating nuclear power programs around the world and monitoring the production of materials—enriched uranium and plutonium—that can be used to manufacture bombs. But they have done nothing to control their own use of nuclear threats as an instrument of policy, which is probably the most significant factor in the decision by other countries to obtain nuclear weapons in the first place. The lack of significant cuts in U.S.–Soviet arsenals—the 1988 INF Treaty cut superpower arsenals by only 5 percent—also makes many countries suspicious of superpower claims that they want to control the spread of nuclear arms. After China took a seat in the United Nations in 1971, its delegates called superpower arms control efforts "a hoax."[81]

The United States failed to prevent its allies—Israel and Pakistan —from developing nuclear weapons; the Soviet Union could not prevent its allies—China and India—from doing the same. The two superpowers, however, have successfully forestalled the development of nuclear weapons by other divided-state allies.

After the United States abandoned its effort to prevent the reunification of Vietnam by the North and withdrew completely in 1975, South Korean leaders became concerned that the United States might eventually withdraw, in a similar fashion, from Korea. Only a month after the fall of Saigon, President Park declared, "If the U.S. nuclear umbrella were to be removed, we [would] have to start developing our nuclear capability."[82] Intense U.S. diplomatic pressure persuaded the South Koreans not to begin such a program, though they already possessed complex nuclear power facilities. A South Korean agreement to purchase a French reprocessing plant was canceled in 1976 after the U.S. objected.[83]

President Carter's announcement in 1977 that he planned to withdraw all U.S. ground forces from the peninsula over a four-to-five-year period rekindled South Korean interest in nuclear development. Foreign Minister Tong-jin Park told the National Assembly that the government would proceed with weapons development "if it is necessary for national security interests and people's safety."[84] And the government subsequently released a report that expressed support for the idea of a South Korean nuclear deterrent.[85] The implicit threat to develop nuclear weapons if U.S. policy was not changed may have been the first time a non-nuclear state has used the prospect of atomic weapons to threaten a nuclear power. In 1979, Carter suspended the plan to withdraw U.S. troops. It is not clear what role South Korea's threat to go nuclear played in this decision, or whether there was a *quid pro quo*—the United States agreeing to stay if the South Koreans agreed not to develop nuclear arms—but both countries returned to the pre-1977 status quo.

In North Korea, the Soviets (at U.S. urging) pressured the Communist government to ratify the non-proliferation treaty in 1985. The North Koreans had previously built a large research reactor at Yong Bong, which might have been used as the basis for a nuclear weapons program.[86] Vietnam, on the other hand, withdrew from the non-proliferation treaty in 1975, but the Vietnamese do not possess any nuclear facilities that might be used for weapons development.[87]

Taiwan, fearing U.S. abandonment (like South Korea), twice began developing an independent nuclear weapons program. The with-drawal of the U.S. fleet from the strait in 1969; U.S. recognition of China in 1971, which resulted in Taiwan's ouster from the United Nations, and the seating of the Chinese Communist delegation; the alteration of U.S. security commitments and aid to Taiwan in the 1970s; the withdrawal of U.S. forces from Vietnam—these events undoubtedly played a role in the decision by Kuomintang officials to embark on covert attempts to develop nuclear arms in 1975–77 and again in 1987.[88] When U.S. officials discovered these secret facilities, they successfully persuaded government officials to halt and disman-tle their clandestine operations.

In Europe, despite the introduction of U.S. and Soviet nuclear weapons into Germany, the superpowers have prevented either Ger-man state from acquiring nuclear weapons, though both possess the means to do so. The United States has occasionally discussed pro-viding nuclear weapons to German NATO forces, but neither super-power has been eager to put nuclear arms in German hands and, because they retain their authority as occupation forces, could prob-ably prevent the Germans from doing so.

The introduction of nuclear weapons in the divided states, where sibling states are prone to irregular and conventional war, where the acquisition of nuclear weapons is itself regarded as a threat, and where the norm of international behavior is to use them against non-nuclear opponents, is, in President Kennedy's prescient words, "an increas-ingly dangerous situation."

In this context the concept of "deterrence" also acquires a different meaning. As Hans Spier wrote in 1957: "A government that is exposed to atomic threats in peacetime readily regards them as 'blackmail' whereas the threatening power is likely to call them 'deterrence.' "[89] Indeed, this is precisely how the Soviets use the term. Richard Betts has noted that in describing their own use of nuclear weapons to deter the West, "the Soviets most commonly use the term *sderzhivaniye* ('restraining')," but in describing the West's use of nuclear weapons as a deterrent, "they use the word *ustrasheniye*, which comes very close to meaning 'intimidation.' "[90] In the divided states, nuclear weapons acquire both meanings. And because they are used both to restrain and to threaten, or as Mao said, "to boost our courage and scare others," the presence of nuclear weapons stimulates the ac-quisition of more nuclear weapons by others.

As it is employed by superpower strategists, deterrence—the use of massive nuclear arsenals to prevent the use of other massive nuclear arsenals—is supposed to keep the peace and prevent the outbreak of war. In the context of U.S.–Soviet relations, large arsenals have generally deterred U.S. and Soviet officials from threatening or attacking each other. It is also true that the superpowers frequently share a common interest in preserving the interstate system and have been reluctant to depart from it.

But if deterrence can be said to "work" or have a restraining influence on superpower relations, it has had the *opposite* effect in the divided states. The acquisition of nuclear weapons by divided states, ostensibly to "deter" superpower nuclear threats, encourages their neighbors to develop their own nuclear weapons. This development promotes both regional and global insecurity and tension. It puts countries at odds with their neighbors and with their allies and superpower enemies. And it permits countries that have regularly engaged in irregular and conventional wars to express their conflicts in nuclear terms.

Ironically, the superpowers, which attempted to use nuclear weapons to assert their mastery over others, have found themselves, "willy-nilly, for better or worse, the masters and the servants of the weird and terrifying warriors who have grown up in their pasture." The eruption of conflict in nuclear-capable divided states is today capable of turning local and regional conflicts into global, nuclear conflicts. As Soviet General Secretary Mikhail Gorbachev observed in his speech to the United Nations in December 1988, "The bell of regional conflict tolls for all of us."[91]

· 12 ·

The Next Generation

Partition, as we have seen, leads to social conflict and war. But despite its sorry history, it continues to be advanced as a solution to political problems around the world—not because people are ignorant of its history, but because powerful states and contemporary independence movements find it in their interest to promote it. To a certain extent, partition has become "institutionalized," an accepted political practice within the interstate system. The subdivision of Pakistan in 1971, the partition of Cyprus in 1974, the *de facto* partition of Lebanon, Sri Lanka, and Ethiopia, and the incipient redivision of Israel/Palestine demonstrate that partition remains vigorous around the world.

This does not mean that partition is everywhere the preferred solution to social conflict, only that it is a likely solution, depending on the circumstances. The United Nations, for instance, has adopted a resolution on self-determination that opposes "any action which would impair, totally or in part, the territorial integrity or political unity of sovereign and independent states."[1] But in practice, the United Nations has actively participated in the division of states (Korea, Palestine) or acquiesced to partition and admitted divided states as members (Germany, India, Pakistan, Bangladesh). The interstate system, which was designed by the United States and the Soviet Union to encourage the emergence of independent nation-states, can accommodate this practice. There is, after all, no upward limit set on the number of states that can participate in the system. And from the superpowers' point of view, the proliferation of small states increases the relative power of large states.

The superpowers are ambivalent about the utility of partition. Neither the United States nor the Soviet Union endorses partition as a solution to problems in Africa—they both opposed it in Nigeria and Ethiopia—and they are opposed to partition in their own countries or immediate spheres of influence. Nonetheless, they have both practiced partition and view it as a legitimate practice. In 1988, for instance, former President Jimmy Carter stated that he thought partition might be a "good solution" to the political problems in Somalia.[2]

Although no state, except perhaps South Africa, advances the division of itself, many states are willing to promote the partition of other states. China, India, Israel, Syria, and Turkey have participated in the division of neighboring states as a means of securing their own regional interests. Moreover, a growing number of independence movements around the world have come to see partition as a way to secure state power for themselves. Although some movements promote the unification of separate states, these are now relatively few in number. One such movement, the right-wing Cypriots that sought to unify Cyprus with Greece, took measures that resulted in partition, not unification. Independence movements have thus increasingly adopted a secessionist orientation as the shortest, surest way to achieve state power on their own terms.

After the first wave of partitions following World War II, there was a pause. No countries were divided during the 1960s, though secessionist movements in the Congo, Nigeria, and Ethiopia attempted to divide these countries along ethnic lines. But after this hiatus, partition resumed as a political practice in the 1970s, with the divisions of Pakistan and Cyprus.

Although the course of partition in these countries proceeded along now-familiar lines, these second-generation divisions differed from those of the first generation in two important respects. Unlike first-generation partitions, in which great and superpower states played a decisive role, Pakistan and Cyprus were divided, in the main, by regional powers—India, Greece, and Turkey. The superpowers played important roles (indeed, it is unlikely that Cyprus would have been divided without U.S. assent), but they did not initiate or manage the process as they had done earlier.

The independence movements that pressed for state power in Pakistan and Cyprus also assumed rather different roles. Previously, majority movements tended to be unificationist and minority movements secessionist. But in Pakistan, the secessionist Bengali movement, led by the Awami League, actually represented a slight majority of Pakistan's total population.[3] And in Cyprus, the movement of unificationist Greek Cypriots represented only a minority of the island's population. In the second round of partition, then, majority movements could be secessionist and minority movements unificationist.

However, neither the changing and variable character of dividing states nor that of independence movements within divided states altered the fundamental dynamic of partition, though it did complicate it.

In 1971, Pakistan became the first divided state to be subdivided. In a geographic sense, it had been subdivided from the outset, since East and West Pakistan were separated by a thousand miles of Indian territory. But geography alone does not explain why the populations in the two Pakistani territories waged a bloody civil war that resulted in the creation of an independent Bangladesh in the east. The rise of Bengali separatism owes more to the disenfranchisement of eastern Bengalis by western Punjabis during the years following independence and partition in 1947.[4]

When the British divided India in 1947, they devolved power in Pakistan to the Muslim League, whose power base was strongest in West Pakistan. Jinnah established Karachi (in the West) as the capital of Pakistan, and his successors pressed for the adoption of Urdu as the language of state, despite the fact that Bengali was spoken by more people. The military coup in 1958 disenfranchised the citizenry in both East and West, but the impact of military rule was felt more strongly in the East. Opposition to the military regime formed in both East and West during the 1960s, but opposition parties in each region took rather different forms. In West Pakistan, Zulfikar Ali Bhutto pressed for an end to military rule, but did so as a kind of loyal opposition—with Bhutto even serving for a time as the junta's Foreign Minister. In the East, the Awami League, led by Sheik Mujibur Rahman, pressed for an end to military rule and for greater autonomy for Bengal.

Although the two major opposition movements shared a common antipathy to military rule and a common identity as Moslems in an Islamic state, they mobilized along different lines. Bhutto organized along populist, relatively secular class lines; Mujibur, along ethnic, regional lines. The result was the creation of a relatively secular unificationist movement in the West and an ethnic secessionist movement in the East. This latter movement created a new ethnic identity based on Bengali regionalism. Although Bengalis constituted a majority of Pakistan's population, they organized as if they were a disenfranchised minority, complaining about their minority status in the government and the military and their unequal treatment in economic and political affairs. They adopted self-determination, or greater self-determination, as their goal. While Bhutto wanted to assume state power within the existing framework of government, Mujibur sought to change the constitutional character of the state so that Bengalis could exercise greater power within it. As a consequence, when the military government decided in 1969 to hold elections and to devolve power to civilian authorities, the two independence movements began to diverge, just as the Muslim League and the Indian National Congress had taken different roads as the devolution of British power approached. Because the military government agreed to use the elections to revamp the constitution—to facilitate the return of civilian authority—the Awami League was in a position to campaign on the basis of more radical, thoroughgoing demands than Bhutto's Pakistan People's Party.

The elections, originally scheduled for October 1970, were postponed until late December after a cyclone and heavy flooding struck East Pakistan. When the disaster devastated the countryside, it undermined confidence in the government and assisted the Awami League, which captured virtually the entire Bengali vote and gained an absolute majority in the newly created constituent assembly. (The Pakistan People's Party won a majority of the West Pakistani vote, but secured only half as many seats as the Awami League.) The election provided an opportunity for the Awami League to press its program, which called for a directly elected federal government (dominated by the more numerous Bengalis) that would have responsibility for foreign affairs and defense, while East and West

Pakistan would each be permitted to establish its own currency, conduct its own trade, and maintain its own militia or paramilitary force. Because the Awami League platform stopped short of demanding full autonomy and provided for continued ties with the West, it resembled the position taken by the moderate wing of Sinn Fein on the eve of British devolution. (Sinn Fein moderates originally accepted devolution on British terms—that Ireland remain within the commonwealth and that Britain retain some control over defense and foreign policy.) This moderately secessionist agenda was opposed by both the outgoing military regime and by the Pakistan People's Party. As the prospect of Bengali-majority rule approached, the military regime postponed the opening of the constituent assembly and, as negotiations between the two civilian political parties deadlocked, prepared to crush the burgeoning Bengali independence movement by force. Although Bhutto's party did not join the military government as it prepared its coup from above, it obstructed the Awami League's ascent to power and supported the military's attempt to suppress it in the East.[5]

On March 25, 1971, Pakistani military forces, which had been built up in East Pakistan following the election, launched a preemptive coup, attacking the civilian population, seizing Mujibur, arresting opposition leaders, and slaughtering hundreds of thousands, Moslems and Hindus alike. The regime imposed martial law, banned all political activity, and set out to destroy all Bengali opposition to West Pakistani rule.[6]

The West Pakistani attack on the East forced the unarmed opposition to take up arms and to begin conducting an irregular guerrilla war. The irregulars were now determined to campaign for the creation of a completely separate state, not just a relatively autonomous one. Just before he was captured, Mujibur announced, "Bangladesh is a Sovereign and Independent People's Republic."[7] The nucleus of the armed irregulars—the Mukti Bahini—consisted of Bengali members of the army and police who had escaped the army's initial attack. And a provisional government-in-exile was formed in India.[8]

By August some 8 million refugees had fled to India, nearly 10 million by mid-November.[9] Indian officials permitted Mukti Bahini irregulars to use bases in India. Having failed to wipe out the opposition or defeat the irregulars, West Pakistani forces began making incursions into Indian territory and then widened the war by launching preemptive attacks on Indian airfields. This too failed. Indian forces intervened in the war and, with the Mukti Bahini, quickly defeated the West Pakistani Army and seized Dacca. Although Indian assistance made it possible for the Bengali independence movement to achieve its secessionist aims, the Awami League was strong enough in its own right to dissuade India from attempting to annex Bengal and reunite this part of the subcontinent. The Indian government thus recognized Bangladesh as an independent state in December 1971; Pakistan became a subdivided divided state.

India had made the partition of Pakistan possible, but both super-powers had knowingly permitted division to occur. The Soviets signed a security treaty with India in August 1971 and used their UN Security Council veto to block all attempts to impose a cease-fire before Indian and insurgent forces could defeat West Pakistani forces in Bengal. Although U.S. officials sided with West Pakistan—President Nixon sent nuclear-capable naval forces into the Bay of Bengal in an attempt to prevent India from widening the war and pressing its advantage in the West—they also imposed an arms embargo on both sides, hurting West Pakistan more than India, which continued to receive military aid from the Soviet Union. The United States eventually agreed to recognize Bangladesh and admit it to the United Nations in 1974. Humanitarian concerns, aroused by natural disaster, widespread starvation, and attacks on civilian populations by the West Pakistani Army, together with the fact that neither the insurgent secessionist movement nor its Indian ally was Communist, made it difficult for the United States to take steps to prevent the partition. So while the United States did not initiate or endorse partition, it did permit division to harden.

For a time, West Pakistan adopted its own version of the Hallstein Doctrine and severed diplomatic relations with any state that recognized Bangladesh. But this effort only deepened its political isolation. After a few years, Pakistani officials abandoned this self-defeating policy and in 1975 recognized Bangladesh.[10]

Natural disaster, civil war, and partition had devastating social and political consequences. Some 10 million Bengalis fled the country and 15 million more were displaced within the country.[11] Many of these refugees returned to their homes after the war, but many also stayed in India, leading to social conflict in Indian provinces over the years. Some Indian leaders have called for the expulsion of Bengali refugees: in Tripura, an Indian state east of Bangladesh, indigenous movements have alternatively demanded the repatriation of Bengali refugees and the creation of a separate state within India, which would presumably expel them on its own authority.[12]

The advance of Mukti Bahini insurgents during the civil war also created a second, though much smaller, wave of migration—that of Eastern supporters of West Pakistan, who had fled at the approach of Mukti Bahini and Indian forces. Some 250,000 Biharis, for instance, still live in refugee camps within Bangladesh. The Biharis were Moslems who had fled India in 1947 and who remained loyal to Pakistan during the 1971 civil war. When the Bengali independence movement came to power, many were killed, and tens of thousands were uprooted and herded into refugee camps, where they remain to this day.[13] These various displacements and migrations have strained the economic capacity of India and Bangladesh. Starvation was widespread after the war, and human and economic displacements made economic recovery and self-sufficiency difficult to achieve. A telling measure of this difficulty was the government's announcement in 1986 that it would offer a bounty for every rat killed by its citizenry, offering 50 poish per rat, or the equivalent of 20 cents per dozen. Rats consume as much as 20 million tons of grain per year, or one-tenth of the country's annual crop. Agriculture minister Abdul Munim said that "this is almost the quantity we need to import annually to meet our food shortage."[14] Devastating floods in the fall of 1988 further undermined the agricultural capacity of this delta country. Because it is on its own as an independent nation-state, it does not receive the kind of aid that a larger, more diverse, governmental entity might provide.

The political consequences of partition have also been pronounced. Sheik Mujibur Rahman and the Awami League assumed power after the war, but their attempts to strengthen the League's one-party rule antagonized opposition parties and the army. Mujibur was murdered along with eighteen family members in a military coup in 1975. His oldest daughter, Hasina Wajed, was studying abroad at the time and escaped the massacre. She now leads one of the two major opposition parties in Bangladesh.[15]

A second coup brought General Ziaur Rahman to power three months after Mujibur's death. He headed a military junta for three years, then reintroduced "civilian" rule with himself as President. He survived twenty coup attempts before he was assassinated in an abortive coup in 1981. His widow, Khaled Zia Rahman, now heads the other major opposition party.

The current leader of Bangladesh, President Hossain Mohammad Ershad, came to power in a military coup in 1982. He has suppressed opposition parties, several times arresting their "dynastic" leaders, and has effectively disenfranchised the electorate by rigging elections. A number of protesters were shot and killed by the army and police during election riots in 1987.

The derogation of citizenship by military regimes has also led to the organization of ethnic and separatist movements in Bangladesh. In May 1988, for instance, Hindus, Buddhists, and Christians, who make up a small minority (13 percent) of the country's population, marched together to protest legislation that would make Islam the official state religion. And the predominantly Buddhist inhabitants of the Chittagong Hill Tracts, in southeast Bangladesh, have protested the settlement of Moslem Bengalis in this area and have organized an irregular militia, the Shanti Bahini ("Peace Force"), to attack settlers and government troops. They have a separatist orientation.

Political developments in West Pakistan have followed similar lines, though coups and political assassinations have been less frequent. The partition of Pakistan was an immediate disaster for the military leaders that had initiated civil war in Bengal and interstate war with India. Partition so discredited the regime that it quickly devolved power to Bhutto, who, like Mujibur, attempted to consolidate power at the expense of other political parties and the army, and who met much the same fate. In 1977, General Muhammad Zia ul-Haq deposed Bhutto in a military coup and subsequently had him hanged. Bhutto's daughter Benazir, like Mujibur's oldest daughter, assumed the leadership of his party.

Zia ruled for the next decade. He pressed ahead with the Islamization of the country and disenfranchised secular opposition movements (like Bhutto's People's Party) and the Pathan and Baluchi secessionist movements that resisted the ascent of Punjabis within the army and the government. These developments closely resembled those in Bangladesh during the same period, but after Zia was killed in an airplane crash in 1988, the military authorities held elections (previously called by Zia) that returned power to civilian parties. Benazir Bhutto's party won an electoral majority and she became Prime Minister in December 1988. So while Bangladesh continues to be ruled by a military regime, Pakistan has returned power to civilian authorities. But both continue to face opposition parties and ethnic secessionist movements.

* * *

Cyprus was divided in 1974, three years after Pakistan. In Cyprus, partition advanced in waves, on a rising tide. Partition was first tentatively advanced in the late 1950s, before the British devolved power to an indigenous independence movement. It gained a beachhead in the mid-1960s, and finally swamped the island in 1974. Neighboring Turkey and Greece played principal roles in the division, though Great Britain, the United States, and the Soviet Union also assisted the process.

Cyprus was a British colony. Unlike India and Palestine, however, Cyprus was not made independent, nor was it divided after World War II, in part because of the turn of events in these other colonies. As the British retreated from India and Palestine, their hold on Cyprus tightened; Cyprus's importance as a British naval and military base increased as Great Britain abandoned other strategic possessions. As Prime Minister Clement Attlee wrote in 1947: "[Our] position in Palestine and Egypt has deteriorated and it is now more than ever necessary from the strategic aspect to keep our foothold in the Eastern Mediterranean in Cyprus."[16]

British rejection of Cypriot independence in the 1940s fostered the creation of Cypriot independence movements in the 1950s. Three different movements emerged, and although they all pressed for the devolution of British authority, each sought to obtain devolved power on different terms. Two movements organized the Greek Cypriot majority, some 80 percent of the island's population, and one organized the Turkish Cypriot minority. The National Organization of Cypriot Fighters (EOKA), led by Colonel George Grivas, pressed for devolution and unification (*enosis*) with Greece. Grivas sought to organize the Greek Cypriot majority along right-wing ethnic lines based on Cypriots' identity as Greeks. He conducted an irregular war against the British and the Turkish Cypriots, and received considerable support from Greek officials and citizens, who viewed *enosis* favorably.

Archbishop Makarios III organized his Greek Cypriot movement along relatively secular lines, despite being head of the Greek Orthodox Church in Cyprus. He was less interested in unification with Greece and preferred independence for Cyprus. Makarios had initially supported *enosis*, but in 1958, as the prospect of devolution approached, he began pushing for independence. He did not want to subordinate his movement to Greek authority or antagonize Turkey and the Turkish Cypriot minority.

A third movement arose among the Turkish Cypriot minority. Within it, political organizations such as the Turkish Defense Organization (TMT) were much like the EOKA. These clandestine organizations pressed for devolution and union with Turkey, which would be achieved through partition. These groups were supported by Turkish state officials and sympathetic populations in mainland Turkey.[17]

The EOKA's irregular war against British rule and against Turkish Cypriot communities led to British reprisals and intercommunal violence between 1955 and 1959.[18] The outbreak of war on the island, coupled with Britain's ill-fated Suez adventure in 1956, forced the British to open negotiations with Greece and Turkey, and then with the Cypriot independence movements themselves. The British considered partition as a solution but rejected it; they wanted to keep large military bases on the island after devolving power, and thus were not eager to admit other countries—Greece or Turkey—onto the island (a likely scenario in the wake of any ethnic partition). Instead, the British preferred to devolve power to the indigenous independence movement led by Makarios, which at the time was the largest and most moderate of the three movements. They believed that Makarios was not strong enough to challenge a continued British presence on the island but was strong enough to defuse conflict between Greek and Turkish Cypriots. The British thus devolved power to an independence movement in a unified state. Greek and Turkish officials accepted these terms because the British agreed to stay on and keep the peace, and on August 16, 1960, Cyprus became an independent republic and Makarios became its first President.

But the other independence movements were frustrated by these developments. Greek Cypriot unificationists and Turkish Cypriot secessionists began to clash violently in 1963. Makarios was forced to ask for British intervention to contain rioting and irregular civil war. The British responded by establishing a "Green Line" between Greek and Turkish Cypriot communities in Nicosia, the capital. But, as in Palestine, the British soon tired of a protracted peacekeeping role. So in 1964 they asked that their responsibility devolve to the United Nations. For all practical purposes, this meant devolving power to the superpowers, particularly the United States.

The United States and the Soviet Union supported the introduction of UN peacekeeping forces in the spring of 1964. The Soviets supported UN intervention because they wanted the left-leaning Makarios government to remain independent, and they did not want

Cyprus annexed by one or both of its NATO neighbors.[19] But in spite of UN intervention, the fighting escalated as Greece and Turkey began assisting their respective allies in Cyprus. Turkish officials even threatened to invade Cyprus to protect the Turkish minority.

President Johnson then ordered the Sixth Fleet into the area—much as Truman had done with the Seventh Fleet in the Taiwan Strait in 1950—to prevent a Turkish invasion of the island, which is located only eighty miles off Turkey's southern coast.[20] Johnson acted not because he was eager to preserve an independent and non-aligned Cyprus (in fact, U.S. officials detested Makarios, whom they regarded as a Communist), but because he did not want to risk war between two NATO allies—Greece and Turkey—at a time when the United States was trying to drum up support for the escalating war in Vietnam. U.S. officials therefore advanced a plan that they thought would placate both parties—divide the island and award a chunk of the north to Turkey and the bulk of the south to Greece.[21] But the Greek officials and Makarios rejected this proposal: the Greeks, because it did not go far enough; Makarios, because it went much too far. President Johnson then threatened to withdraw NATO aid from Greece and allow the Turks to invade the island if the Greeks did not accept this plan. But in the end, U.S. officials did not permit Turkey to invade in 1964 (or again in 1967), nor did they force Greece to accept partition. They did, however, force Greece to remove troops that it had landed on the island after the outbreak of the conflict in 1963.[22]

Although support for unification with Greece or partition and annexation by Turkey declined within Cyprus during the late 1960s (Makarios was reelected by majorities in both the Greek and Turkish communities), *enosis* and partition were gaining powerful adherents outside the island. Greek military leaders renewed their support for *enosis* with Cyprus, in part because they wanted to eliminate Makarios, who was a vocal and effective critic of the military dictatorship in Greece. They sponsored the return to Cyprus of Colonel Grivas, who in 1969–70 announced the creation of a new insurgent independence movement: EOKA-B. The EOKA-B then began conducting an irregular war against the government and planned a coup to overthrow Makarios.[23]

On July 15, 1974, Greek-supported, pro-unificationist insurgents attacked the presidential palace, seized control of the island, and established a military government headed by Nikos Sampson, EOKA-B's new leader (Grivas had died earlier that year). But Makarios escaped the attempt on his life and fled to London. This bald effort to impose *enosis* by force prompted Turkish intervention, and three days later Turkish paratroopers began landing on the island. This time, however, the United States did not move to block the Turkish intervention, forcing Greek military leaders to surrender power to civilian authorities there. And the collapse of Sampson's military backers led to the collapse of his own regime.

In many respects, the Greek junta's actions were similar to those of the West Pakistani junta in Bangladesh. In Pakistan, the military tried to maintain unification by force; in Cyprus, the Greek military tried to obtain unification by force. Both took the initiative and both were rebuffed, in the first instance by indigenous forces—the Mukti Bahini in Bengal and Makarios's supporters in Cyprus—and in the second instance by neighboring states that intervened in the conflict—India and Turkey. In both cases, the attempt to maintain or obtain national unity led to war and partition.

In Cyprus, neither the United States nor the Soviet Union opposed partition. The United States did not because the EOKA-B coup and Turkish intervention achieved what the United States had earlier proposed: the partition of the island and the diminution of Makarios's authority over it. The Soviet Union did not oppose partition because the conflict over Cyprus divided two NATO allies, resulting in the collapse of an anti-Communist dictatorship in Greece and the eventual restoration of an independent Cypriot state, albeit a smaller one.[24]

In the end, partition did not result in "double *enosis*"—the unification of Turkish Cyprus with Turkey and Greek Cyprus with Greece—but it came close. Had Makarios been killed in the coup, Sampson could have established himself as Makarios's legitimate successor and then managed to cede his authority to Greece. But Makarios survived. Sampson could not quickly obtain the legitimacy he needed, and the unificationist putsch failed, toppling juntas in both Greece and Cyprus. The irony is that *enosis*, long advocated by state officials in Greece and by some indigenous Cypriots, was instead realized by state officials in Turkey and the Turkish Cypriot minority. The coup left Cyprus divided—something that unificationist Greeks and Cypriots always opposed—but also independent, at an even greater distance from Greece than before.

As in other divided states, partition had disruptive social consequences. Nearly 180,000 Greek Cypriots and 37,000 Turkish Cypriots fled their homes as Turkish forces advanced. Five thousand were killed. After the war, a massive population "swap" took place: 20,000 Turkish Cypriots went north; 200,000 Greek Cypriots headed south.[25] Few Cypriots today remain on the wrong side of the border. And some 65,000 settlers from Turkey have moved into the northern zone.[26]

The Greek Cypriot government has demanded that Turkish settlers and troops be withdrawn and the country reunited. But the Turkish government has rejected these demands and moved to solidify Turkish rule in the north. In 1975, Turkish officials announced that northern Cyprus had become the Turkish Federated State of Cyprus, which placed Turkish-occupied Cyprus in an ambiguous position, since federation fell short of either annexation or independence.[27] The government attempted to resolve this ambiguity in 1983 by sponsoring elections that resulted in the creation of a government led by Rauf Denktash, a former Prime Minister of Turkey. This government then declared itself to be the independent Turkish Republic of North Kibris.[28] But as with other divided states, sovereignty is a problematic thing. Turkey's Prime Minister Turgut Ozal said in 1986 that other states would eventually recognize North Kibris's independence, but so far, only Turkey itself has recognized it as an independent state.[29]

In southern Cyprus, partition completely discredited the enosis-minded independence movement. The secular independence movement led by Makarios returned to power, supported by a coalition of parties that included the Communist Party. In 1988, George Vassiliou, a millionaire businessman supported by the Communists, became President.

Since partition, successive governments have pressed for reunification with the north, but negotiations have repeatedly collapsed. And the country remains deeply divided. There is only one civilian crossing point along the 118-mile frontier,[30] and separate currencies circulate in the north and the south. They even use different standards of time. Clocks in the north have been set back one hour, as Christopher Hitchens observes, "so that the north of Cyprus beats time, literally as well as metaphorically, with Anatolia," not its island neighbors.[31] And the two communities stage rival rallies every year on July 20 to mark the anniversary of Turkey's 1974 invasion. People attending events in the south mourn; those in the north celebrate.[32]

The practice of dividing states did not end with the partition of Pakistan and Cyprus. Partition is already well advanced, though not yet complete, in a number of other countries. It is incipient in many others. Of course, many may never be fully divided or redivided. But the possibility exists.

Partition is already well advanced in Lebanon. Without some decisive shift in the strength and character of existing social and political forces, Lebanon will probably be divided into two states, one Christian and one Moslem. The outlines of this division are already drawn. Although none of the parties to the conflict in Lebanon favors partition (each would prefer a unitary state controlled by itself), none opposes it decisively, because it appears to offer at least something for everyone.[33]

The Lebanese parliament's inability to choose a successor to outgoing President Amin Gemayel in the fall of 1988 led to the creation of two rival cabinets: a Christian one headed by Major General Michel Aoun and a Moslem one led by Prime Minister Selim al-Hoss. These two overall groupings are themselves composed of rival factions that regularly battle each other in the streets and hills of Lebanon. But their animosity toward ethnic-religious enemies (Christian vs. Moslem) is stronger than their hatred of ethnic-religious rivals (Sunni vs. Shiite, Maronite vs. Druse). Although the two sides say they oppose any solution that would result in partition—one of General Aoun's favorite sayings is "Lebanon is too big to swallow and too small to partition"[34]—the Christian leader frequently compares Lebanon to a troublesome marriage and admits that "a marital dispute ends with reconciliation or divorce."[35] In Lebanon, however, the "marital" dispute is also a "martial" dispute, and any divorce of Lebanese political partners will be difficult, bloody, and protracted. As one Druse leader has remarked, "With everything heading to formal partition, the divorce is still not easy."[36] Both sides, in fact, have already begun to petition for divorce. Each cabinet has announced that it is the only legitimate authority in the country and has begun to seek international recognition for its claims.[37]

International recognition by the principal external actors in Lebanon—Israel and Syria—may not be long in coming. Both Israel and Syria have invaded Lebanon and have tried to establish unitary regimes favorable to themselves. They have failed to do so because the other power was adamantly opposed to this project and because indigenous opposition was too strong to subdue unilaterally. In this regard, General Aoun is probably right: Lebanon is too big to swallow. Instead, Israel and Syria occupy parts of the country and assist indigenous allies. But they probably could accept the creation of sympathetic states, which they would regard as defensive buffers, on their own frontiers. If either Israel or Syria recognizes one of the two Lebanese governments, the other will probably follow suit and the *de facto* partition of Lebanon will become *de jure*. As yet, they have not done so, because political advantage goes to the state that acts last—the first will be blamed for partition—and because neither wants to act without its superpower ally's tacit or explicit consent.

The superpowers' keen interest in the Middle East must also be taken into account, but the U.S. position on partition in Lebanon has been increasingly ambiguous. In 1958 and again in 1982–83, U.S. military forces were dispatched to Lebanon to preserve its sovereign unity. But the bombing of the U.S. Embassy and Marine barracks in 1983, the taking of American hostages, and the seemingly intractable internecine violence of the last decade has dampened U.S. enthusiasm for this project, much as it did for the British in the years preceding partition in Palestine. As U.S. officials tire, they may increasingly be amenable to partition as a way of making the best of a bad situation. And if the United States is willing to consider it, the Soviet Union will probably agree, as they have in the past. Partition would probably assist their Syrian ally, which could withdraw the bulk of its costly occupation army in Lebanon, and a Moslem Lebanese government would probably become a Soviet ally. As for Aoun's claim that Lebanon is too small to partition, he need only look eighty miles to the west. Cyprus, now divided into two states, is roughly the same size as Lebanon.

This does not mean that partition would be easy. Ethnic militias and neighboring states occupy patchwork territories. The Syrians control the north and west, a Christian ally of Syria occupies a chunk along the north coast, with a Maronite ally of Israel to the south of it. Beirut is divided between Christian and Moslem forces, east and west, and Druse militia control a section of the coast to the south of the city. Various Shiite militias allied with Iran occupy the area to the south, and the Israelis, together with a Christian militia, occupy the southernmost part of the country.[38]

These sedimentary layers would no doubt be a partition cartographer's nightmare. Any serious partition would require prodigious gerrymandering and demand substantial population shifts, as other partitions have. The centerpiece of any partition would be Beirut, which has already been divided, like Nicosia, along a "Green Line."

Partition in Lebanon, as elsewhere, will be a protracted, uneven process. Over time, though, it will probably deepen.

All the conditions for partition now exist. Various cosmopolitan-parochial independence movements have been created by the derogation of citizenship and sovereignty in Lebanon that accompanied the widening of the conflict over Palestine. These movements, which seek to take state power by force, have waged relentless irregular wars against indigenous rivals and external enemies. This has ground down indigenous institutions and unitary identities and made neighboring and superpower states party to domestic social and political struggles. After a decade of civil and interstate war, the parties to this conflict might well regard partition as a relief, as an end to the nightmare that is conjured up by the word "Beirut." But if the history of partition is any indication, the end of the present conflict would merely mark the beginning of another.

To talk of partition in Israel and Sri Lanka is to step back in time to the pre-partition forties. Then, independence movements agitated violently for the devolution of state power to ethnic minorities. Partition emerged as a possible political solution, and powerful states implemented it as a way to keep the peace. This is familiar historical territory.

In Israeli-occupied Palestine, the Arab Palestinian uprising has renewed talk of implementing the United Nations partition plan of 1947–48, albeit along revised geographic lines. Forty years have passed, years visited by massive migrations and repeated war, yet the political solution being advanced is essentially the same plan. Only the sides have changed. In 1948, Arab Palestinians rejected partition and Zionists accepted it. Today, Arab Palestinians accept it and the Israeli government rejects it. Both parties look to the past to guide them into the future.

In Sri Lanka, an ethnic independence movement led by the Liberation Tigers of Tamil Eelam has been engaged in a furious irregular war with the Sinhalese majority and the armies of Sri Lanka and, recently, India. The conflict echoes the pre-partition history of India, Pakistan, Cyprus, and Ireland. Reading the newspapers, one is struck by the sense that Sri Lanka is merely the latest chapter of subdivision on the subcontinent, and that whether or not it is divided, it will contribute to secessionist impulses in India, Pakistan, Bangladesh, and even Burma.

At the same time, to speak of partition in Israel and Sri Lanka is to talk about the future. Things today are not as they once were. Several important developments have changed the context in which partition would occur. The most important is that partition will no longer be associated with devolution from colonial European empires. The reason, of course, is that there are few colonial empires left. The Kanak independence movement in French New Caledonia, an island group in the South Pacific, shares much in common with first-generation independence movements. Conflict between the Kanak movement and French colonial settlers may lead to partition, but this is now an atypical case. For the most part, secession and partition arise within the context of already independent nation-states: Basques may attempt to secede from Spain or France, Croatians from Yugoslavia, Eritreans from Ethiopia, Sikhs from India, and Tibetans from China.

This development is important because it changes the role of the superpower states. The United States and the Soviet Union supported self-determination, secession, and partition when it resulted in the breakup of European colonial empires. In the postwar context, this contributed to the creation of independent nation-states, which were to become the constituent units of the new interstate system, simultaneously diluting the influence of colonial empires within the system. But the superpowers are reluctant to support secession from independent nation-states. They may do so on a case-by-case basis, as in Pakistan, Cyprus, and perhaps Lebanon, but they do not want to endorse it as a rule. To do so would undermine not only the legitimacy of the interstate system but also their own legitimacy as multi-ethnic states. All the great and superpower states are composed of diverse social and political groups, some of which have had their citizenship abrogated: African Americans in the United States, Estonians and Armenians in the Soviet Union, Welsh and Scots in the United Kingdom, Basques and Corsicans in France, and Tibetans in China. These groups have formed movements seeking to recover their rights and have claimed self-determination as a right; some have even pressed for secession as a way to achieve state power on their own terms.

Because great and superpower states view the division of independent nation-states as problematic, they are reluctant to advance partition as a solution to conflict in many regions around the world. The Soviet Union and the United States have refused to endorse or support partition in Africa, even though some secessionist independence movements there can justifiably claim that their struggle is as deserving of superpower support as those of Koreans, Indians, Zionists, or Irish. The superpowers supported UN intervention in the Congo in 1960 to prevent the secession of Katanga province, they supported the Nigerian government in its war against Ibo secessionists in Biafra from 1966 to 1970, and they support the Ethiopian government in its long-running war with Eritrean secessionists. African states themselves support the superpower opposition to secession in Africa because they fear that once secession is admitted to the continent—which is composed almost exclusively of multi-ethnic nation-states—there will be no end to partition and secession.

The superpowers have also been opposed to secessionist movements within their European spheres of influence, in part because they view nascent independence movements as a threat to indigenous states, and in part because they view them as a threat to the integrity of their own political-military blocs.

The history of partition will also shape its future. Ireland was a precedent for many of the partitions that took place after World War II, and each succeeding partition has had a cumulative effect. The experience of first-generation partitions will almost certainly affect the character of second-generation partitions, as has been the case in Pakistan and as is likely to occur in Lebanon, Israel, and Sri Lanka.

This will no doubt complicate matters for states and for independence movements within states. During partition's first generation, Great Britain, the United States, and the Soviet Union were the principal dividers. They devolved and divided power between independence movements directly. Other states, such as France and China (as well as the United Nations), participated, but they did so as junior partners. However, during second-generation partitions, as in Pakistan and Cyprus, regional powers played the important roles in the partition process; the superpowers remained on the sidelines. In the future, the number of actors will probably increase. Partition in Lebanon, for example, may involve a wide assortment of competing independence movements (not just two, as was common in first-generation partitions), Lebanese state officials (their counterparts did not exist or, if they did, did not usually participate in first-generation partitions), neighboring states, great and superpower states—the United States and the Soviet Union as well as Great Britain and

France—and the United Nations. Partition will consequently be a more complex political process in the future than it has been in the past.

The history of partition will also complicate matters for independence movements as well. First-generation independence movements were usually organized along either ethnic or ideological lines. But today, because leaders of movements are now more easily exposed to a wider variety of cosmopolitan ideologies, they combine them in novel ways, mixing ethnic and religious identities with political ideologies, so that their movements defy easy categorization.

Take Velupillai Prabakaran. In 1971, at seventeen years of age, Prabakaran organized a band of teenagers who later became the Liberation Tigers of Tamil Eelam. He devised an effective political practice based on diverse social and ideological currents. He is something of a Marxist who has organized the Tamil population of Sri Lanka along ethnic lines, and he takes his inspiration from Clint Eastwood movies, which he watches on videocassettes.[39] Mary Anne Weaver, a writer for *The New Yorker*, has said of him, "Prabakaran is not a Marxist in the traditional sense. In fact, his political thinking seems a bit muddled, and the labels pinned on him have ranged from extreme rightist to extreme leftist. All that can be said for certain is that he is an extremely militant and angry Tamil nationalist. He and his men wear cyanide capsules around their necks as a special badge of membership and determination—and, of course, as a means of avoiding interrogation under arrest."[40]

Whatever their eclectic ideology, the Tigers have battled the armies of both Sri Lanka and India (50,000 strong in 1988) to a standstill and have driven the country toward war and partition. The Tigers' counterparts, extremist Sinhalese organizations such as the People's Liberation Front, also defy easy categorization. Founded in the 1960s by Rohana Wijeweera (then a medical student at Patrice Lumumba University in Moscow), the PLF also advances a Marxist politics, as its name, redolent with associations of movements past, suggests. But its Marxism is a curious amalgam. Sinhalese militants idolize Lenin, but they are anti-Soviet and anti-Chinese. They couch this cosmopolitan ideology in a parochial, Sinhalese supremacist vernacular that draws on Buddhist religious identities.[41] Former Sri Lankan President Junius R. Jayewardene, a Sinhalese who narrowly escaped a PLF attack on the parliament in 1987, said of them, "Watch out. Be careful. They are ruthless. They have no humanity."[42]

The social and political amalgamations of contemporary independence movements may be more complicated or diverse than first-generation movements, but they can nonetheless be understood in much the same terms. They fuse cosmopolitan and parochial orientations and portray themselves as simultaneously traditional and modern political practitioners in a determined effort to organize an effective movement that can seize state power. Categories like "right" and "left" do not mean very much in this context because the axes (cosmopolitan-parochial, traditional-modern) are different.

Stepping back from the divided and soon-to-be divided states, one can identify a great many movements around the world that have organized along similar lines and that press for self-determination and state power: Polisario guerrillas in Western Sahara; Eritreans in Ethiopia; Kurds in Turkey, Iraq, and Iran; Basques in Spain and France; German-speaking Tyroleans in northern Italy; Corsicans in France; Karens in Burma; Melanesians in New Caledonia and Fiji; Papuans and Timorese in Indonesia; Québecois in Canada; Hutus in Burundi—not to mention the Armenians, Lithuanians, Moldavians, and other nationalities within the Soviet Union itself.

By and large, the movements that organize these groups are secessionist, because they see secession as the only way that these typically minority populations can assume state power. They do not believe they can do so in a unitary state. Unificationist movements, meanwhile, have generally been subsumed by the state, which has taken on the role previously played by those independence movements representing majority populations.

Many of these secessionist movements have long-standing claims and have conducted protracted political and military campaigns to achieve their ends. Basque and Eritrean independence movements have done so for decades. With some justification they demand the same rights—state power—accorded to Zionist Jews, Moslem Indians, and Bengali Pakistanis. But they do not seem to be very near achieving their ends. Given that majority populations and state officials are hostile to this project, and that the superpowers are reluctant to support their independence, they will probably not be able to achieve their independence any time soon. This does not mean that they will go away or give up, but it does mean that their struggle, whether successful or unsuccessful, will be long and difficult. They hope that state officials and majority populations will tire of irremediable conflict and that superpower officials will step in and advance partition as a solution. This is not a blind ambition. Thomas Melady, the former U.S. ambassador to Burundi, has said of recent ethnic conflict between majority Hutus and minority Tutsis, who control the army and state power:

> To prevent further ethnic bloodbaths, both communities must be separated . . . the predominantly Tutsi area of Gilega should be designated as the Tutsi part of the country and the rest of Burundi should be assigned to the Hutus.
> Toward that end, the United States should recruit European, Asian and African countries to co-sponsor a call for a meeting of the United Nations Security Council to consider instructing the United Nations to establish a framework of partition and to administer partition. . . .
> The Hutu-Tutsi alienation resulting from a variety of historic forces has resulted in a genocide prone culture in both tribal communities. Separation is the only solution that will prevent further ethnic slaughter.[43]

This is the kind of response indigenous militants hope to produce by slaughtering civilians and waging irregular wars against the state. By provoking their opponents to retaliate in kind, thus raising the level of internecine violence, they can create a "genocide prone culture" in which partition will appear as a great relief, the only sane way to end the savagery. This is what Velupillai Prabakaran and the Liberation Tigers of Tamil Eelam, and their numerous counterparts around the world, hope to accomplish by dragging women and children off buses and murdering them. The slaughter of innocent civilians rouses the majority population to fury. Majority extremists, paramilitary forces, or the state then visits its fury on the minority population, and the descent into violence, the deepening of division, and the creation of a "genocide prone culture" begins. In this context, ruthless irregular war is an effective tactic because it advances the movement's strategic goal. Contemporary independence movements use violence in this fashion because it works.

And this is the dilemma. Violence is used to advance partition, which is seen as a solution to violence. But partition, in turn, produces new conditions that lead to violence and war, where partition can again be advanced as a solution.

· 13 ·

Self-Determination or Democracy?

Partition is a failed political policy. It was advanced by great and superpower states as a peaceful, equitable means of devolving political power to competing independence movements. By dividing power between indigenous rivals, internecine social conflict would be avoided and these groups would exercise self-determination and democracy within independent nation-states. But the promise of this policy remains unfulfilled. Instead, partition has led to the displacement of indigenous populations, disenfranchisement of ethnic and secular minorities, frustration of empowered majorities, internecine social conflict, and interstate war. These developments, which were institutionalized by state officials, defended by social movements within divided states, and protected by superpower allies, have further divided peoples and polities. Despite its sorry history, its tragic human consequences, partition is still being promoted as a political solution to conflict in countries around the world.

As a policy, partition owes much to the concept of self-determination, for it was advanced under that rubric. The failure of partition, then, suggests that self-determination is also a failed concept. This may seem heretical. After all, there are few cosmopolitan ideas more universally accepted than self-determination. Leaders of capitalist,

Communist, religious, and military states adopt the principle of self-determination as a right and endorse it in global political forums like the United Nations. But its application in the divided states has been a disaster. As noted in Chapter 3, Secretary of State Robert Lansing concluded in 1919 that self-determination was "one of those declarations which sounds true . . . but which, when the attempt is made to apply it . . . becomes a source of political instability and domestic disorder and not infrequently a cause of rebellion." He also warned that it is "a phrase simply loaded with dynamite."[1] Lansing was right. In the divided states, self-determination detonated with disastrous results. This suggests that the idea should be critically reassessed.

Self-determination was first advanced by Wilson and Lenin during World War I to express their support for the secession of colonies from European empires. They believed that colonies had a right to become independent nation-states, which could then participate as equals in a new, collective-security interstate system. In this context, self-determination became a progressive rallying cry for would-be superpowers and for indigenous independence movements in colonies around the world. After World War II, the superpowers set about constructing this new interstate system, European empires devolved power in their colonies to indigenous movements, and power in some countries was divided between competing independence movements.

In divided states, power was devolved and boundaries drawn so that the "nation"—a homogeneous group of people who shared ethnic or ideological characteristics—and the "state" would be synonymous. Because "majority" and "minority" alike would assume state power over a given territory, they could each separately realize self-determination and pursue democracy without the constraints imposed by contentious, non-national groups within each state. Because partition aimed to create relatively homogeneous nation-states, one might have expected that self-determination and democracy would be more fully realized in the divided states than in multi-ethnic, multi-"national" nation-states. But just the opposite occurred. It turned out that no country could be completely homogeneous; despite massive voluntary and involuntary migrations, minority populations remained behind. And they made it impossible for majority populations to exercise self-determination without some constraint. In this context, self-determination acquired two unintended, self-destructive meanings.

First, partition established the right to rule without regard for "others" who were not part of the "nation." State officials did not provide constitutional protection for the civil rights of minority populations, or if they did, these safeguards were quickly eroded by the assertion of majority rights. State officials and majority populations assumed that disenchanted, disenfranchised minorities could find protection in neighboring states, where their compatriots had assumed state power. Protection for minorities, what may be called civil rights, was derogated. Instead of being the responsibility of all states, the civil rights of a given group became the responsibility of a particular state. So, for example, when Israel declared its independence as a Jewish state, many neighboring states decided that they could abdicate responsibility for the civil rights of Jews within their countries.

Partition presented a choice to minority populations. They could either migrate to the particular state where their compatriots had assumed power or they could seek state power on their own terms, in their own land. Self-determination thus began to acquire a second meaning: the right of minority populations to secede from independent nation-states when their civil rights were denied. The self-determination of the majority population legitimized the pursuit of self-determination by minority populations.

In this context, the pursuit of self-determination is based on a chimera. The identity of majority and minority groups is, after all, a social construction. Nationalist independence movements create these identities in an effort to mobilize popular support that can help them seize or assume state power. But as these *ad hoc* social constructions change over time, the meaning of self—of national identity— changes as well. Thus the realization of self-determination by a particular people or nation in a given state is itself problematic, even utopian.

The pursuit of self-determination in the divided states has led away from democracy and toward apartheid. The social construction of political systems that divide and disenfranchise the citizenry has led to the rise of second-generation movements that claim secession as their right. Social conflict over majority and minority rights has led to internecine and interstate war, which has further divided and embittered people. Although the pursuit of self-determination does not always lead toward apartheid, it has not enriched the meaning of democracy in the modern world. Instead, it has impoverished it.

After this review of the causes and consequences of partition in the divided states, it seems appropriate to discuss an alternative to partition or at least to recommend ways to resolve the problems endemic to divided states. As a practical matter, however, it would take another book to weigh possible solutions that have a realistic chance of being implemented. As a matter of principle, it would be irresponsible to advance particular policy solutions. Partition is a social problem, and durable solutions must be advanced by the people who are affected by it. But it would be equally irresponsible not to suggest a perspective that might assist social movements that are attempting to wrestle with the problems endemic to divided states (and also to many undivided states). As an alternative to self-determination, let us consider a return to the principles articulated in the United States by Abraham Lincoln and by Dr. Martin Luther King, Jr.

The United States fought a bloody civil war in the mid-nineteenth century. This conflict might have ended in partition, North and South, but the Northern unionist majority defeated the Southern secessionist insurgency and the Union survived.

During the course of the Civil War, President Abraham Lincoln advanced two arguments to rebut the claims of the secessionist minority. He argued that democracy is nothing if not majority rule, and he asserted that minority civil rights should be protected by the federal Constitution, not by the states. To achieve the first, he waged a relentless military campaign to crush the secessionist insurgency. And to achieve the second, he sought to guarantee civil rights for minority populations, both white Southerners and, later, black slaves.

In his inaugural address on the eve of war, Lincoln agreed that minorities possessed the right to revolt if "a majority should deprive a minority of any clearly written constitutional right." But, he argued, no such right had been denied the Southern minority: "All the vital rights of minorities and of individuals are so plainly assured to them by affirmations and negations, guarantees and prohibitions, in the Constitution, that controversies never arise concerning them." He said that since the extension of slavery to new territories was not expressly protected by the Constitution, Southern slaveholders could not claim this as their "right" or as justification for revolt. "If the minority will not acquiesce [in non-constitutional issues], the majority must or the government must cease. There is no alternative; for continuing the government is acquiescence of one side or the other."

Lincoln then pointed to the danger inherent in a minority, secessionist conception of democracy (a theme that would later be reiterated by Secretary of State Lansing): "If a minority in such case will secede rather than acquiesce, they make a precedent which in turn will divide and ruin them; for a minority of their own will secede from them whenever a majority refuses to be controlled by such minority." And he asked, "Why may not any portion of the confederacy a year or two hence arbitrarily secede again, precisely as portions of the present Union now claim to secede from it? All who cherish disunion sentiments are now being educated to the exact temper of doing this. . . .

"Plainly," Lincoln argued, "the central idea of secession is anarchy." As an alternative, he argued that the majority—a constantly shifting majority—should rule. "A majority held in restraint by constitutional checks and limitations, and always changing easily with deliberate changes of popular opinion and sentiments, is the only true sovereign of a free people. . . . The rule of a minority, as a permanent arrangement, is wholly inadmissible; so that, rejecting the majority principle, anarchy or despotism in some form is all that is left."

Anticipating the practical problem of dividing peoples and building walls between them, Lincoln said, "Physically speaking, we cannot separate. We cannot remove our respective sections from each other, nor build an impassable wall between them. A husband and wife may be divorced, and go out of the presence and beyond the reach of the other; but the different parts of the country cannot do this. They cannot but remain face to face, and intercourse, either amicable or hostile, must continue between them."[2] This, of course, is exactly what divided states have attempted to do, without success, despite Lenin's argument that the right of secession was akin to the right to divorce.

Lincoln's determination to preserve majority rule as the cornerstone of democracy was evident during the protracted Civil War. Although he was willing to concede to the South many issues, even the right to own slaves, he brooked no compromise on the principle of majority rule, even if it meant burning Southern cities to the ground.

Had his conception of democracy remained fixed only on majority rule, Lincoln might be regarded as a despot. But it was not. Lincoln's necessary complement to majority rule was his insistence on minority civil rights guaranteed by the Constitution. During the war, Lincoln moved to secure the civil rights of the enslaved black minority. A series of wartime measures, leading up to the Emancipation Proclamation of 1863, extended the promise of freedom to slaves, and after the war, the Constitution was amended to secure freedom and civil rights for blacks and other minorities; the civil rights of insurgent secessionists were restored soon thereafter.

Lincoln's conception of democracy—majority rule, minority civil rights—is not the same as Wilson's or Lenin's. At bottom, self-determination is a secessionist principle and owes more to Confederate conceptions of democracy than to Unionist Republican ideals. As a practical matter, however, Lincoln's conception of democracy did not immediately triumph in the United States. Secessionist political forces were not completely destroyed by the war, and they re-emerged after Reconstruction. Southern whites rolled back many of the gains made by the black minority and constructed systems of apartheid, what came to be known as "Jim Crow," on a state-by-state basis, effectively disenfranchising blacks and derogating their civil rights.

Nearly one hundred years after the Civil War, the black minority revolted against segregation systems developed by Southern states and organized a movement that sought to realize democracy in Lincoln's terms. Dr. Martin Luther King, Jr., was a cosmopolitan parochialist much like the leaders of independence movements around the world. He took cosmopolitan ideologies about religion and politics and injected them into a parochial Southern setting. From cosmopolitan, socially conscious, liberal religious intellectuals like Reinhold Niebuhr and Paul Tillich, he borrowed the concept of *agape*, and from Gandhi he borrowed the politics of non-violence.[3] In King's view, "*Agape* is disinterested love. It is a love in which the individual seeks not his own good, but the good of his neighbor. . . . *Agape* is love seeking to preserve and create community. . . . *Agape* is a willingness to go to any length to restore community. . . . He who works against community is working against the whole of creation. Therefore, if I respond with a reciprocal hate, I do nothing but intensify the cleavage in broken community. I can only close the gap in broken community by meeting hate with love [*agape*]."[4]

For King, segregation divided people and broke up the national community. By restoring lost civil rights, the movement hoped to restore community for both minority and majority alike. This approach contrasts sharply with insistence on self-determination and the creation of separate communities. King, profoundly influenced by Gandhi, believed that community could best be restored by non-violent means. He advanced non-violent direct action as a way of achieving community both as a practical matter and as a matter of conscience. He said that a violent struggle for civil rights would "mislead Negroes . . . and place them as a minority in a position where they confront a far larger adversary than it is possible to defeat in this form of combat."[5] As a matter of principle, King argued that "the end of violence or the aftermath of violence is bitterness. The aftermath of non-violence is reconciliation and the creation of a beloved community."[6]

King understood that democracy could not be advanced by claiming separate rights for minority or majority, that neither majority nor minority can insist on democracy only on its own terms. Democracy must be inclusive, not exclusive. That is why King placed such great emphasis, throughout his life, on community. To achieve community he sought to deconstruct apartheid, to deconstruct the ethnic social identity given to the black minority by social, political, and economic institutions in the United States and to reconstruct this identity so that blacks could join the national community on an egalitarian basis. King sought nothing less than the transformation of the "Negro" minority into a majority made up of other disenfranchised minorities—the young, the old, the poor, women, white and black.

The development of a new minority consciousness in the 1940s and 1950s made this transformation possible. "Once plagued with a tragic sense of inferiority, resulting from the crippling effects of slavery and segregation," King noted, "the Negro has been driven to reevaluate himself."[7] This is where the movement came in. By mobilizing the black community through parochial institutions like the black church, and by using a parochial religious vernacular, where appeals for *agape* and non-violence were accompanied by a chorus of slave spirituals, King helped construct a new social identity. According to King, the civil rights movement enabled blacks to develop a "new sense of 'somebodyness' and self-respect. [A] new Negro has emerged with a new determination to achieve freedom and dignity whatever the cost may be."[8] In this context, "somebodyness" becomes the American equivalent of *doc lap*, *swaraj*, or *sinparam*.

But unlike some contemporary movements, which seek only to create an exclusive ethnic or ideological identity that is limited to people with certain given attributes, King sought not only to construct a positive identity for the black minority but also to create a wider identity that could transform minority into majority. This is why King emphasized integration and not self-determination as the goal. Integration would make it possible for blacks to join with other groups, participate in the democratic community, and possibly forge a majority politics based on economic and social equality and justice.

King reached out to the country's poor and to whites. "Having faith that the white majority is not an undifferentiated whole," he said in 1960, "Negro leaders have welcomed a moral appeal which can reach the emotions and intellects of significant white groups."[9] The ability to transform minority and majority alike lay at the center of his organizing strategy and at the heart of his philosophy. As he said on the steps of the Lincoln Memorial in 1963, "I have a dream that one day on the red hills of Georgia, sons of former slaves and sons of former slave-owners will be able to sit down together at the table of brotherhood. . . . And when we allow freedom to ring, when we let it ring from every village and hamlet, from every state and city, we will be able to speed up that day when all of God's children—black men and white men, Jews and Gentiles, Catholics and Protestants— will be able to join hands and to sing in the words of the old Negro spiritual, 'Free at last, free at last; thank God Almighty, we are free at last.' "[10]

During its first decade, the civil rights movement succeeded in dismantling formal segregation in states across the South and was beginning to attack *de facto* economic, political, and social segregation throughout the rest of the country. But in the mid-1960s, some sections of the movement, impatient with the pace of change and led by people borrowing cosmopolitian ideologies of a different character—that of Third World nationalism—turned away from the principles advanced by Lincoln and King and began pursuing a separatist-secessionist politics based on self-determination and its indigenous parochial expression: "Black Power."

King criticized such separatist politics:

> Beneath all the satisfaction of a gratifying slogan, Black Power is a nihilistic philosophy born out of the conviction that the Negro can't win. It is, at bottom, the view that American society is so hopelessly corrupt and enmeshed in evil that there is no possibility of salvation from within. . . . [The Black Power movement] claims to be the most revolutionary wing of the social revolution taking place in the United States. Yet it rejects the one thing that keeps the fire of revolution burning: the

ever-present flame of hope. When hope dies, a revolution degenerates into an undiscriminating catchall for evanescent and futile gestures. The Negro cannot entrust his destiny to a philosophy nourished solely on despair, to a slogan that cannot be implemented into a program. . . . In a multi-racial society no group can make it alone. It is a myth to believe that the Irish, the Italians and the Jews—the ethnic groups that Black Power advocates cite as justification for their views—rose to power through separatism. . . . To succeed in a pluralistic society, and an often hostile one at that, the Negro obviously needs organized strength, but that strength will only be effective when it is consolidated though constructive alliances with the majority group. . . . The cooperation of Negro and white based on the solid ground of honest conscience and proper self-interest can continue to grow in scope and influence. It can attach the basic strength to alter basic institutions by democratic means. Negro isolation can never approach this goal. . . . There is no separate black path to power and fulfillment that does not intersect white paths, and there is no separate white path to power and fulfillment, short of social disaster, that does not share that power with black aspirations for freedom and human dignity. We are bound together in a single garment of destiny.[11]

King's assassination in 1968 weakened the section of the movement supporting a democratic politics based on majority rule and minority civil rights. It strengthened support for a separatist politics, in which blacks and other disenfranchised minorities would independently pursue their self-determination and work together only in coalitions, in what might be called a "confederate" politics. The movement splintered and newly emerging women's, gay, and environmental movements organized around given social identities. The fragmentation of disenfranchised minorities in the late 1960s and 1970s, moreover, made it possible for a conservative minority, defined along white-ethnic and middle-class lines, to establish political and social hegemony during the late 1970s and 1980s.

Lincoln and King's conception of politics advanced democracy in the United States, but the projects they began remain incomplete. Nonetheless, they have been exemplary for some social movements around the world, even in divided states, that have pressed for a democratic politics based on majority rule and minority civil rights. Students in West Germany and South Korea and women in Cyprus have demanded that the walls dividing their countries be torn down and their countries reunited on a democratic basis. The Catholic civil rights movement in Northern Ireland during the late 1960s and early 1970s was self-consciously modeled on the U.S. civil rights movement. And various political parties, social movements, and dissident intellectuals have emerged to press (from within and without) for the democratization of countries subject to one-party or military rule.

Although these movements practice a politics that attempts to realize democracy, not self-determination, they are relatively weak. Compared with separatist movements, they have set themselves a more difficult task, since they must deconstruct and reconstruct not only their own identity but that of the majority as well, while explicitly eschewing violence as a means of attaining their goals. Theirs is not an impossible task, however, because ethnic and ideological identities are themselves socially constructed, which means that they can and do change. And non-violence can play an important and effective role in changing social and political institutions, as they have in South Korea and Pakistan.

Recent political events at the interstate level might also assist the advance of democracy in divided states. The United States and the Soviet Union—responding to defeat in Vietnam and Afghanistan, economic difficulties resulting from attempts to maintain overextended spheres of influence, and the emergence of regional powers —have recently begun to resolve some long-standing disagreements. This superpower accord may make it easier for them to resolve conflicts within and between divided states or to adopt a collective approach to regional conflict.

Regional powers have also shown renewed interest in common-security approaches to regional conflict. The Arias Plan, put together by Costa Rican President Oscar Arias Sánchez, is an attempt to establish a common-security regime in Central America. Parties to the plan agreed to withhold support for irregular insurgents in other countries, to ask the superpowers not to intervene in the region, and to democratize the political process—allowing the press to operate freely, permitting opposition political parties to form, conducting regular elections, and guaranteeing human rights—so that domestic problems can be resolved without resort to insurrection and to interstate war. Leaders in India and Pakistan have discussed the adoption of non-proliferation accords to stave off a nuclear arms race and the threat of nuclear war in the subcontinent. And there is widespread interest in the United Nations playing a constructive, non-partisan role in the resolution of regional conflicts. Many states—some non-aligned and some allied with the superpowers—would like to see the interstate system become more egalitarian, with the superpowers devolving some of their authority to the United Nations. This may become more possible as U.S.–Soviet conflict diminishes.

These developments may make it easier in the future to resolve conflicts within and between divided states. But the forces are still relatively weak. The United Nations itself, for instance, played an active role in the partitions of Korea, Palestine, and Cyprus, and will probably play a role in any formal division of Lebanon. The impulse to divide remains strong, not only for great and superpower states, but for regional powers as well.

Unless social movements and government officials find a way to promote democracy in heterogeneous nation-states, to deconstruct social identities defined by animosity, and to find peaceful solutions to social and political conflict within and between states, the divisions created by partition will sharpen and the walls dividing people will continue to rise.

Bibliographic Essay

The literature on partition is as divided as the states themselves. Few books cover both the periods before and after partition, and most post-partition studies treat divided states separately. Consequently, there are few books comparing developments in North and South Korea or East and West Germany. This makes it difficult to trace the causes and consequences of partition or to examine it as a general phenomenon.

The only general discussion of partition is Gregory Henderson, R. N. Lebow, and J. G. Stroessinger, *Divided Nations in a Divided World* (New York: David McKay, 1974), which examines some of the divided states. The fine concluding essay by Richard Lebow reaches some of the conclusions made here. But because the book is organized as a series of separate case studies, it cannot integrate the separate histories into a comprehensive analysis.

The literature on partition is very uneven. As one might expect, there are more books written about India than about Cyprus. But size is not always a guide. Though it is a small country, work on Palestine/Israel takes up many shelves in most libraries. The volume of work is a reflection of partisan interest and attests to the strength of the Zionist movement and the importance attached to its history by Jewish scholars around the world. Arab writers have only recently begun to compete for space on library shelves. Likewise, the study of Ireland is voluminous and partisan. Most of the work on Northern Ireland is written by scholars sympathetic to the plight of the minority Catholic population. As Sarah Nelson has pointed out in *Ulster's Uncertain Defenders* (Syracuse, N.Y.: Syracuse University Press, 1984), "Everyone in the research and journalism business was doing 'the Catholics' " (p. 9). By contrast, Communist Parties in Asian states have produced partisan works in small numbers, preferring to revise the history of the pre- and post-partition period rather than writing a lot of separate histories.

In general, the former British colonies—Ireland, India, and Palestine— have benefited from the work of fine British scholars who have written extensively about matters relating to Empire. Reginald Coupland, in *The Indian Problem* (London: Oxford University Press, 1944), provides an unparalleled work about the pre-partition period. Unfortunately, the interest of formidable British scholars falls off considerably after the devolution of power. There is consequently no literary equal to Coupland's work in the post-partition period, though R. F. Holland, *European Decolonization, 1918–1981* (New York: St. Martin's Press, 1985), provides a comprehensive description of that process.

While British interest fell off, U.S. scholarly interest picked up after the United States became involved in Asia and Europe. Most of the good work has been done in the last two decades. Joyce and Gabriel Kolko, *The Limits of Power* (New York: Harper & Row, 1972), is the first, and perhaps most important, work on U.S. participation in postwar partition. The defeat and retreat from Vietnam stimulated an intense U.S. interest in divided states, particularly Korea and Vietnam. Bruce Cumings, *The Origins of the Korean War* (Princeton: Princeton University Press, 1981), and Stanley Karnow, *Vietnam: A History* (New York: Viking Press, 1983), stand out as exemplary. Curiously, there is no equivalent work in English on China or Germany. For these countries, the scholarly literature remains divided by geography and by period.

The literature on partition is divided not only by volume, perspective, geography, and period but by quality as well. One can read ten essential texts before finding a well-written and compelling book. Despite these difficulties, there are a few books that are both reliable and readable. These provide useful starting points for further research.

In addition to Cumings, Bong-youn Choy, *A History of the Korean Unification Movement* (Peoria, Ill.: Institute of International Studies, Bradley University, 1984), is essential to any study of Korea. Choy's work spans the pre- and post-partition period, and both Choy and Cumings examine the struggles between and among independence movements and superpower states.

Although the literature on China is extensive, there is little on partition or on the relation between China and Taiwan. June M. Grasso, *Truman's Two-China Policy* (Armonk, N.Y.: M. E. Sharpe, 1987), provides a point of departure into a dispersed literature. Because the partition of China was caught up with partition and war in Korea, most of the best material is to be found in the margins of work on the Korean War, for example in Rosemary Foot, *The Wrong War* (Ithaca, N.Y.: Cornell University Press, 1985), and Ralph Clough, *Embattled Korea* (Boulder, Colo.: Westview Press, 1987).

On Vietnam, in addition to Karnow's work, two books stand out: Jean Lacouture's biography *Ho Chi Minh* (New York: Random House, 1968) and Huynh Kim Khanh, *Vietnamese Communism, 1925–45* (Ithaca, N.Y.: Cornell

University Press, 1982), are both excellent, the latter providing one of the best detailed examinations of an emerging independence movement in the pre-partition period.

Works on partition in India must begin with Coupland, which ends during World War II. H. V. Hodson, *The Great Divide* (Oxford: Oxford University Press, 1985), picks up where Coupland leaves off and covers the period up through 1947. Salman Rushdie's early fiction, *Midnight's Children* (New York: Avon Books, 1980) and *Shame* (New York: Aventura, 1984), provides fictional accounts of post-partition developments in India and Pakistan that surpass most non-fiction treatments of the period.

The literature on Palestine and Israel, as noted above, is extensive. Walter Laqueur, *A History of Zionism* (New York: Schocken Books, 1976), is an indispensable analysis of the movement before partition. Michael J. Cohen, *The Origins and Evolution of the Arab-Zionist Conflict* (Berkeley: University of California Press, 1987), is an excellent primer, and Amos Perlmutter, *Israel: The Partitioned State* (New York: Charles Scribner's Sons, 1985), provides a useful account of both the pre- and post-partition period. Sabri Jiryis, *The Arabs in Israel, 1948–1966* (Beirut: Institute for Palestine Studies, 1967), examines Arab-Jewish relations from partition to the Six-Day War. Geoffrey Aronson, *Creating Facts* (Washington, D.C.: Institute for Palestine Studies, 1987), picks up where Jiryis leaves off, examining post-1967 developments. Benny Morris, *The Birth of the Palestinian Refugee Problem* (Cambridge: Cambridge University Press, 1988), is probably the most important book to be published on this subject in recent years. His detailed account of the partition process is essential to any understanding of contemporary problems.

Christopher Hitchens, *Cyprus* (New York: Quartet Books, 1984), now reissued as *Hostage to History* (New York: Noonday Press, 1989), is a singular work on partition in Cyprus.

Scholarly work on Germany remains riveted to the Nazi era, but in the postwar period, Bruce Kuklick, *American Policy and the Division of Germany* (Ithaca, N.Y.: Cornell University Press, 1972), and the Kolkos' work provide the best accounts of the partition process, though neither extends much beyond 1953. The subsequent history of the two Germanys, like that of the two Chinas, is best found elsewhere, in books on the Cold War and U.S.–Soviet relations. Diana Johnstone, *The Politics of Euromissiles: Europe's Role in America's World* (London: Verso, 1984), is an absorbing account of contemporary developments.

Arthur Balfour was an important figure in the partition of Ireland, India, and Palestine. Catherine B. Shannon, *Arthur J. Balfour and Ireland, 1874–1922* (Washington, D.C.: Catholic University of America Press, 1988), provides an excellent political biography of the man and the partition process in Ireland. Much of the literature on Ireland concentrates on the period before partition, followed by a hiatus of several decades before scholarship resumes with intensity in the 1970s. Michael Farrell, *Northern Ireland: The Orange State* (London: Pluto Press, 1980), is one of the only works that provides continuous coverage throughout the post-partition period. And John Conroy, *Belfast Diaries: War as a Way of Life* (Boston: Beacon Press, 1987), provides a compelling account of life in a divided state at war. His superb account describes how social divisions are created and deepened.

In addition to books on particular countries, there are works that address themes related to war, independence movements, and superpower relations. Daniel Ellsberg's essay "Call to Mutiny," in E. P. Thompson and Dan Smith, *Protest and Survive* (New York: Monthly Review Press, 1981), ignited my interest in the relation between the threat of nuclear war and partition. This essay should be read in conjunction with more detailed treatments of the history of nuclear threats—such as Richard Betts, *Nuclear Blackmail and Nuclear Balance* (Washington, D.C.: Brookings Institution, 1987), and Morton Halperin, *Nuclear Fallacy* (Cambridge, Mass.: Ballinger, 1987)—and of nuclear proliferation—Leonard S. Spector, *Going Nuclear* (Cambridge, Mass.: Ballinger, 1987) and *The Undeclared Bomb* (Cambridge, Mass.: Ballinger, 1988). Spector monitors proliferation in divided states on an annual basis. John Lewis and L. Xue, *China Builds the Bomb* (Stanford: Stanford University Press, 1988), offer a first-rate analysis of the tortuous course of proliferation in China.

An examination of the superpowers' role in partition should begin with Richard W. Van Alstyne's "Woodrow Wilson and the Idea of the Nation State," *International Affairs* 37, no. 3 (July 1961), which examines the simultaneous emergence of the "new diplomacy" in the United States and the Soviet Union. Jean-Baptiste Duroselle, *From Wilson to Roosevelt* (New York: Harper & Row, 1963), covers the interwar period. Fernando Claudin, *The Communist Movement* (Harmondsworth, England: Penguin, 1975), provides a comprehensive treatment of the Soviet Union and its relation to Communist movements around the world during this period. In the postwar period, John L. Gaddis's *The United States and the Origins of the Cold War* (New York: Columbia University Press, 1972) and his book of essays, *The Long Peace* (New York: Oxford University Press, 1987), are valuable works. But as an antidote to Gaddis's Kennanesque interpretation of postwar events, it is extremely useful to read Walter Lippmann's prescient critique of George Kennan and containment, *The Cold War* (New York: Harper & Brothers, 1947), which anticipates many of the problems that the United States would eventually face in divided states.

While reading hundreds of books, I came across two oddities that deserve mention. Sigmund Freud and William Bullitt (a disenchanted member of Woodrow Wilson's entourage who later became U.S. ambassador to the Soviet Union) co-authored a psychological-political profile, *Woodrow Wilson: A Psychological Study* (Boston: Houghton Mifflin, 1967), which is memorable, though disturbing and unfair. An equally disturbing book is Shai Feldman, *Israeli Nuclear Deterrence* (New York: Columbia University Press, 1982), which attempts to find a way for Israel to use its nuclear weapons to deter conventional war with its Arab neighbors. To accomplish this, Feldman suggests that the Arabs acquire nuclear weapons so that an effective deterrence regime—like that developed by the United States and the Soviet Union—can be established. This work is proof that the proliferation of nuclear weapons in divided states is an extremely dangerous development.

Finally, as I became disenchanted with self-determination as a political guide, a perspective perhaps best explored in Lee Burcheit, *Secession: The Legitimacy of Self-Determination* (New Haven: Yale University Press, 1978), I began casting around for an alternative formulation. Coincidentally, Gore Vidal's novel *Lincoln* (New York: Ballantine Books, 1984) led me to a more serious study of Lincoln's views on democracy. Many of Lincoln's speeches, letters, and other writings are found in Carl Sandburg's four-volume study, *Abraham Lincoln* (New York: Harcourt, Brace and Company, 1939). My inquiry into democratic theory along Lincolnian lines led straight to its contemporary proponents in the U.S. civil rights movement and the work of Dr. Martin Luther King, Jr. In *A Testament of Hope: The Essential Writings of Martin Luther King, Jr.* (San Francisco: Harper & Row, 1986), James M. Washington collects most of King's important speeches, essays, and selections from his books. Finally, Taylor Branch, *Parting the Waters* (New York: Simon and Schuster, 1988), offers an extraordinary portrait of King and the civil rights movement.

Notes

The epigraph is from a speech given by Conor Cruise O'Brien in 1958, as the Ambassador of the Republic of Ireland to the United Nations, during a UN debate about the future of Cyprus. Quoted in Stephen George Xydis, *Cyprus: Conflict and Conciliation, 1954–1958* (Columbus: Ohio State University Press, 1967), p. 405.

Introduction

1 Barry Blechman and S. Kaplan, *Force Without War* (Washington, D.C.: Brookings Institution, 1981), pp. 48, 51, 100; Morton Halperin, *Nuclear Fallacy* (Cambridge, Mass.: Ballinger, 1987), p. 24; Richard Betts, *Nuclear Blackmail and Nuclear Balance* (Washington, D.C.: Brookings Institution, 1987), pp. 7–8.

2 The post-World War I division of the Austro-Hungarian Empire very nearly qualifies as a "partition" in this sense. In many ways, its partition created problems that led to war, much as the other partitions have. But the history of "partition" in Eastern Europe, its prewar roots and postwar consequences, which contributed to World War II and its redivision afterward, has been explored extensively by others.

3 George William Russell, *The living torch* (New York: Macmillan, 1938), p. 134.

4 *The New York Times*, February 28, 1988.

5 Stanley Karnow, *Vietnam: A History* (New York: Viking Press, 1983), pp. 179–80.

6 Michael Sturmer, "The Evolution of the Contemporary German Question," pp. 21–32, in *Germany Between East and West*, ed. Edwina Moreton (Cambridge: Cambridge University Press, 1987), p. 21.

1. The Independence Movements

1 Stanley Karnow, *Vietnam: A History* (New York: Viking Press, 1983), p. 121.

2 Jean Lacouture, *Ho Chi Minh* (New York: Random House, 1968), pp. 27–28.

3 He later recalled that the "Third International is putting considerable attention to the colonial problem. It has promised to help oppressed people to recover their freedom and independence, while the Second International has not even mentioned the fate of the colonies. That is why I voted for the Third International." Huynh Kim Khanh, *Vietnamese Communism: 1925–45* (Ithaca, N.Y.: Cornell University Press, 1982), pp. 278–79.

4 Lacouture, *Ho Chi Minh*, p. 122.

5 Ibid., p. 51.

6 Karnow, *Vietnam*, p. 123. On his journeys, Ho used many names. Although he was born Nguyen Sinh Cung, his mother renamed him Nguyen Tat Thanh when he turned eleven. He took the name Nguyen Ai Quock, which means Nguyen Who Loves His Country, when living in France. He adopted Ho Chi Minh, or Bringer of Light, in the 1940s. One historian says he has discovered thirty-two aliases for the Vietnamese leader; historians in Hanoi claim to have found seventy-six. Perhaps he should have called himself Nguyen of Many Names.

7 See Lacouture's discussion of "Ho's Lincolnism" in *Ho Chi Minh*, pp. 264–65.

8 Ibid., p. 262; Karnow, *Vietnam*, p. 135.

9 Douglas Pike, *Vietnam and the Soviet Union* (Boulder, Colo.: Westview Press, 1987), p. 12. And Ho remembered the source of his ideas. During the war he lived in a mountain hideaway near the Chinese border, where he camped by a stream. He called the mountain "Karl Marx" and the stream that flowed beside his camp "Lenin." Ivan Illich notes that the word "memory" is based on the Greek word *mnemos*, which is also the word for river. And in Freudian terms, consciousness is often referred to as a "stream." It is not surprising, then, that Ho would call a stream, a source of his ideas, "Lenin." Lacouture, *Ho Chi Minh*, p. 74.

10 Robert T. Oliver, *Syngman Rhee* (New York: Dodd, Mead, 1954), pp. 118–19.

11 Bruce Cumings, *The Origins of the Korean War* (Princeton: Princeton University Press, 1981), p. 431.

12 John King Fairbank, *The United States and China* (Cambridge, Mass.: Harvard University Press, 1983), pp. 205–6.

13 Ibid., pp. 252–53.

14 Nehru was not a lawyer. He was influenced by liberal democratic and Communist ideologies. "As between fascism and communism," he wrote in his autobiography, "my sympathies are entirely with communism . . . [but] I'm very far from being a communist. My roots are still perhaps in the nineteenth century, and I have been too much influenced by the humanist liberal tradition to get out of it completely. This bourgeois background follows me around and is naturally a source of irritation to many communists." Jawaharlal Nehru, *Toward Freedom* (New York: John Day, 1942), p. 231.

15 Chaim Weizmann, *Trial and Error* (London: Hamish Hamilton, 1949), pp. 220–22.

16 William Quandt, F. Jabber, and A. Mosley, *The Politics of Palestinian Nationalism* (Berkeley: University of California Press, 1973), p. 20.

17 Mary C. Bromage, *De Valera and the March of a Nation* (New York: Noonday Press, 1956), p. 15.

18 Tom Nairn, *The Break-up of Britain* (London: New Left Books, 1977), p. 340.

19 Khanh, *Vietnamese Communism*, pp. 278–79.

20 Pike, *Vietnam and the Soviet Union*, p. 10.

21 Khanh, *Vietnamese Communism*, p. 80. In his biography of Ho Chi Mihn, Jean

Lacouture describes Ho as "the man who remains awake when everyone else is asleep," *Ho Chi Minh*, p. 4.

22 Khanh, *Vietnamese Communism*, p. 260. This metaphor had widespread appeal for those writing about independence movements. In his epic study of the Zionist movement, Walter Laqueur says of its early years, "Zionism, in brief, was comatose when in 1896 Theodor Herzl appeared." *A History of Zionism* (New York: Schocken Books, 1976), p. 83.

23 The manifesto continues: "Do not allow an oppressive tyrant who has only disdain for you to remain in your country; cleanse your country from those who show their enmity to you, to your race and to your language." Michael J. Cohen, *The Origins and Evolution of the Arab-Zionist Conflict* (Berkeley: University of California Press, 1987), pp. 137–38.

24 Verney Lovett, *A History of the Indian Nationalist Movement* (New York: Augustus M. Kelley, 1969), pp. 106–7. And when the British ceded independence to India, Nehru referred again to this imagery: "At the stroke of the midnight hour, when the world sleeps, India will awake to life and freedom." Michael Edwardes, *Nehru: A Political Biography* (New York: Praeger, 1971), p. 214.

25 Nicholas Mansergh, *The Irish Question* (London: George Allen and Unwin, 1975), p. 41.

26 Edwardes, *Nehru*, p. 26.

27 Lacouture, *Ho Chi Minh*, p. 129. Lacouture says that "some translated 'Doc Lap' as 'freedom,' others as 'independence'—Ho and his colleagues clearly favored the second interpretation." He adds: "Linguistically, they were certainly right. *Doc Lap* means 'to stand alone.' "

28 John Eglinton, *Ideals in Ireland* (London, 1901), p. 65. When Arthur Griffith introduced the Gaelic term "Sinn Fein," which means "ourselves," he sought to describe a people able to stand apart from other people, the British in particular, but also other nations. Belinda Probert, *Beyond Orange and Green* (Dublin: Academy Press, 1978), p. 38.

29 Nehru, *Toward Freedom*, p. 75.

30 Cumings, *Korean War*, p. 68.

31 Nehru, *Toward Freedom*, p. 65.

32 Ibid., p. 79. *Swaraj* means "self-government" as well as freedom or independence. But because the British believed that India might be given self-government or "home rule" and still remain within the Commonwealth (not severing colonial ties completely), the Indian National Congress began using the phrase *purna swaraj*, or "complete independence," to distinguish its meaning of independence from British usage. See the pledge taken by the Indian National Congress on January 26, 1930. Ibid., p. 388. In general, British officials and their colonial subjects gave the same meaning to the term "independence," but they gave different meanings to its vernacular equivalent.

33 As Benedict Anderson says, "No nation imagines itself as coterminous with mankind. The most messianic nationalists do not dream of a day when all the members of the human race will join their nation in a way that it was possible, in certain epochs, for, say, Christians to dream of a wholly Christian planet." *Imagined Communities* (London: Verso, 1983), p. 16. At the same time, no nation imagines that it is not part of mankind.

34 See Reginald Coupland, *The Indian Problem* (London: Oxford University Press, 1944), vol. 1, pp. 15–16.

35 Fairbank, *United States and China*, pp. 231–32.

36 Benedict Anderson, "Narrating the Nation," *The Times Literary Supplement*, June 13, 1986.

37 Weizmann, *Trial and Error*, pp. 41–42.

38 Laqueur, *History of Zionism*, p. 96. See also Laqueur's identification of three basic anti-Zionist positions within the Jewish community: "the assimilationist, the orthodox-religious, and the left-wing revolutionary." Ibid., p. 385.

39 Ibid., pp. 408–9.

2. The Uses of History

1 I am indebted to Benedict Anderson for his work on this subject. In "Narrating the Nation," *The Times Literary Supplement*, June 13, 1986, he explores the simultaneous newness and oldness of nationalist movements. In *Imagined Communities* (London: Verso, 1983), p. 65, he notes that "it is instructive that the Declaration of Independence in 1776 speaks only of 'the people,' while the word 'nation' makes its debut only in the Constitution of 1787."

2 B. N. Pandey, *The Breakup of British India* (New York: St. Martin's Press, 1969), p. 42. At the first session of the Congress in 1885, Subramania Ayar praised the British for unifying India and therefore making a nationalist movement possible: "For the first time in the history of the Indian populations there is to be beheld the phenomenon of national unity among them, of a sense of national existence" Reginald Coupland, *The Indian Problem* (London: Oxford University Press, 1944), vol. 1, p. 23. It was only in 1905 that the Congress declared its aim to be "the form of government [that] exists in the self-governing Colonies of the British Empire." Ibid., p. 37. And it was not until 1920 that Gandhi persuaded the Congress to adopt *swaraj*, or independence, as its goal. Pandey, *Breakup of British India*, p. 114.

3 Indeed, Coupland says that between 1919 and 1924 the League "was virtually merged in the Congress" and did not even meet as a separate body." *Indian Problem*, p. 74.

4 Lawrence McCaffrey, *The Irish Question, 1800–1922* (Lexington: University of Kentucky Press, 1968), p. 152.

5 Bong-youn Choy, *A History of the Korean Reunification Movement* (Peoria, Ill.: Institute of International Studies, Bradley University, 1984), p. 18. Choy says the movement "was originally promoted by two social forces, one composed of intellectual middle-class patriots, including former government officials of the Yi Dynasty and neo-Confucian scholars, and the other composed of leftist intellectuals, including communists influenced by the Russian Bolshevik revolution." The Young Men's Christian Association was itself another institution that provided the Korean independence movement considerable support during the early part of the century. American missionaries active in the YMCA were sympathetic to Korean anti-colonial activists and were viewed with hostility by Japanese colonial administrators.

6 Ibid., p. 29.

7 Pandey, *Breakup of British India*, p. 30.

8 Verney Lovett, *A History of the Indian Nationalist Movement* (New York: Augustus M. Kelley, 1969), p. 107.

9 Ibid.

10 As Benedict Anderson says, "Thus for all the newness of the moment of national consciousness, the nation's most prized possessions are always 'long there.' Hence, in so many nationalist narratives, the trope of a brilliant 'awakening' from an historic sleep." "Narrating the Nation."

11 Walter Laqueur, *A History of Zionism* (New York: Schocken Books, 1976), pp. 95–96. Chaim Weizmann, who succeeded Herzl as leader of the Zionist movement, said of *Der Judenstaat* that it "contained not a single new idea for us." He belittled Herzl's claim as founder of Zionism because he "made no allusion in his little book to his predecessors in the field . . . [and] he apparently did not know of the existence of

Chibath Zion; he did not mention Palestine; he ignored the Hebrew language." *Trial and Error* (London: Hamish Hamilton, 1949), p. 61. But this is only part of Weizmann's argument that Zionism has an ancient legacy. As Laqueur notes, "The term Zionism appeared only in the 1890s, but the cause, the concept of Zion, has been present throughout Jewish history." Laqueur, *History of Zionism,* p. 40.

12 At the Sixth Zionist Congress, a map of Palestine that had hung behind the president's chair at previous congresses was replaced with a map of Uganda, a move that filled Weizmann with "foreboding." Herzl presented the case for Jewish settlement in Uganda, which caused great dissension. At one point in the debate, Weizmann recalls, "a young woman ran up on to the platform, and with a vehement gesture tore down the map of Uganda which had been suspended there in the place of the usual map of Zion." *Trial and Error,* pp. 110–11, 113. At the congress Weizmann argued, "If the British Government and people are what I think they are, they will make us a better offer." Ibid., p. 114.

13 Ibid., pp. 143, 144.

14 Huynh Kim Khanh, *Vietnamese Communism: 1925–45* (Ithaca, N.Y.: Cornell University Press, 1982), pp. 81–82.

15 Nguyen Trian celebrated the victory with this poem:

> *Henceforth our country is safe.*
> *Our mountains and rivers begin life afresh.*
> *Peace follows war as day follows night.*
> *We have purged our shame for a thousand centuries,*
> *We have regained tranquillity for ten thousand generations.*

Stanley Karnow, *Vietnam: A History* (New York: Viking Press, 1983), p. 104.

16 Khanh, *Vietnamese Communism,* p. 82.

17 Robert T. Oliver, *Syngman Rhee* (New York: Dodd, Mead, 1954), pp. 138–39. The 1919 uprising was ruthlessly suppressed by Japanese colonial administrators; 7,500 Koreans were killed. Jon Halliday, *A Political History of Japanese Capitalism* (New York: Pantheon Books, 1975), p. 94. The *mansei* demonstrations, moreover, preceded Gandhi's non-violent campaign in India by a year. Choy, *Korean Reunification Movement,* pp. 30–31.

18 Khanh, *Vietnamese Communism,* pp. 100–1.

19 Catherine B. Shannon, *Arthur J. Balfour and Ireland, 1874–1922* (Washington, D.C.: Catholic University of America Press, 1988), pp. 167–68.

20 Anderson, "Narrating the Nation." Anderson also notes that the name Vietnam was invented by a scornful nineteenth-century Manchu dynast. It means land to the south of China, "a realm conquered by the Han . . . and reputed to cover today's Chinese provinces of Kwangtung and Kwangsi, as well as the Red River valley." *Imagined Communities,* pp. 143–44.

21 Walter Benjamin wrote of the Angel of History: "His face is turned towards the past. Where we perceive a chain of events, he sees one single catastrophe which keeps piling wreckage upon wreckage and hurls it in front of his feet. The angel would like to stay, awaken the dead, and make whole what has been smashed. But a storm is blowing from Paradise; it has got caught in his wings with such violence that the angel can no longer close them. This storm irresistibly propels him into the future to which his back is turned, while the pile of debris before him grows skyward. This storm is what we call progress." *Illuminations* (London: Fontana, 1973), p. 259.

22 Karl Marx, *The 18th Brumaire of Louis Bonaparte* (New York: International Publishers, 1963), p. 15.

23 Tim P. Coogan, *The I.R.A.* (New York: Praeger, 1970), p. 19.

24 Marx, *18th Brumaire,* p. 18.

25 George William Russell, *The living torch* (New York: Macmillan, 1938), p. 134.

26 Frank Ninkovich, *Germany and the United States* (Boston: Twayne, 1988), p. 25.

27 James Joll, *The Second International* (New York: Harper Colophon, 1966), p. 56.

28 This is not to say that leaders of independence movements did not organize in secret, apply strict membership tests, and impose an iron discipline on their members. Sinn Fein organizers advocated creation of a non-violent, public political party, with nominal membership restrictions. Yet, after he joined the public Sinn Fein, Eamon De Valera, who would become Ireland's first Prime Minister, discovered that a secret "oath-bound" brotherhood existed within the organization. The "physical force party" recruited him to join a covert, paramilitary apparatus composed of Sinn Fein members. Mary C. Bromage, *De Valera and the March of a Nation* (New York: Noonday Press, 1956), p. 38.

29 Pandey, *Breakup of British India*, p. 42.

30 Amos Perlmutter, *Israel: The Partitioned State* (New York: Charles Scribner's Sons, 1985), p. 21.

31 Among independence movements in the not-yet-divided states, only the Indian National Congress eschewed the use of force as a means to its ends, though for a brief time Gandhi helped organize some provincial militias and paramilitary defense organizations. He soon gave this up and attempted to organize a Peace Army designed to combat communal disorders, but this too failed to attract widespread support. See Coupland, *Indian Problem*, pp. 105–6. Parties of force did exist in India and in exile communities overseas. For example, the Ghadr Party, founded in San Francisco in 1913, attempted to send arms to India and organize a rebellion there in 1915. It failed miserably. Pandey, *Breakup of British India*, pp. 102–3.

The conspicuous absence of a military arm of the Indian National Congress is a testament to Gandhi's influence on Indian politics and his ability to disassociate the movement from violence by its supporters who, on a number of occasions, participated in riots against British rule. In a 1920 article, "The Doctrine of the Sword," Gandhi distinguished non-violent methods from the methods used by Irish revolutionaries against British rule: "I isolate this non-cooperation from Sinn Feinism, for it is so conceived as to be incapable of being offered side by side with violence. And I invite even the school of violence to give this peaceful non-cooperation a trial." Quoted in Jawaharlal Nehru, *Toward Freedom* (New York: John Day, 1942), p. 82. Aside from the Indian National Congress, which eschewed the use of force, all the other independence movements took up arms, though they did not do so as the only means to their ends. Syngman Rhee and other Korean nationalists organized non-violent demonstrations against Japanese colonial rule in 1919, a year or so before Gandhi introduced his first non-violent campaign in India, but they later took up arms during World War II. The Indian National Congress is the only movement to abstain from the use of force during peace *and* war.

The Muslim League turned to the use of force in 1946, when it organized a "Direct Action Day" to convince British authorities that they were determined to secure a separate Moslem state in Pakistan. This led to massive rioting in Calcutta, in which 5,000 died. But the League relied in this instance on extracurricular violence from which it could disassociate itself. Tariq Ali, *Can Pakistan Survive?* (London: New Left Books, 1983), p. 34; Pandey, *Breakup of British India*, p. 184.

32 Perlmutter, *Israel*, pp. 84–85; William Quandt, F. Jabber, and A. Mosley, *The Politics of Palestinian Nationalism* (Berkeley: University of California Press, 1973), pp. 32–33; Bromage, *De Valera*, p. 51; McCaffrey, *Irish Question*, p. 156.

33 As John King Fairbank says, "Mao's guerrilla style had ancient roots. The Sun-tzu says, 'By discovering the enemy's disposition and remaining invisible ourselves, we can keep our forces concentrated while the enemy is divided. We can form a single

united body, while the enemy must be split into fractions.' " He then compares this to Mao's writing in 1936: "We can turn a big 'encirclement and suppression' campaign waged by the enemy against us into a number of small, separate campaigns of encirclement and suppression waged by us against the enemy. . . . We can use the few to defeat the many—this we say to the rulers of China as a whole." *The United States and China* (Cambridge, Mass.: Harvard University Press, 1983), p. 286.

34 Jean Fritz, *China's Long March: 6,000 Miles of Danger* (New York: G. P. Putnam's Sons, 1988), p. 55.

35 Jean Lacouture, *Ho Chi Minh* (New York: Random House, 1968), p. 92.

36 Michael J. Cohen notes, "As a people without a territory who sought to return to their ancient homeland, now occupied by an Arab majority and still in 1917 under Turkish suzerainty, the Jews had since 1897 avoided the demand for a Jewish state. In 1917 the use of the euphemism 'Jewish national home' compromised the Zionist cause. The very term was unknown in international usage and was therefore open to different interpretations according to one's persuasion." *The Origins and Evolution of the Arab-Zionist Conflict* (Berkeley: University of California Press, 1987), pp. 54–55.

37 Perlmutter, *Israel*, pp. 67–68.

38 Joll, *Second International*, p. 22.

3. Self-Determination

1 Richard W. Van Alstyne, "Woodrow Wilson and the Idea of the Nation State," *International Affairs* 37, no. 3 (July 1961): 307. Van Alstyne argues, "It is a remarkable fact—one, I think, of tremendous historical significance—that the concept of the 'New Diplomacy' emerged simultaneously from Washington and Petrograd. Although only dimly realized at that time, the U.S.A. and the U.S.S.R. were already rivals in 1918. Wilson and Lenin are the prophets of the new international order. Each in his own way, but in fulfilment of the peculiar mission of his respective nation, struck a mortal blow at the classical system of nation States. Lenin conspired to extirpate the nation State and erect a wholly new type of society resting on the Communist revolution. Wilson was a Christian crusader, the author of a creed for a vague new international order wherein America would interpret the rules and the other nations merely signify their assent." Ibid. In the main, Van Alstyne is right, except that their shared perspective made them partners, not rivals. See also Geoffrey Barraclough, *An Introduction to Contemporary History* (New York: Penguin Books, 1967), pp. 118–19; Rudolph Von Albertini, *Decolonization* (Garden City, N.Y.: Doubleday, 1971), p. 8; Paul Kennedy, *The Rise and Fall of the Great Powers* (New York: Random House, 1987), p. 287; Gordon Levin, Jr., *Woodrow Wilson and World Politics* (New York: Oxford University Press, 1968), p. 1.

2 W. Ofuatey-Kodjoe, *The Principle of Self-Determination in International Law* (New York: Nellen Publishing, 1977), p. 79.

3 Jean-Baptiste Duroselle, *From Wilson to Roosevelt: Foreign Policy of the United States* (New York: Harper & Row, 1963), p. 37.

4 Ibid., p. 75.

5 V. I. Lenin, *National Liberation, Socialism and Imperialism* (New York: International Publishers, 1968), p. 80; Ofuatey-Kodjoe, *Self-Determination*, pp. 198–99.

6 See the collection of Lenin's essays on the subject in *National Liberation*.

7 Lee Burcheit, *Secession: The Legitimacy of Self-Determination* (New Haven: Yale University Press, 1978), pp. 115, 114; David Cronon, *The Political Thought of Woodrow Wilson* (New York: Bobbs-Merrill, 1965), p. 455.

8 Lenin, *National Liberation*, pp. 113, 47.

9 Branko Lazitch and M. Drachkovitch, *Lenin and the Comintern* (Stanford: Hoover

Institution Press, 1972), p. 369. Lenin's lieutenant Joseph Stalin argued that the "right of self-determination means that a nation can arrange its life according to its own will. It has the right to arrange its life on the basis of autonomy. It has the right to enter into federal relations with other nations. It has the right to complete secession. Nations are sovereign and all nations must be equal." *Marxism and the National Question* (New York: International Publishers, 1972), p. 23. And the modern Soviet constitution provides in Article 17 that "the right to secede from the U.S.S.R. is reserved to every union republic." Burcheit, *Secession*, p. 100.

10 Cronon, *Political Thought of Woodrow Wilson*, p. 455.

11 Burcheit, *Secession*, pp. 65–66.

12 Ibid., p. 115.

13 Lenin, *National Liberation*, p. 72.

14 Neil Harding, *Lenin's Political Thought* (London: Macmillan, 1983), pp. 65–66; Burcheit, *Secession*, pp. 118–19.

15 Alfred Cobban, *The Nation State and National Self-Determination* (New York: Thomas Crowell, 1970), p. 76.

16 Phillip Darby, *Three Faces of Imperialism* (New Haven: Yale University Press, 1987), p. 169.

17 He went on to say, "[It would be absurd] to imagine that it has made a number of brilliant discoveries and has introduced a heap of socialist innovations. I have not heard anybody make this claim, and I assert that we shall not hear anybody make it. We acquired practical experience in taking the first step towards destroying capitalism in a country where specific relations exist between the proletariat and the peasants. Nothing more." Harding, *Lenin's Political Thought*, p. 236.

18 Ibid., pp. 241, 329.

19 Franz B. Gross, *The United States and the United Nations* (Norman: University of Oklahoma Press, 1964), p. 46.

20 Lenin, *National Liberation*, p. 114.

21 Neil MacFarlane, *Superpower Rivalry and Third World Radicalism: The Idea of National Liberation* (Baltimore: Johns Hopkins University Press, 1985), p. 30.

22 Lazitch and Drachkovitch, *Lenin and the Comintern*, p. 53.

23 The Comintern's World Congress was supposed to meet annually. But after meeting five times in its first six years, it met only twice more during its next eighteen. Gunter Nollau, *International Communism and World Revolution* (New York: Praeger, 1961), pp. 53–54. See also Fernando Claudin, *The Communist Movement: From Comintern to Cominform* (Harmondsworth, England: Penguin, 1975), p. 18.

24 The Bolsheviks argued, "The Soviet power considers diplomatic relations necessary not only with governments, but also with revolutionary socialist parties seeking the overthrow of existing governments." Lazitch and Drachkovitch, *Lenin and the Comintern*, p. 30. Not surprisingly, few existing governments were willing to extend recognition to the Soviet government on this basis. The League of Nations refused admission to the Soviet Union until 1933, the same year the United States recognized the Soviet Union.

25 Duroselle, *From Wilson to Roosevelt*, pp. 121–22.

26 Nollau, *International Communism*, pp. 38, 51.

27 Hashim S. H. Behbahani, *The Soviet Union and Arab Nationalism, 1917–1966* (London: KPI, 1986), pp. 17–18.

28 Nollau, *International Communism*, p. 58.

29 Arthur Walworth, *Wilson and His Peacemakers* (New York: W. W. Norton, 1986), p. 63.

30 R. F. Holland, *European Decolonization, 1918–1981* (New York: St. Martin's Press, 1985), p. 1.

31 J. N. Saxena, *Self-Determination: From Biafra to Bangladesh* (Delhi: University of Delhi Press, 1978), p. 10; Burcheit, *Secession*, pp. 71–72.

32 Nollau, *International Communism*, p. 70.

33 Duroselle, *From Wilson to Roosevelt*, p. 137.

34 Nollau, *International Communism*, p. 89; Isaac Deutscher, *Stalin* (New York: Oxford University Press, 1969), p. 392.

35 Nollau, *International Communism*, p. 94.

36 Ibid., pp. 78–79.

37 Claudin, *Communist Movement*, p. 254.

4. Dominion and Union

1 Edward Grierson, *The Death of the Imperial Dream* (New York: Doubleday, 1972), p. 274.

2 Lord Curzon remarked that it was amazing that this architecture held together at all: "An Empire like our own, which has overrun the world, which embraces hundreds of races and scores of States, many of which were claiming, and rightly, to be counted as nations themselves—that such an Empire should voluntarily hold together when there is no force to compel it to do so, when the forces that are working in the direction of separation are so strong, when separation itself is so easy—will be an unparalleled and magnificent achievement." He did not mention, of course, the unifying role of the Royal Navy, or that of British manufactures and the imperial bureaucracy, of which he was part. Rudolf Von Albertini, *Decolonization* (Garden City, N.Y.: Doubleday, 1971), pp. 35–36.

3 U.S. public opinion was sharply critical of British colonial policy, especially in the wake of the 1916 Easter Rebellion. Lloyd George, then Minister of Munitions in the Asquith cabinet, warned his colleagues in 1916, "The Irish American vote will go over to the German side, the Americans will break our blockade, and force an ignominious peace on us, unless something is done even provisionally to satisfy America [on the Irish Question]." Catherine B. Shannon, *Arthur J. Balfour and Ireland, 1874–1922* (Washington, D.C.: Catholic University of America Press, 1988), p. 216.

4 Balfour continued: "I would add that progress in this policy can only be achieved by successive stages. The British Government and the Government of India . . . must be the judges of the time and measure of each advance, and they must be guided by the cooperation received from those upon whom new opportunities of service will thus be conferred and by the extent to which it is found that confidence can be reposed in their sense of responsibility." Reginald Coupland, *The Indian Problem* (London: Oxford University Press, 1944), vol. 1, pp. 52–53.

5 Michael J. Cohen, *The Origins and Evolution of the Arab-Zionist Conflict* (Berkeley: University of California Press, 1987), pp. 143–44.

6 Robert M. Dawson, *The Development of Dominion Status* (London: Frank Cass, 1965), p. 35.

7 Albertini, *Decolonization*, p. 54.

8 Grierson, *Imperial Dream*, p. 251.

9 Oscar Janowsky, *Nationalities and National Minorities* (New York: Macmillan, 1945), p. 10.

10 Alfred Cobban, *The Nation State and National Self-Determination* (New York: Thomas Crowell, 1970), p. 87.

11 Southern Rhodesia was granted "responsible" government in 1923, but it was a spin-off of white settler rule in South Africa. Albertini, *Decolonization*, p. 78.

12 Ibid., p. 55.

13 Ibid.

14 Ibid., p. 85.

15 Blanche E. C. Dugdale, *Arthur James Balfour* (New York: G. P. Putnam's Sons, 1937), p. 280.

16 Even the British Labour Party, which in 1918 denounced "the Imperialism that seeks to dominate other races or to impose our will on other parts of the British Empire," did not advocate independence or self-determination. Rather, it said, "The Labour Party stands for [the British Empire's] maintenance and progressive development on the lines of local autonomy and Home Rule All Round; the fullest respect for the rights of each people, whatever its colour, to all the democratic Self-Government to which it is capable." Albertini, *Decolonization*, p. 116.

17 Coupland, *Indian Problem*, p. 26.

18 Ibid., p. 81.

19 Ibid., p. 132.

20 Ibid., pp. 143–46.

21 Grierson, *Imperial Dream*, p. 234.

22 Albertini, *Decolonization*, p. 74.

23 Ibid., p. 266; see also pp. 277–78.

24 Ibid., p. 372.

25 Bruce D. Marshall, *The French Colonial Myth* (New Haven: Yale University Press, 1973), p. 7.

26 Ibid., p. 102.

27 W. Ofuatey-Kodjoe, *The Principle of Self-Determination in International Law* (New York: Nellen Publishing, 1977), p. 132.

28 Albertini, *Decolonization*, p. 392.

29 Marshall, *French Colonial Myth*, pp. 210–11.

30 Jon Halliday, *A Political History of Japanese Capitalism* (New York: Pantheon Books, 1975), p. 141.

31 John Dower, *War Without Mercy* (New York: Pantheon Books, 1986), p. 8.

32 Ibid., pp. 280–81.

33 Ibid., pp. 279, 203, 226.

34 Ibid., p. 277.

35 Halliday, *Japanese Capitalism*, pp. 147–48.

36 Ibid., p. 149.

37 Ibid., pp. 158–59. "In these countries," Halliday argues, "the Japanese behaved very much like the European imperialists." Ibid., p. 152.

38 Much the same was true in Europe. The combined American, British, and French forces in the Western European theater faced some 50 German divisions, while the Soviets faced some 200 German, Eastern European, and Italian divisions.

39 See Alan S. Milward, *War, Economy and Society, 1939–1945* (Berkeley: University of California Press, 1977); Alan S. Milward, *The New Order and the French Economy* (Oxford: Clarendon Press, 1970).

5. A New Interstate System

1 Richard M. Nixon, *RN: The Memoirs of Richard Nixon* (New York: Warner Books, 1978), p. 461.

2 Roger W. Louis, *Imperialism at Bay* (New York: Oxford University Press, 1978), p. 200.

3 Edward Grierson, *The Death of the Imperial Dream* (New York: Doubleday, 1972), p. 252.

4 Malcolm Chalmers, *Paying for Defense* (London: Pluto Press, 1985), p. 37.

5 Paul Kennedy, *The Rise and Fall of the Great Powers* (New York: Random House,

1987), p. 366; Fred L. Block, *The Origins of International Economic Disorder* (Berkeley: University of California Press, 1977), p. 62.

6 Block, *International Economic Disorder*, p. 64.

7 Kennedy, *Rise and Fall*, p. 358.

8 Walter LaFeber, *America, Russia and the Cold War, 1945–85* (New York: Alfred A. Knopf, 1985), p. 18.

9 Robert Divine, *Roosevelt and World War II* (Baltimore: Johns Hopkins University Press, 1969), pp. 54, 55.

10 Louis, *Imperialism at Bay*, pp. 226, 121. Roosevelt once told Churchill that "the British would take land anywhere in the world, even if it were only a rock or a sand bar." Ibid., p. 26. Naturally, this attitude infuriated Churchill.

11 Ibid., pp. 154–55.

12 Ibid., p. 284.

13 Ibid., p. 28; John Foster Dulles and Gerald Ridinger, "The Anti-Colonial Policies of F.D.R.," *Political Science Quarterly* 70 (March 1955): 10.

14 Louis, *Imperialism at Bay*, p. 356.

15 Bruce D. Marshall, *The French Colonial Myth* (New Haven: Yale University Press, 1973), p. 182.

16 I. Brownlie, "An Essay in the History of the Principle of Self-Determination," in *Grotian Society Papers 1968*, ed. C. H. Alexandrowicz (The Hague: Martinus Nijhoff, 1970), p. 97.

17 Franz B. Gross, *The United States and the United Nations* (Norman: University of Oklahoma Press, 1964), p. 30.

18 Brownlie, "Self-Determination," p. 98; Marshall, *French Colonial Myth*, p. 182.

19 R. F. Holland, *European Decolonization, 1918–1981* (New York: St. Martin's Press, 1985), p. 53.

20 Louis, *Imperialism at Bay*, p. 458. During this outburst, Stalin got up from the table and walked around the room, smiling.

21 Ibid., p. 148.

22 Ralph B. Clough, *Embattled Korea* (Boulder, Colo.: Westview Press, 1987), p. 3.

23 "[Secretary of State] Sumner Welles later described Roosevelt's faith in plebiscites as one example of the President's tendency to rely 'upon a few favorite panaceas for problems that were actually too basic and far-reaching in their origins and nature to admit of any easy solutions.' " John L. Gaddis, *The United States and the Origins of the Cold War* (New York: Columbia University Press, 1972), p. 12.

24 Divine, *Roosevelt and World War II*, p. 52; Diane S. Clemens, *Yalta* (London: Oxford University Press, 1970), p. 53.

25 It could be argued that Stalin had a point: the Soviet constitution did permit its constituent republics the right to secede, whereas the forty-eight American states could not, by virtue of the decision reached by the Civil War.

26 Richard Fenno, *The Yalta Conference* (Boston: D. C. Heath, 1955), pp. 12–13.

27 Divine, *Roosevelt and World War II*, p. 62.

28 Clemens, *Yalta*, p. 48.

29 Ibid., p. 130.

30 LaFeber, *Cold War*, p. 22.

31 Kennedy, *Rise and Fall*, p. 389.

32 Chalmers, *Paying for Defense*, p. 43.

33 LaFeber, *Cold War*, p. 70.

34 The global system of time and space is another example of an egalitarian hierarchy. See Robert Schaeffer, "The Standardization of Time and Space: Longitude and the Greenwich Meridian," in *Ascent and Decline in the World-System*, ed. Edward Friedman (Beverly Hills: Sage, 1982), pp. 69–90.

6. The British Balancing Act

1 Catherine B. Shannon, *Arthur J. Balfour and Ireland, 1874–1922* (Washington, D.C.: Catholic University of America Press, 1988), p. 19. Salisbury was Arthur J. Balfour's uncle and mentor.

2 Ibid., p. 182.

3 Ibid., p. 243.

4 Ibid., p. 261.

5 Reginald Coupland, *The Indian Problem* (London: Oxford University Press, 1944), vol. 1, pp. 52–53.

6 M. J. Akbar, *India: The Siege Within* (New York: Penguin, 1985), p. 27.

7 B. N. Pandey, *The Breakup of British India* (New York: St. Martin's Press, 1969), p. 160. As Gandhi said in 1940, "The Congress claims for itself the right to protect civil liberty in this country, but must have the right to state freely what we feel about the war. . . . I claim the liberty of going through the streets of Bombay saying that I shall have nothing to do with this war, because I do not believe in this war and in the fratricide that is going on in Europe." Coupland, *Indian Problem*, p. 247.

8 Pandey, *Breakup of British India*, p. 166.

9 Coupland, *Indian Problem*, p. 206.

10 Pandey, *Breakup of British India*, p. 167.

11 Ibid., p. 183.

12 H. V. Hodson, *The Great Divide* (Oxford: Oxford University Press, 1985), p. 166.

13 Ibid. "If the Muslims gave the provocation and started the holocaust, they were certainly its worst victims, for they were a minority in the city. . . . The police were inadequate and not wholly reliable." Ibid., pp. 166–67.

14 Michael J. Cohen, *The Origins and Evolution of the Arab-Zionist Conflict* (Berkeley: University of California Press, 1987), pp. 90–93.

15 Amos Perlmutter, *Israel: The Partitioned State* (New York: Charles Scribner's Sons, 1985), pp. 82–83.

16 Ibid., p. 55.

17 R. F. Holland, *European Decolonization, 1918–1981* (New York: St. Martin's Press, 1985), p. 114.

18 Michael J. Cohen, *Palestine and the Great Powers, 1945–48* (Princeton: Princeton University Press, 1982), pp. 9, 11.

19 William R. Louis, *The British Empire in the Middle East* (Oxford: Clarendon Press, 1984), p. 383.

20 Shannon, *Balfour and Ireland*, p. 215.

21 Ibid., p. 216.

22 Ibid., p. 226.

23 Ibid., p. 227.

24 Ibid., p. 232.

25 Ibid., p. 228.

26 Pandey, *Breakup of British India*, pp. 161, 165.

27 Holland, *European Decolonization*, p. 281.

28 Shannon, *Balfour and Ireland*, p. 232.

29 As colonial secretary, Churchill played an important role in drafting these promises and he wrote the official explanation of the second Balfour Declaration. Louis, *Middle East*, p. 385.

30 Tom Nairn, *The Break-up of Britain* (London: New Left Books, 1977), p. 223.

31 Pandey, *Breakup of British India*, pp. 157–58.

32 Coupland, *Indian Problem*, pp. 336–37.

7. "Divide and Quit"

1 Catherine B. Shannon, *Arthur J. Balfour and Ireland, 1874–1922* (Washington, D.C.: Catholic University of America Press, 1988), pp. 65, 178.

2 Reginald Coupland, *The Indian Problem* (London: Oxford University Press, 1944), vol. 1, p. 244.

3 Michael J. Cohen, *The Origins and Evolution of the Arab-Zionist Conflict* (Berkeley: University of California Press, 1987), p. 154.

4 Coupland, *Indian Problem* p. 201. And Jinnah said that democracy based on majority rule could not work in India. Ibid., p. 310.

5 Mary C. Bromage, *Churchill and Ireland* (Notre Dame, Ind.: University of Notre Dame Press, 1964), p. 42.

6 Nicholas Mansergh, *The Irish Question, 1840–1921* (London: George Allen and Unwin, 1975), p. 229.

7 M. J. Akbar, *India: The Siege Within* (New York: Penguin, 1985), p. 25.

8 William J. Barnds, *India, Pakistan and the Great Powers* (New York: Praeger, 1972), p. 16; B. N. Pandey, *The Breakup of British India* (New York: St. Martin's Press, 1969), p. 47.

9 Akbar, *India*, p. 35.

10 As the historian B. N. Pandey notes, "The British Raj was not the originator of communalism. But it did nourish Muslim separatism as a useful ally against Congress nationalism. . . . British policy made Pakistan feasible and Congress, by lacking a definite policy towards the League, made it attainable." *Breakup of British India*, pp. 215–16.

11 Shannon, *Balfour and Ireland*, p. 176.

12 Ibid., p. 286.

13 Ibid., p. 206.

14 Ibid., p. 254.

15 John Bowman, *De Valera and the Ulster Question* (Oxford: Clarendon Press, 1982), p. 40.

16 Pandey, *Breakup of British India*, p. 198.

17 H. V. Hodson, *The Great Divide* (Oxford: Oxford University Press, 1985), pp. 367–68.

18 Pandey, *Breakup of British India*, p. 177.

19 At a cabinet meeting in which British officials discussed what the imposition of full-scale martial law would mean, General Neville MacCready said that one hundred rebels would be shot the first week. Shannon, *Balfour and Ireland*, p. 274.

20 Michael Farrell, *Northern Ireland: The Orange State* (London: Pluto Press, 1980), p. 47.

21 Coupland, *Indian Problem*, p. 121.

22 Akbar, *India*, p. 20.

23 C. H. Philips and M. D. Wainwright, *The Partition of India* (Cambridge, Mass.: MIT Press, 1970), p. 209.

24 Ibid.

25 Ibid., p. 210.

26 Coupland, *Indian Problem*, vol. 2, p. 298.

27 R. F. Holland, *European Decolonization, 1918–1981* (New York: St. Martin's Press, 1985), p. 75.

28 Philips and Wainwright, *Partition of India*, p. 219. Nehru indicated, however, that he had reached this conclusion earlier, in 1944.

29 Ibid., p. 20.

30 A. Jeyartnam Wilson and D. Dalton, *The States of South Asia* (Honolulu: University of Hawaii Press, 1982), p. 51. Other leaders agreed. "V. P. Menon urged [Nehru] to accept quick partition in order to avert the further spread of communal bitterness and to prepare for later reunification." Ibid.

31 Philips and Wainwright, *Partition of India*, p. 220.

32 Amos Perlmutter, *Israel: The Partitioned State* (New York: Charles Scribner's Sons, 1985), p. 56.

33 Ibid., p. 70.

34 Ibid.

35 Ibid., pp. 58–73. The day after the United Nations approved partition in Palestine, Dr. Magnes predicted, "It looks like trouble." Walter Laqueur, *A History of Zionism* (New York: Schocken Books, 1976), p. 582.

36 Ibid., p. 546.

37 Perlmutter, *Israel*, p. 111.

38 Cohen, *Arab-Zionist Conflict*, p. 160.

39 J. C. Hurewitz, *The Struggle for Palestine* (New York: Schocken Books, 1976), p. 245.

40 Ritchie Ovendale, *The Origins of the Arab-Israeli Wars* (London: Longman Group, 1984), p. 97; Laqueur, *History of Zionism*, p. 573.

41 Laqueur, *History of Zionism*, pp. 577–78.

42 Ibid., p. 577. The British government did not recommend to the United Nations either the conclusions of the Peel Commission or the White Paper or the Anglo-American Commission, because it was of two minds about partition.

43 Holland, *European Decolonization*, p. 120.

44 Hurewitz, *Struggle for Palestine*, p. 296.

45 Compare the 1937 Peel partition plan (Cohen, *Arab-Zionist Conflict*, p. 94) with the UN plan (Hurewitz, *Struggle for Palestine*, p. 297).

46 William R. Louis, *The British Empire in the Middle East* (Oxford: Clarendon Press, 1984), p. 475. On August 9, 1947, *The Economist* had suggested, "In any situation of complete deadlock, the only hope is to introduce a completely new factor—a catalyst—such as was found in India [and for that matter Ireland] when the Government announced a date for the transfer of power. If the policy of catalyst worked there, could it not work in Palestine?" Ibid., p. 476.

47 Holland, *European Decolonization*, p. 118.

48 Cohen, *Arab-Zionist Conflict*, pp. 126–27. See also Louis, *Middle East*, p. 387.

49 Gromyko said this on April 18, 1948, after the UN vote but before partition went into effect. Hashim S. H. Behbahani, *The Soviet Union and Arab Nationalism, 1917–1966* (London: KPI, 1986), pp. 58–59.

50 Laqueur, *History of Zionism*, p. 586; Avi Shlaim, *Collusion Across the Jordan* (New York: Columbia University Press, 1988), p. 386.

51 Holland, *European Decolonization*, p. 113.

52 Barnds, *Great Powers*, pp. 38–43.

53 Ovendale, *Arab-Israeli Wars*, p. 123.

8. Cold War Partition

1 See Audrey Kurth Cronin, *Great Power Politics and the Struggle over Austria, 1945–1955* (Ithaca, N.Y.: Cornell University Press, 1986).

2 Walter LaFeber, *America, Russia and the Cold War, 1945–85* (New York: Alfred A. Knopf, 1985), p. 13.

3 John L. Gaddis, *The United States and the Origins of the Cold War* (New York: Columbia University Press, 1972), p. 100.

4 Gabriel Kolko, *The Politics of War* (New York: Vintage, 1968), p. 316.

5 Bruce Kuklick, *American Policy and the Division of Germany* (Ithaca, N.Y.: Cornell University Press, 1972), p. 25.

6 Kolko, *Politics of War*, p. 316; Kuklick, *Division of Germany*, p. 25.

7 Truman would later claim that he always wanted "a unified Germany with a centralized government in Berlin." John L. Snell, *Dilemma over Germany* (New Orleans: Phauser Press, 1959), p. 200.

8 Ibid., p. 49.

9 Kuklick, *Division of Germany*, p. 30; Snell, *Dilemma over Germany*, pp. 125, 142.

10 Snell, *Dilemma over Germany*, p. 109.

11 Ibid., p. 55.

12 Ibid., pp. 75–76.

13 Ibid., p. 79. Morgenthau told White during their deliberation, "I don't care what happens to the population. . . . I would take every mine, every mill and factory and wreck it. . . . Steel, coal, everything. Just close it down." Gaddis, *Origins of the Cold War*, p. 120.

14 Gaddis, *Origins of the Cold War*, p. 119.

15 Ibid., p. 120.

16 Kuklick, *Division of Germany*, pp. 22–23, 69.

17 Gaddis, *Origins of the Cold War*, p. 236.

18 Bong-youn Choy, *A History of the Korean Reunification Movement* (Peoria, Ill.: Institute of International Studies, Bradley University, 1984), p. 10.

19 Ibid.; see also Joyce and Gabriel Kolko, *The Limits of Power* (New York: Harper & Row, 1972), p. 278.

20 Peter Lowe, *The Origins of the Korean War* (London: Longman, 1986), p. 14; James I. Matray, "Captive of the Cold War: Decision to Divide Korea at the 38th Parallel," *Pacific Historical Review* 5, no. 2 (May 1981): 164; John Sullivan, *Two Koreas—One Future?* (Lanham, Md.: University of America Press, 1987), p. 7; Choy, *Korean Reunification Movement*, p. 12.

21 Coincidentally, Russia and Japan had twice discussed dividing Korea at the 38th parallel, first in 1896 and again in 1903. Choy, *Korean Reunification Movement*, p. 13.

22 Matray, "Captive of the Cold War," p. 166.

23 Lowe, *Origins of the Korean War*, pp. 90–91; LaFeber, *Cold War*, p. 107.

24 John T. McAlister, *Vietnam* (New York: Alfred A. Knopf, 1970), p. 275.

25 LaFeber, *Cold War*, p. 107; Andrew J. Rotter, *The Path to Vietnam* (Ithaca, N.Y.: Cornell University Press, 1987), p. 93.

26 Stanley Karnow, *Vietnam: A History* (New York: Viking Press, 1983), p. 137.

27 Ibid., p. 147.

28 Ibid., p. 152.

29 John King Fairbank, *The United States and China* (Cambridge, Mass.: Harvard University Press, 1983), pp. 341–42.

30 LaFeber, *Cold War*, pp. 30–31.

31 Kolko, *Limits of Power*, p. 255; Lowe, *Origins of the Korean War*, pp. 99–100.

32 Kolko, *Limits of Power*, p. 255.

33 Frank Ninkovich, *Germany and the United States* (Boston: Twayne, 1988), p. 58.

34 Snell, *Dilemma over Germany*, p. 227.

35 LaFeber, *Cold War*, p. 75.

36 Ninkovich, *Germany and the United States*, p. 60.

37 Snell, *Dilemma over Germany*, p. 224.

38 Ninkovich, *Germany and the United States*, p. 60.

39 Ibid., pp. 43, 62.

40 Ibid., p. 69.

41 John L. Gaddis, *The Long Peace* (New York: Oxford University Press, 1987), p. 64.

42 Ibid.

43 Ninkovich, *Germany and the United States*, p. 71.

44 Ibid., p. 72; Henry Ashby Turner, Jr., *The Two Germanies Since 1945* (New Haven: Yale University Press, 1987), p. 50.

45 Gaddis, *Long Peace*, p. 54.

46 Ibid., p. 55.

47 Ibid., p. 62.

48 Lawrence S. Kaplan, *NATO and the United States* (Boston: Twayne, 1988), pp. 17–30, 33.

49 LaFeber, *Cold War*, p. 83.

50 Ibid.

51 Rotter, *Path to Vietnam*, p. 99.

52 LaFeber, *Cold War*, p. 84.

53 Rotter, *Path to Vietnam*, pp. 14–15; see also Kaplan, *NATO*, p. 33.

54 LaFeber, *Cold War*, pp. 69, 70.

55 See Kolko, *Limits of Power*, pp. 33, 56; Ralph B. Clough, *Embattled Korea* (Boulder, Colo.: Westview Press, 1987), p. 20; Turner, *Two Germanies*, p. 36.

56 Choy, *Korean Reunification Movement*, pp. 41–42.

57 Ibid., p. 45.

58 Ibid., pp. 46–48.

59 Ibid., p. 49.

60 Ibid., pp. 50–51.

61 Ibid., p. 52.

62 Ibid., pp. 52, 54.

63 Ibid., p. 55.

64 Bruce Cumings, *The Origins of the Korean War* (Princeton: Princeton University Press, 1981), p. 211; Lowe, *Origins of the Korean War*, p. 35.

65 Lowe, *Origins of the Korean War*, pp. 48, 49; Bruce Cumings, *Child of Conflict: The Korean-American Relationship* (Seattle: University of Washington Press, 1983), p. 189. The initial decision to withdraw was made in the fall of 1947, when the U.S. asked the UN to supervise the devolution process. Gaddis, *Long Peace*, p. 94.

66 Clough, *Embattled Korea*, p. 20; Gaddis, *Long Peace*, p. 94.

67 Robert Blum, *Drawing the Line* (New York: W. W. Norton, 1982), p. 71.

68 Seymour Topping, *Journey Between Two Chinas* (New York: Harper Colophon, 1972), p. 54; Roy Medvedev, *China and the Superpowers* (London: Basil Blackwell, 1986), p. 90.

69 Lowe, *Origins of the Korean War*, p. 114.

70 Topping, *Journey Between Two Chinas*, p. 53.

71 Lowe, *Origins of the Korean War*, p. 108.

72 Gaddis, *Long Peace*, p. 81. George Kennan, for instance, argued that "Formosan separatism is the only concept which has sufficient grassroots appeal to resist communism." Ibid. And Secretary of State Dean Acheson hoped to satisfy "the legitimate demands of indigenous Formosans for self-determination either under a U.N. trusteeship or through independence." Cumings, *Child of Conflict*, p. 47. But these schemes foundered because the Kuomintang was strong, Taiwanese independence movements weak, and the U.S. had already agreed to return Taiwan to China. A State Department memo warned that an attempt to detach the island "would outrage *all* Chinese elements and as a resort to naked expediency would destroy our standing with the smaller countries of the world [emphasis added]." Gaddis, *Long Peace*, p. 83.

73 Medvedev, *China and the Superpowers*, p. 21.

74 The Soviet historian Roy Medvedev observes: "No personal letter to Mao Zedong . . . came from Stalin . . . whose silence was all the more unusual in that only ten days later, on the occasion of the proclamation of the German Democratic Republic, he would send a long personal letter to the first President of the GDR, Wilhelm Pieck, and to the Prime Minister, Otto Grotewohl." Ibid.

75 Gaddis, *Long Peace*, p. 78.

76 June M. Grasso, *Truman's Two-China Policy* (Armonk, N.Y.: M. E. Sharpe, 1987), p. 113.

77 Lloyd C. Gardner, *Approaching Vietnam* (New York: W. W. Norton, 1988), p. 62.

78 Karnow, *Vietnam*, p. 152.

79 Blum, *Drawing the Line*, p. 106.

80 Gardner, *Approaching Vietnam*, p. 75.

81 Blum, *Drawing the Line*, p. 107. Bao Dai was a notorious playboy. Following his return to Vietnam, the Emperor took up with a blonde who was supposedly part of a documentary film crew. When officials told him they doubted she could use a camera and was merely masquerading as part of the crew, Bao Dai replied, "Yes, I know. But really that girl is quite extraordinary in bed." Then he added, "She is only plying her trade. Of the two I am the real whore." Rotter, *Path to Vietnam*, p. 95.

82 Rotter, *Path to Vietnam*, p. 96.

83 Ibid., p. 113.

84 Ibid., pp. 169–70.

85 Lowe, *Origins of the Korean War*, p. 119; Grasso, *Truman's Two-China Policy*, 127.

86 Lowe, *Origins of the Korean War*, p. 156; Ralph B. Levering, *The Cold War, 1945– 87* (Arlington Heights, Ill.: Harlan Davidson, 1988), p. 44.

87 LaFeber, *Cold War*, p. 103.

88 Melvin Gurtov and Byong-Moo Huang, *China Under Threat* (Baltimore: Johns Hopkins University Press, 1980), p. 54.

89 LaFeber, *Cold War*, p. 99.

90 Choy, *Korean Reunification Movement*, p. 61.

91 Ibid.; Kolko, *Limits of Power*, p. 568.

92 Choy, *Korean Reunification Movement*, p. 61.

93 Cumings, *Child of Conflict*, p. 187.

94 LaFeber, *Cold War*, p. 105.

95 Grasso, *Truman's Two-China Policy*, pp. 128, 141.

96 U.S. conservatives, who opposed the Truman Administration's policy of placing Korea and Taiwan outside the U.S. defensive perimeter in Asia, welcomed this policy change. Senator H. Alexander Smith said of Truman's action, "It was all very wonderful and an answer to prayer. The saving of Formosa was clearly God guided." Gaddis, *Long Peace*, p. 87.

97 Karnow, *Vietnam*, p. 177.

98 Rotter, *Path to Vietnam*, p. 104.

99 More than 50,000 Chinese troops assigned to the invasion-of-Taiwan army were moved north to the Korean frontier. Gurtov and Huang, *China Under Threat*, p. 49.

100 Eisenhower said that the "Seventh Fleet [should] no long[er] be employed to shield Communist China." Gardner, *Approaching Vietnam*, p. 129. This was a neat reversal. When Truman first sent the fleet into the straits, he did so to protect Taiwan from mainland attack and also to halt Kuomintang raids on the mainland, which had caused considerable damage. So to assuage congressional critics of the move, Eisenhower claimed he was removing the fleet so that it would no longer protect the mainland from Nationalist attack. But this was a thin charade.

101 Medvedev, *China and the Superpowers*, p. 85; Ilpyong Kim, *The Strategic Alliance* (New York: Paragon House, 1987), p. 185.

102 Medvedev, *China and the Superpowers*, p. 87.

103 Gaddis, *Long Peace*, p. 185.

104 Ibid.

105 Kim, *Strategic Alliance*, p. 196.

106 Gardner, *Approaching Vietnam*, p. 116.

107 Karnow, *Vietnam*, p. 191.

108 Gardner, *Approaching Vietnam*, p. 153.

109 R. F. Holland, *European Decolonization, 1918–1981* (New York: St. Martin's Press, 1985), p. 100; Gardner, *Approaching Vietnam*, p. 179.

110 Rotter, *Path to Vietnam*, p. 215.

111 Karnow, *Vietnam*, p. 202.

112 Gardner, *Approaching Vietnam*, p. 316.

113 Karnow, *Vietnam*, pp. 202, 201.

114 Ibid., pp. 202–4.

115 Ibid., p. 204.

116 Gardner, *Approaching Vietnam*, p. 284.

117 Ibid., p. 313.

118 Ibid., p. 281.

119 Topping, *Journey Between Two Chinas*, p. 151; Gardner, *Approaching Vietnam*, p. 298.

120 Malcolm Chalmers, *Paying for Defense* (London: Pluto Press, 1985), p. 83.

121 Gardner, *Approaching Vietnam*, p. 298.

122 Ibid., p. 340.

123 Gabriel Kolko, *The Roots of American Foreign Policy* (Boston: Beacon Press, 1969), p. 111; Topping, *Journey Between Two Chinas*, p. 151.

124 Rotter, *Path to Vietnam*, p. 180. As the historian Andrew Rotter notes, "A strong France [was] a prerequisite to an integrated Europe that included West Germany. The Americans pursued [this objective] . . . with increasing vigor in the spring of 1950, but it quickly became clear to them that this goal was incompatible with the continuation of the French military effort in Indochina." Ibid., p. 166.

125 Ibid., p. 217.

126 Ibid., p. 184.

127 Ibid., p. 211.

128 LaFeber, *Cold War*, p. 109.

129 Kaplan, *NATO*, p. 44.

130 Ninkovich, *Germany and the United States*, pp. 84–85.

131 Rotter, *Path to Vietnam*, pp. 218–19.

132 Gardner, *Approaching Vietnam*, p. 189.

9. Citizenship Diminished

1 A. Jeyartnam Wilson and D. Dalton, *The States of South Asia* (Honolulu: University of Hawaii Press, 1982), p. 20.

2 Gregory Henderson, R. N. Lebow, and J. G. Stroessinger, *Divided Nations in a Divided World* (New York: David McKay, 1974), p. 208; Sarah Nelson, *Ulster's Uncertain Defenders* (Syracuse, N.Y.: Syracuse University Press, 1984), p. 31.

3 John Sullivan, *Two Koreas—One Future?* (Lanham, Md.: University of America Press, 1987), p. 100; Henderson, Lebow, and Stroessinger, *Divided Nations*, pp. 60–61.

4 Henderson, Lebow, and Stroessinger, *Divided Nations*, p. 61.

5 Ibid., p. 100.

6 Ibid., p. 138.

7 Ibid., p. 28. See Frank Ninkovich, *Germany and the United States* (Boston: Twayne, 1988), p. 123; Henry Ashby Turner, Jr., *The Two Germanies Since 1945* (New Haven: Yale University Press, 1987), p. 130.

8 Ninkovich, *Germany and the United States*, p. 108.

9 Turner, *Two Germanies*, p. 130.

10 R. F. Holland, *European Decolonization, 1918–1981* (New York: St. Martin's Press, 1985), p. 80.

11 H. V. Hodson, *The Great Divide* (Oxford: Oxford University Press, 1985), p. 411.

12 Holland, *European Decolonization*, p. 80.

13 Hodson, *Great Divide*, p. 404.

14 Ibid.

15 Edward Said and Christopher Hitchens, *Blaming the Victims* (London: Verso, 1988), pp. 213, 236.

16 Ibid., p. 4; Holland, *European Decolonization*, p. 120; Benny Morris, *The Birth of the Palestinian Refugee Problem, 1947–1949* (Cambridge: Cambridge University Press, 1988), p. 8.

17 Morris, *Palestinian Refugee Problem*, pp. 297–98.

18 Milton J. Esman and Itamar Rabinovich, *Ethnicity, Pluralism and the State in the Middle East* (Ithaca, N.Y.: Cornell University Press, 1988), p. 97; J. C. Hurewitz, *The Struggle for Palestine* (New York: Schocken Books, 1976), p. 321; Said and Hitchens, *Blaming the Victims*, p. 266.

19 Said and Hitchens, *Blaming the Victims*, p. 74.

20 Quoted in ibid., p. 75.

21 Morris, *Palestinian Refugee Problem*, pp. 155–69.

22 Ibid., p. 141.

23 Ibid., p. 174.

24 Ibid., p. 240.

25 Ibid., p. 255.

26 Holland, *European Decolonization*, p. 121; Ritchie Ovendale, *The Origins of the Arab-Israeli Wars* (London: Longman Group, 1984), p. 124.

27 Said and Hitchens, *Blaming the Victims*, pp. 268, 252.

28 Ibid., p. 261.

29 Ibid.

30 Morris, *Palestinian Refugee Problem*, pp. 28, 280.

31 Michael Farrell, *Northern Ireland: The Orange State* (London: Pluto, 1980), p. 221.

32 Esman and Rabinovich, *Ethnicity, Pluralism and the State*, p. 27.

33 Werner Hulsberg, *The German Greens* (London: Verso, 1988), p. 19.

34 Ibid., pp. 20–21.

35 Henderson, Lebow, and Stroessinger, *Divided Nations*, p. 66.

36 Ibid., p. 64.

37 Ralph B. Clough, *Embattled Korea* (Boulder, Colo.: Westview Press, 1987), p. 33; Henderson, Lebow, and Stroessinger, *Divided Nations*, pp. 65–66.

38 Sullivan, *Two Koreas*, pp. 110–11.

39 Henderson, Lebow, and Stroessinger, *Divided Nations*, pp. 304–5.

40 *The New York Times*, October 3, 1988; *The Washington Post*, June 22, 1988.

41 Uri Davis, *Israel* (London: Zed Books, 1987), pp. 34–35.

42 Geoffrey Aronson, *Creating Facts* (Washington, D.C.: Institute for Palestine Studies, 1987), p. 12.

43 Sabri Jiryis, *The Arabs in Israel, 1948–1966* (Beirut: Institute for Palestine Studies, 1967), pp. 131, 133.

44 Ibid., pp. 133–34.

45 *The New York Times*, October 6, 1988.

46 Davis, *Israel*, p. 9.

47 Reported on the CBS Evening News, November 2, 1988.

48 Farrell, *Northern Ireland*, p. 83.

49 Ibid., p. 84.

50 Ibid., pp. 211–12.

51 Henderson, Lebow, and Stroessinger, *Divided Nations*, p. 212. See also Farrell, *Northern Ireland*, p. 84; Belinda Probert, *Beyond Orange and Green* (Dublin: Academy Press, 1978), p. 60.

52 Henderson, Lebow, and Stroessinger, *Divided Nations*, p. 211; Farrell, *Northern Ireland*, p. 85.

53 Farrell, *Northern Ireland*, p. 120.

54 Ibid., p. 145. Sinn Fein, the political wing of the illegal Irish Republican Army, ended a twenty-five-year electoral boycott in Northern Ireland in 1986. *Bangor* [Maine] *Daily News*, November 3, 1986.

55 Ninkovich, *Germany and the United States*, p. 113.

56 Thomas Omestad, "Dateline Taiwan: A Dynasty Ends," *Foreign Policy*, no. 71 (Summer 1988): 184.

57 Ibid., 179.

58 Selig S. Harrison, "Taiwan After Chiang Ching-kuo," *Foreign Affairs* 66, no. 4 (Spring 1988): 794.

59 Omestad, "Dateline Taiwan," 181.

60 Ibid., 185.

61 Ibid., 186.

62 Gabriel Kolko, *The Roots of American Foreign Policy* (Boston: Beacon Press, 1969), p. 112.

63 Henderson, Lebow, and Stroessinger, *Divided Nations*, p. 145.

64 Jiryis, *Arabs in Israel*, p. 2.

65 Ibid., pp. 7–9.

66 Ibid., p. 67.

67 Ibid., p. 15.

68 Farrell, *Northern Ireland*, p. 50.

69 Lynne Shivers and D. Bowman, *More Than the Troubles* (Philadelphia: New Society Publishers, 1984), p. 81.

70 Farrell, *Northern Ireland*, pp. 94–95.

71 Probert, *Beyond Orange and Green*, p. 126; Farrell, *Northern Ireland*, p. 96.

72 Douglas Mendel, *The Politics of Formosan Nationalism* (Berkeley: University of California Press, 1970), p. 46.

73 Tariq Ali, *Can Pakistan Survive?* (London: New Left Books, 1983), p. 45.

74 Henderson, Lebow, and Stroessinger, *Divided Nations*, p. 303. "Bengali was spoken by 56 percent of Pakistan's population, Punjabi by 37 percent, and the remainder spoke Pustu, Sindhi, Baluchi and Urdu." Ali, *Can Pakistan Survive?*, pp. 44–45.

75 Ali, *Can Pakistan Survive?*, p. 45.

76 Henderson, Lebow, and Stroessinger, *Divided Nations*, p. 303.

77 Ali, *Can Pakistan Survive?*, p. 47.

78 M. J. Akbar, *India: The Siege Within* (New York: Penguin, 1985), p. 44; Henderson, Lebow, and Stroessinger, *Divided Nations*, p. 303.

79 Ali, *Can Pakistan Survive?*, p. 42.

80 Akbar, *India*, p. 42.

81 *The New York Times*, August 10, 1986.

82 Ibid.

83 *The Washington Post,* October 17, 1988.
84 *The New York Times,* August 10, 1988.
85 Ibid.
86 Ibid.
87 *The New York Times,* November 11, 1988.
88 *The New York Times,* June 29, 1987.
89 Norman Zucker, *The Coming Crisis in Israel* (Cambridge, Mass.: MIT Press, 1973), pp. 79, 108.
90 Ibid., p. 108.
91 *The New York Times,* June 15, 1988.
92 *The New York Times,* November 8, 1988.
93 *The Village Voice,* May 2, 1986.
94 *The New York Times,* November 11, 1988.
95 Padraig O'Malley, *The Uncivil Wars: Ireland Today* (Boston: Houghton Mifflin, 1983), pp. 62–63.
96 *The New York Times,* June 28, 1986.
97 Stanley Karnow, *Vietnam: A History* (New York: Viking Press, 1983), p. 278.
98 Ibid., p. 279.
99 Ibid., p. 281. Diem's older brother, the archbishop of Hue at the time, was "later excommunicated by the Vatican for religious extremism." Ibid., p. 691.
100 Davis, *Israel,* p. 18.
101 Ibid., pp. 19, 20.
102 Aronson, *Creating Facts,* p. 88.
103 Gerard Chaliand, *Revolution in the Third World* (New York: Penguin, 1977), p. 139.
104 Ibid., p. 95.
105 Karnow, *Vietnam,* p. 231.
106 Davis, *Israel,* p. 35.
107 Clough, *Embattled Korea,* p. 58; *The New York Times,* December 3, 1988.
108 *The New York Times,* November 9, 1988.
109 See Norman Gelb, *The Berlin Wall* (New York: Times Books, 1986), p. 4; *The New York Times,* November 13, 1987.
110 Peter Schneider, "Is There a Europe?," *Harper's,* September 1988, p. 56.
111 *San Francisco Chronicle,* October 19, 1988.
112 *The New York Times,* August 13, 1988; Aronson, *Creating Facts,* p. 53.
113 John Conroy, *Belfast Diaries: War as a Way of Life* (Boston: Beacon Press, 1987), p. 113.
114 Ibid., p. 114.
115 Ibid., p. 117.
116 Ibid., p. 108.

10. Sovereignty Denied

1 Gerard Chaliand, *Guerrilla Strategies* (Berkeley: University of California Press, 1982), p. 311.
2 Bernard Fall, *Two Vietnams* (New York: Frederick A. Praeger, 1964), p. 409.
3 Ibid., p. 428.
4 Gregory Henderson, R. N. Lebow, and J. G. Stroessinger, *Divided Nations in a Divided World* (New York: David McKay, 1974), p. 35.
5 Immanuel Wallerstein, *Historical Capitalism* (London: Verso, 1983), p. 49.
6 Henderson, Lebow, and Stroessinger, *Divided Nations,* p. 36; Henry Ashby Turner, Jr., *The Two Germanies Since 1945* (New Haven: Yale University Press, 1987), p. 87.

7 Edwina Moreton, *Germany Between East and West* (Cambridge: Cambridge University Press, 1987), p. 110.

8 Ibid., p. 164.

9 Henderson, Lebow, and Stroessinger, *Divided Nations*, p. 147.

10 As of 1989, only twenty-three countries recognize Taiwan. *The Washington Post*, April 7, 1989.

11 Honecker finally made the trip in 1987. *The New York Times*, July 19, 1987.

12 *The New York Times*, September 19, 1988.

13 *The Washington Post*, July 5, 1987.

14 Tariq Ali, *Can Pakistan Survive?* (London: New Left Books, 1983), p. 51.

15 Ibid., pp. 51–52.

16 Ibid., p. 52.

17 *The New York Times*, December 23, 1987.

18 Bong-youn Choy, *A History of the Korean Reunification Movement* (Peoria, Ill.: Institute of International Studies, Bradley University, 1984), p. 123.

19 Ibid., pp. 123–24.

20 See Eisenhower's and Dulles's critical views of Indian "neutralism" and their attempt to undermine the non-aligned movement and India's leadership role in it. Joann Krieg, *Dwight D. Eisenhower* (New York: Greenwood Press, 1987), pp. 200–4.

21 Lynn Shivers and D. Bowman, *More Than the Troubles* (Philadelphia: New Society Publishers, 1984), p. 97.

22 *The New York Times*, December 2, 1985.

23 The Cypriots have a similar set of stamps. One depicts the island set in a blue sea, with the northern, Turkish-occupied half of the island engulfed in flames. Above it, the 1984 stamp notes: "Ten years of Occupation of Cyprus Territory by Turkey." Other Cypriot stamps feature children or groups of men encircled by rolls of barbed wire.

11. States of War

1 John L. Gaddis, *The Long Peace* (New York: Oxford University Press, 1987), p. 151.

2 Christopher Hitchens, "Wanton Acts of Usage," *Harper's*, September 1987, p. 66.

3 "The Second Coming of Pol Pot," *World Press Review*, October 1988, p. 25.

4 John Lewis and L. Xue, *China Builds the Bomb* (Stanford: Stanford University Press, 1988), p. 66.

5 Ibid., p. 72.

6 Ibid., p. 40.

7 Peter Merkl, *Political Violence and Terror* (Berkeley: University of California Press, 1986), pp. 94–95.

8 One Irish minister was forced to resign in 1970 after his participation in an IRA gunrunning scheme was revealed. Michael Farrell, *Northern Ireland: The Orange State* (London: Pluto, 1980), p. 269.

9 Quoted in Frances FitzGerald, *Fire in the Lake* (Boston: Atlantic Monthly Press–Little, Brown, 1972), p. 176.

10 See Bruce Cumings, *Child of Conflict: The Korean-American Relationship* (Seattle: University of Washington Press, 1983), pp. 3–56.

11 Tom Hartman and J. Mitchell, *A World Atlas of Military History, 1945–1984* (New York: Da Capo Press, 1985), p. 78.

12 Ibid., p. 53.

13 Ibid., p. 54.

14 The recent wars in Afghanistan and the Persian Gulf killed a fraction as many. Only the Nigerian-Biafran war killed people on the same scale as wars in Korea,

Vietnam, and India, in which more than 2 million people died. Ruth Sivard, *World Military and Social Expenditures, 1987–88* (Washington, D.C.: World Priorities, 1987), p. 31.

15 Hartman and Mitchell, *Atlas of Military History*, p. 11.

16 Stephen Kaplan, *Diplomacy of Power* (Washington, D.C.: Brookings Institution, 1981), p. 1.

17 Yaacov Bar-Siman-Tov, *Israel, the Superpowers and the War in the Middle East* (New York: Praeger, 1987), p. 50.

18 Stephen Ambrose, *Eisenhower: The President* (New York: Simon and Schuster, 1984), p. 361.

19 Kaplan, *Diplomacy of Power*, p. 187.

20 Carnegie Task Force on Non-Proliferation and South Asian Security, *Nuclear Weapons and South Asian Security* (Washington, D.C.: Carnegie Endowment for International Peace, 1988), p. 30. Hereafter cited as Carnegie Report.

21 Ibid.

22 Marc Trachtenberg, "A Wasting Asset," *International Security* 13, no. 3 (1988/89): 28.

23 Gaddis, *Long Peace*, p. 100. General MacArthur's unwillingness to accept these more limited objectives led Truman to dismiss him in April 1951. Ibid. MacArthur had expressed a desire to abandon the UN's "tolerant effort" to limit the fighting to Korea. Trachtenberg, "Wasting Asset," 70.

24 Kaplan, *Diplomacy of Power*, p. 652.

25 Douglas Pike, *Vietnam and the Soviet Union* (Boulder, Colo.: Westview Press, 1987), pp. 87–88.

26 Quoted in Keenen Peck, "First Strike, You're Out," *The Progressive*, July 1985, p. 32.

27 Barry Blechman and S. Kaplan, *Force Without War* (Washington, D.C.: Brookings Institution, 1981), pp. 48, 51, 100; Morton Halperin, *Nuclear Fallacy* (Cambridge, Mass.: Ballinger, 1987), p. 24; Richard K. Betts, *Nuclear Blackmail and Nuclear Balance* (Washington, D.C.: Brookings Institution, 1987), pp. 7–8.

28 Blechman and Kaplan, *Force Without War*, pp. 48, 51, 100; Irving Kristol, "Does NATO Exist?" in *Reflections of a Neo-Conservative* (New York: Basic Books, 1983), pp. 5–6.

29 Trachtenberg, "Wasting Asset," 49; Roger Dingman, "Atomic Diplomacy During the Korean War," *International Security* 13, no. 3 (1988/89): 51–53.

30 Betts, *Nuclear Blackmail*, p. 23.

31 Trachtenberg, "Wasting Asset," 5.

32 McGeorge Bundy, *Danger and Survival* (New York: Random House, 1988), p. 246; Gaddis, *Long Peace*, p. 124.

33 Stephen P. Cohen, *The Pakistani Army* (Berkeley: University of California Press, 1984), p. 153. As the Indians and Pakistanis have observed, the only time nuclear weapons were exploded over civilian populations was when the opponent (Japan) did not possess nuclear weapons.

34 Timothy Botti, *The Long Wait* (New York: Greenwood Press, 1987), p. 111.

35 McNamara says, however, that the Soviets still possessed enough weapons to make nuclear war an unthinkable option. James Blight, unpublished interview with Robert S. McNamara, Washington, D.C., May 21, 1987, pp. 22, 33–34.

36 Rosemary Foot, *The Wrong War* (Ithaca, N.Y.: Cornell University Press, 1985), p. 38.

37 Bar-Siman-Tov, *Israel*, p. 57.

38 Kaplan, *Diplomacy of Power*, p. 141.

39 Betts, *Nuclear Blackmail*, p. 79.

40 Leonard S. Spector, *Going Nuclear* (Cambridge, Mass.: Ballinger, 1987), p. 111.

41 Steve Weissman and Herbert Krosney say that the Soviets again threatened the Chinese during the 1971 Indo-Pakistani war. China was warned not to assist its ally Pakistan. *The Islamic Bomb* (New York: Times Books, 1981), p. 57.

42 Betts, *Nuclear Blackmail*, p. 132.

43 Examining the pattern of U.S.–Soviet nuclear confrontations, particularly in the Middle East, James M. McConnell and Anne M. Kelly note that it appears "permissible for one superpower to support a friend against the client of another superpower as long as the friend is on the defensive strategically; the object must be to avert decisive defeat and restore the balance, not assist the client to victory." "Superpower Naval Diplomacy in the Indo-Pakistani Crisis," in *Soviet Naval Developments: Capability and Context*, ed. Michael MccGuire (New York: Praeger, 1973), p. 449.

44 Lewis and Xue, *China Builds the Bomb*, p. 12.

45 William Kincade and C. Bertram, *Nuclear Proliferation in the 1980s* (London: Macmillan, 1982), p. 13.

46 Kaplan, *Diplomacy of Power*, pp. 89–90.

47 Kincade and Bertram, *Nuclear Proliferation*, p. 18.

48 Bundy, *Danger and Survival*, p. 475. Diana Johnstone states that the development of an independent nuclear weapons program "forced a certain national consensus between right and left." *The Politics of Euromissiles: Europe's Role in America's World* (London: Verso, 1984), p. 90.

49 Herzog went on to say, "How vulnerable this actually made Israel was something that could not be determined with certainty at that time. . . . The fact was that a regional conflict . . . escalated overnight into a potential global war." Bar-Siman-Tov, *Israel*, pp. 60–61.

50 Johnstone, *Politics of Euromissiles*, pp. 180, 181.

51 Bundy, *Danger and Survival*, pp. 485–86.

52 Rosemary Foot, "Nuclear Coercion and the Ending of the Korean Conflict," *International Security* 13, no. 3 (1988/89): 99.

53 Bundy, *Danger and Survival*, p. 526; Lewis and Xue, *China Builds the Bomb*, p. 34. The Chinese program, like the Israeli program, was conducted in secret, at least until a bomb was tested.

54 Lewis and Xue, *China Builds the Bomb*, p. 215.

55 Ibid., p. 216.

56 Ibid., p. 130.

57 Ibid., p. 90.

58 Ibid., pp. 154, 159.

59 Ibid., p. 107. Chou announced the successful test at the musical performance of *The East Is Red*. After telling the crowd the news, he said, "You may celebrate all you like. But mind you don't damage the floor." Ibid., p. 189.

60 Mitchell Reiss, *Without the Bomb* (New York: Columbia University Press, 1988), p. 203.

61 Gerald Segal, *Arms Control in Asia* (New York: St. Martin's Press, 1987), p. 103.

62 Reiss, *Without the Bomb*, pp. 215–16.

63 Sumit Ganguly, "Why India Joined the Nuclear Club," *Bulletin of the Atomic Scientists* 39, no. 4 (April 1983): 31.

64 Reiss, *Without the Bomb*, pp. 226–27.

65 Kincade and Bertram, *Nuclear Proliferation*, p. 71.

66 Carnegie Report, p. 35.

67 Spector, *Going Nuclear*, p. 102.

68 Carnegie Report, p. 46; Walter Patterson, *The Plutonium Business* (San Francisco: Sierra Club Books, 1985), p. 86.

69 Spector, *Going Nuclear*, p. 108.

70 Carnegie Report, p. 19.

71 *The Washington Post*, March 24, 1987; see also March 19, 1987.

72 Spector, *Going Nuclear*, p. 87.

73 *The Washington Post*, March 24, 1987.

74 Spector, *Going Nuclear*, p. 83. The construction of new reactors in the mid-1980s greatly increased India's capacity to build bombs. Ibid., p. 77.

75 U.S. officials reportedly considered a preemptive, covert attack on Pakistan's nuclear facilities. Weissman and Krosney, *Islamic Bomb*, p. 193.

76 Spector, *Going Nuclear*, p. 113.

77 Ibid., p. 131; Reiss, *Without the Bomb*, pp. 140, 148.

78 Reiss, *Without the Bomb*, pp. 45–46.

79 Ibid., p. 146.

80 *The New York Times*, November 9, 1986.

81 William Epstein and T. Toyoda, *A New Design for Nuclear Disarmament* (Bristol: J. W. Arrowsmith, 1977), p. 13.

82 Reiss, *Without the Bomb*, p. 93.

83 Kincade and Bertram, *Nuclear Proliferation*, p. 74; Patterson, *Plutonium Business*, p. 115.

84 Reiss, *Without the Bomb*, p. 94.

85 Ibid., pp. 94–95.

86 Leonard S. Spector, *The Undeclared Bomb* (Cambridge, Mass.: Ballinger, 1988), p. 71.

87 William Walker and M. Lonnroth, *Nuclear Power Struggles* (Boston: Allen and Unwin, 1983), p. 119.

88 Patterson, *Plutonium Business*, p. 139; Spector, *Undeclared Bomb*, pp. 75, 77–79.

89 Hans Spier, "Soviet Atomic Blackmail and the North Atlantic Alliance," *World Politics* 9, no. 3 (April 1957): 308. According to Robert Jervis, Richard Lebow, and Janice Stein, "Deterrence has its etymological roots in the Latin term for 'terror.'" *Psychology and Deterrence* (Baltimore: Johns Hopkins University Press, 1985), p. 4.

90 Betts, *Nuclear Blackmail*, p. 5.

91 *The New York Times*, December 8, 1988.

12. The Next Generation

1 Lee Burcheit, *Secession: The Legitimacy of Self-Determination* (New Haven: Yale University Press, 1978), pp. 247–48.

2 Conversation with the author at the "Revolution and War in the World-System" conference, Emory University, March 1988.

3 Bubrata R. Chowdhury, *The Genesis of Bangladesh* (New York: Asia Publishing House, 1972), p. 2.

4 Burcheit, *Secession*, pp. 202–3.

5 J. N. Saxena, *Self-Determination: From Biafra to Bangladesh* (Delhi: University of Delhi Press, 1978), p. 53.

6 Burcheit, *Secession*, p. 206.

7 Ibid.

8 Ibid., p. 207.

9 Ibid.

10 Gregory Henderson, R. N. Lebow, and J. G. Stroessinger, *Divided Nations in a Divided World* (New York: David McKay, 1974), pp. 325–26.

11 Ibid., p. 314.

12 *The New York Times*, August 14, 1988.

13 *The New York Times*, May 18, 1986.

14 *Bangor* [Maine] *Daily News*, October 1, 1986.

15 *The New York Times*, November 14, 1988.

16 William R. Louis, *The British Empire in the Middle East* (Oxford: Clarendon Press, 1984), p. 224.

17 Kyriacos Markides, *The Rise and Fall of the Cyprus Republic* (New Haven: Yale University Press, 1977), p. 23.

18 Robert Stephens, *Cyprus: A Place of Arms* (London: Pall Mall Press, 1966), p. 132.

19 Ibid., p. 190.

20 Ibid., p. 189.

21 Christopher Hitchens, *Hostage to History: Cyprus from the Ottomans to Kissinger* (New York: Noonday Press, 1989), p. 57.

22 Markides, *Cyprus Republic*, p. 134.

23 Ibid., pp. 84–85.

24 Hitchens, *Hostage to History*, p. 90.

25 *The New York Times*, December 20, 1987.

26 *The New York Times*, February 27, 1988.

27 Hitchens, *Hostage to History*, p. 107.

28 Ibid., pp. 139, 179.

29 *The New York Times*, March 30, 1988.

30 *The New York Times*, December 20, 1987.

31 Hitchens, *Hostage to History*, p. 25.

32 *The New York Times*, July 21, 1986.

33 See Milton Viorst, "A Reporter at Large: The Christian Enclave," *The New Yorker*, October 3, 1988, for an excellent description of the problem.

34 *The Washington Post*, October 25, 1988.

35 Ibid.

36 *The New York Times*, October 11, 1988.

37 *The New York Times*, September 27, 1988.

38 *The Economist*, October 11, 1988.

39 Mary Anne Weaver, "A Reporter at Large: The Gods and the Stars," *The New Yorker*, March 21, 1988, p. 41.

40 Ibid., pp. 41–42.

41 *The New York Times*, December 18, 1988.

42 Ibid.

43 *The New York Times*, September 1, 1988.

13. Self-Determination or Democracy?

1 Lee Burcheit, *Secession: The Legitimacy of Self-Determination* (New Haven: Yale University Press, 1978), pp. 65–66.

2 Carl Sandburg, *Abraham Lincoln: The War Years* (New York: Harcourt, Brace and Company, 1939), vol. 1, pp. 131–32, passim.

3 Martin Luther King, Jr., *A Testament of Hope: The Essential Writings of Martin Luther King, Jr.*, ed. James M. Washington (San Francisco: Harper & Row, 1986), pp. 35–36.

4 Ibid., pp. 19–20.

5 Ibid., p. 33. The advocates of violence, he said, "fail to see that no internal revolution has ever succeeded in overthrowing a government by violence unless the government has already lost the allegiance and effective control of its armed forces. Anyone in his right mind knows that this will not happen in the United States." Ibid., p. 249.

6 Ibid., p. 12. "I am convinced that if the Negro succumbs to the temptation of using

violence in his struggle for freedom and justice, unborn generations will be the recipients of a long and desolate night of bitterness." Ibid., pp. 44–45.

7 Ibid., p. 108.
8 Ibid.
9 Ibid., p. 97.
10 Ibid., pp. 219–20.
11 Ibid., pp. 582, 583, 586, 587, 588.

Index

Baghdad Pact, 195
Balfour, Arthur J., 35, 37–39, 62–65, 94,
96–98, 100, 105, 107
Balfour Declarations, 62, 93, 94, 97, 112
Baluchis, 239
Bangladesh, 165, 226–27, 232, 234,
236–39, 243, 247; *see also* Pakistan
Bao Dai, 135–36, 141, 143–44, 147, 169
Basic Law, 126, 191; *see also* West
Germany
Basques, 248, 251
Bavaria, 120
Begin, Menachem, 94, 207
Beirut, 246–47
Belfast, 106, 184, 185
Bengal, 102–3, 156, 165, 234–35, 237,
239, 243, 251
Bengal, Bay of, 226, 237
Ben-Gurion, David, 44, 109–10, 113,
158, 160, 177, 214, 223
Benjamin, Walter, 38
Benvenisti, Meron, 183–85
Berlin, 4, 118, 126–27, 155, 184–85, 215,
218–19, 221; East Berlin, 183; West
Berlin, 127–28, 200
Berlin Airlift, 200
Berlin Wall, 155, 182–83, 200
Besant, Annie, 26, 34
Betar, 41
Betts, Richard, 230
Bevin, Ernest, 94, 127, 129, 215
Bhabha, Homi, 226
Bhutto, Benazir, 165, 239
Bhutto, Zulfikar Ali, 165, 224, 226–27,
234–36, 239
Biafra, 249
Bidault, Georges, 142
Bihar, 106; Biharis, 238
Black and Tans, 90
Black Power, 260–61
Bombay, 40, 91
Bonesteel, C. H. III, 122
Borodin, Mikhail, 21
Boy Scouts, 24
Brandenburg Gate, 200
Brazzaville, 68
Brezhnev, Leonid, 83
Brezhnev Doctrine, 146, 197; *see also*
Monroe Doctrine(s)
Brookings Institution, 218

Buddhists, 37, 179, 188, 239
Bulgaria, 129
Bundestag, 126
Burma, 61–62, 70–71, 96, 100, 247, 251
Burundi, 251–52
Bush, George, 83
Byelorussia, 79

Cairo, 26, 76, 94, 121
Calcutta, 92
Camau, 191
Cambodia, 136, 143, 198, 203, 208–9, 215
Camp David accords, 196, 217
Canada, 48, 61, 64, 251
Carson, Edward, 89, 96
Carter, Jimmy, 83, 229, 233
Catholic Church, 178–79
Catholics, 12, 28–30, 88–90, 94, 95,
102–3, 105, 148, 153, 159–60, 167, 174,
178, 184, 189–90, 206, 208
CENTO, 80, 195
Central America, 262
Central Election Committee (Israel), 166
Central Intelligence Agency, 227, 228
Ceylon, 61, 100; *see also* Sri Lanka
Charney, Marc, 11
Cheju Island, 138
Chen Yi, 222, 225
Chiang Ching-kuo, 169
Chiang Kai-shek, 22–23, 28, 44, 76, 121–23,
132–33, 155, 179, 204, 215
Chief Rabbinical Council (Israel), 177
China, 3–10, 13, 14, 19, 21–22, 29, 33,
41, 42–43, 62, 69, 71, 77–78, 80, 116,
118–19, 122–24, 129–30, 132–34, 136–
42, 146–49, 155, 159–60, 162, 167–68,
173, 179, 183, 187–88, 190–91, 193,
196, 198–99, 203, 211, 213, 216, 220–
22, 224–30, 233, 248–49; Communist
Party, 33; Cultural Revolution, 197; *see
also* Taiwan
Chittagong Hill Tracts, 239
Chong Kyong-mo, 27
Chou En-lai, 142–43, 225
Christian Democrats (West Germany),
163
Christians, 28, 37, 106, 111, 156, 177,
239, 245–46
Chun Doo Hwan, 164, 194